CW01305551

Figure 1. Herman J. Gabryel
(*Building Materials Merchandiser*, March 1964, cover image)

The

Revelations

of

Xxenogenesis

Scott Michaelsen and Louis Kaplan

Copyright©2023 Scott Michaelsen and Louis Kaplan
All rights reserved.
9798863788234

Producer: Sanket Bojewar
Cover Design: Adwait Katkar
Editor: Richard Doyle

InstruXxions

Before reading this book, locate a physical or digital copy of the LP by Xxenogenesis, entitled *SeXxenogenesis #1* (1973).

Please sit as comfortably as you can and relax. Close your eyes and still your consciousness.

Are you ready? Let's have fun and try this and see what you can experience after this revelation.

Now lower the tonearm or just press play.

—

Finished listening? Turn the page….

Contents

InstruXxions i

Contents ii

List of Illustrations iii

1. IntroduXxion 1

2. Self-RefleXxions: A Biographical Timeline in His Own Words 17

3. DiXxionary, From A to Xx 48

4. LP Transcript with Xxegesis 114

5. The Life of Xxenogenesis: A Fantastical Film Treatment in Six Acts 171

Afterword by Gabryel, the son of Herman J. Gabryel, Sr./ Xxenogenesis 196

Acknowledgements 206

List of Illustrations

Figure 1. Herman J. Gabryel --- Frontispiece
Figure 2. Invitation to SeXxy's Chapel, 1984 ------------------------------------- 4
Figure 3. ARC Gallery 1984 Catalogue page for Test Patterns at Raw Space --- 5
Figure 4. The home in which Herman J. Gabryel was raised ------------------ 18
Figure 5. Corpus Christi Church, Buffalo, NY ---------------------------------- 19
Figure 6. Herman's B-17 bomber, damaged by an act of sabotage ----------- 20
Figure 7. Gabryel Lumber in its heyday --- 22
Figure 8. Herman approving his latest astrologically themed ad -------------- 27
Figure 9. Herman standing under his IBM sign --------------------------------- 28
Figure 10. The Mark-Age MetaCenter building -------------------------------- 30
Figure 11. The three directors of early Mark-Age: Wains (aka Jim Speed), Nada-Yolanda (aka Pauline Sharpe), and El Morya (aka Mark aka Charles Boyd Gentzel), 1961 -- 31
Figure 12. "Obelisk" (1969) by Albert Vrana, outside Arlen House ---------- 36
Figure 13. Herman's ad for Mark-Age in *Miami Herald* ------------------------ 38
Figure 14. *Immortality Unveiled* (front cover) -------------------------------------- 43
Figure 15. "The mystery of the perfect atoms" --------------------------------- 52
Figure 16. "The mystery of the carbon 666 atoms" --------------------------- 57
Figure 17. "I am the very much misunderstood crucifixion of man" --------- 61
Figure 18. "Kundalini caduceus serpents/7 chakras – 7 seals – 7 bodies" -- 75
Figure 19. "Seal of Solomon – Star of David – Star in the east ancient Masonic symbol" -- 95
Figure 20. "Universal symbols of 4 gammas forming a gammadion" -------- 96
Figure 21. Front cover of LP, Xxenogenesis, *SeXxenogenesis #1* -------------- 104
Figure 22. Back cover of LP, Xxenogenesis, *SeXxenogenesis #1* --------------- 105
Figure 23. The LP's inner gatefold sermon: Column 1 ------------------------ 106
Figure 24. The LP's inner gatefold sermon: Column 2 ------------------------ 107

Figure 25. The LP's inner gatefold sermon: Column 3 ------------------------ 108
Figure 26. The LP's inner gatefold sermon: Column 4 ------------------------ 109
Figure 27. The LP's inner gatefold sermon: Column 5 ------------------------ 110
Figure 28. The LP's inner gatefold sermon: Column 6 ------------------------ 111
Figure 29. Xxenogenesis Side 1 Record Label ---------------------------------- 112
Figure 30. Pink envelope with inscription included with the LP and to be used for sending a message back to Xxenogenesis ---------------------------- 113

1. IntroduXxion

This is the story of a 40-year obsession and a nearly 50-year-old mystery.

We were disc jockeys at WHRB (Harvard Radio) starting in the late 1970s, and our station "handles" were "Peroxide" (Scott) and "Large Louis" (graphically indicated as capital "L" squared). We co-created the station's first post-punk, new wave, and industrial music program, "Plastic Passions," during the summer of 1980 but soon grew restless spinning records on the two measly turntables in the primary DJ booth. We were budding performance artists with an eye on radio, and we were fascinated by the fact that the station had five separate studios, all of which could be made operational simultaneously. What would happen, we wondered, if we could fill up all the studios with live performers, tape loops, record albums? We could invite Dave Johnson, our brilliant and intrepid engineer, to help us build gigantic tape loops and otherwise figure out the studio logistics, and we'd invite in friends on keyboard (Stephen Drury), guitar (Scott Shershow) and human body percussion (Bob LeVine and Justin Doebele) to add to the mix. Scheduled to get our degrees and therefore be retired or turned into "ghosts" at the end of Spring 1981, we decided to go out with a bang. Harvard Radio was famous for its "orgy" season at the end of every semester, during which time DJs from each of the various station departments proposed multi-hour and sometimes multi-day broadcasts featuring particular artists, genres, or record labels. Our own first orgy, for example, had been quite traditional, devoted to Roxy Music and all of its offshoots. For our final orgy, we began to imagine a six-hour event that we called "Industrial Dinosaurs": a good way to say *au revoir* and good riddance to FM classic rock broadcasting by spinning the classics of hard rock, southern rock, and prog and collaging them with layer upon layer of noises and other intrusions. A real mix-up! As part of our planning for this event, we spent a good deal of time hunting for unusual spoken word albums in the station's vast LP collection. Many of these records had been completely forgotten; most had never been played. Spoken word albums can include recordings of famous speeches, poets reading their poetry, preachers declaiming sermons, and instructional albums (teach your bird to talk, learn to type, explore a foreign language). We were fascinated by this forgotten archive, and there was one record in particular that seemed to be the most unusual and peculiar in the entire collection: a private press recording from 1973 entitled *SeXxenogenesis #1* and seemingly recorded in Miami by a figure known only as "Xxenogenesis."

Put the album on. The first thing you hear is the sound of a needle drop, followed by the opening minute or so of the soundtrack album for *2001: A Space Odyssey* (1968): Strauss' "Also Sprach Zarathustra." Then a greeting from a warm tenor voice with a hint of an Eastern European accent, bathed in a bit of reverb: "And hi everyone! My limitless love unto you, the people of this planet Earth." Wow. Now what? Scads of reverb: "I am that I am," followed by the singing of a few bars from *The Sound of Music*: "mi a name I call myself!" And then our narrator properly introduces himself: "The everlasting, infinite, universal SeXxenogenesis atom of Etcha, from the Sound of Music of all spheres." Wow again. Is this the best record ever?

We thought so. We already knew that preacher records were miserably boring, and that guru LPs were not far behind in terms of promising more than they delivered. But the Xxenogenesis album plays between high-minded theosophical thinking and low-brow comedy as the "Xxenogenesis atom," a mysterious teacher, leads his imaginary flock of initiates along a path of "crazy wisdom" in order to help them to recover their immortal natures and the mystical knowledge that the kingdom of God is within them. To that end, Xxenogenesis sings bits of Broadway songs, tells jokes, quacks like a duck, sings a version of "Ave Maria" and occasionally conjures a thunderstorm. The listener is always on the verge of wondering whether they are listening to a cosmic revelation or to a cockeyed crackpot. For lurking throughout these esoteric teachings is a wavering tonality such that the listener is forced to ask, Who is he kidding? Or, as Xxenogenesis himself asks (and asks himself) at one point, "Hey bud, are you for real?" For the next six or seven years we became avid collectors of spoken word albums and often utilized such recordings in our performances as Test Patterns; and while we amassed mountains of strange and compelling LPs by regularly shopping at Chicago-area Amvets thrift stores, we never found another record that appealed to us as much as *SeXxenogenesis #1*.

We played a portion of the album on the radio for the very first time during "Industrial Dinosaurs" on a memorable May 31, 1981, as part of a mash-up that included, as germ seed, King Crimson's "In the Court of the Crimson King." We saved an aircheck of this moment. Why? It seemed important. Were we the first people on the face of the earth to play this album, or, at least, were we the first DJs to broadcast Xxenogenesis over the airwaves? In any event, we felt that the moment needed to be archived. And we vaguely suspected that we would return to Xxenogenesis.

And indeed, we found our way back to Xxey (as we affectionately refer to him) in 1983 and 1984 when we conceptualized and proposed a month-long art installation in the new Raw Space at the ARC Gallery in Chicago dedicated to the themes of the LP. ARC Gallery was housed in an old, industrial building and Raw Space was their large back room: one doorway, no windows, greasy cement in all directions and completely unfinished. This was a place where anything could happen if you put your mind to it. The show was called, "SeXxenogenesis: Master of the Universe (SeXxy's Chapel)." Xxey's suggestion that electrons are really "cosmic hissing serpents" moving in spiral patterns set the tone for our occupation of Raw Space: bedsprings hung from the ceiling created a kind of cage of coils, slinkies ran from ceiling to floor, and gigantic stuffed snakes slithered through the room. Slideshows created wall size versions of some of the theosophical images from the record album jacket, which transmuted and melted into black white patternings, as Xxenogenesis had specified. (He encourages mankind to "walk in the black-white light equilibrium" among other things.) And didn't Xxey also praise the "electromagnetic spectrum etheric man" on the album? In response, we recorded hours of shortwave radio static that sounded to us like the spiralling cosmos, and we mixed and remixed these shortwave tapes until our fingers bled. Yet other tapes contained specific portions of the LP (sampling Xxey's most mind-blowing spoken words), to be added to the mix during our four live performances in the Raw Space. The last show was organized as a "sleepover" but getting some shuteye in that super-charged sonic environment was not an easy feat. Hand-built "electrocutioners" (hot-wired Radio Shack mics) acted as dangerous guitar picks for strumming on broken, modified instruments, including the "guitar of steel," rewired with different gauges of galvanized steel and the plastic handle of a disposable razor. These were vibrating "extremely very fast" for, after all, we were trying our best to get onto Xxey's wavelength. Bob Puhala, Raul Perez, Antonio Quintanilla, Paul Hagland, and someone's friend named Elton played electrocutioners against the very walls of the coiled cage, while dancer Judy Furton wore a blank, white mask and jumped and darted around our antics. It was all very loud, very scratchy, and very ultra-high frequency.

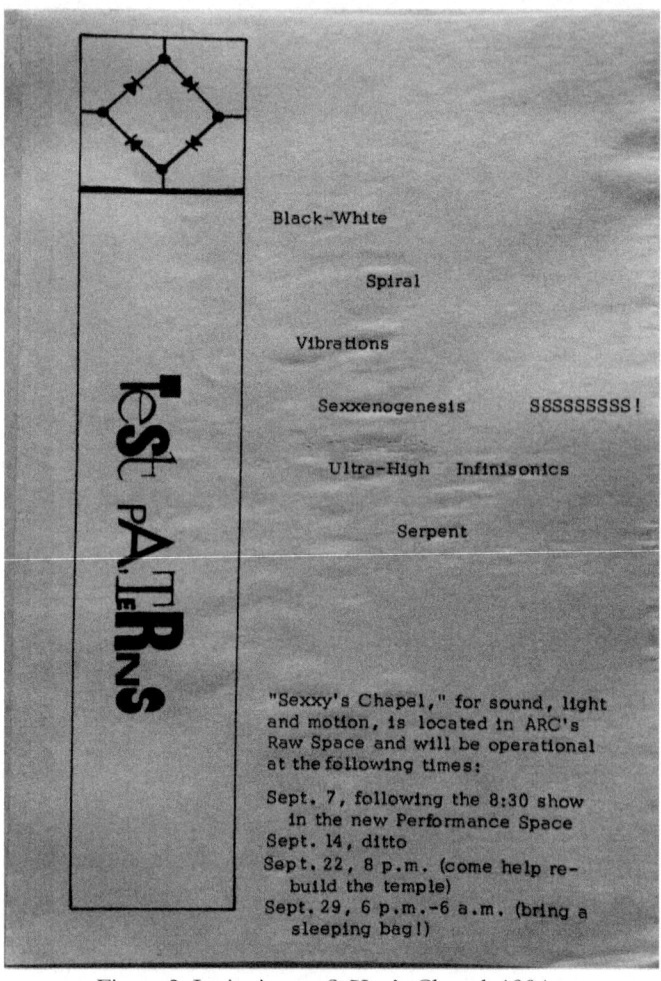

Figure 2. Invitation to SeXxy's Chapel, 1984

"SEXXENOGENESIS"
Installation/
Performance/Sound

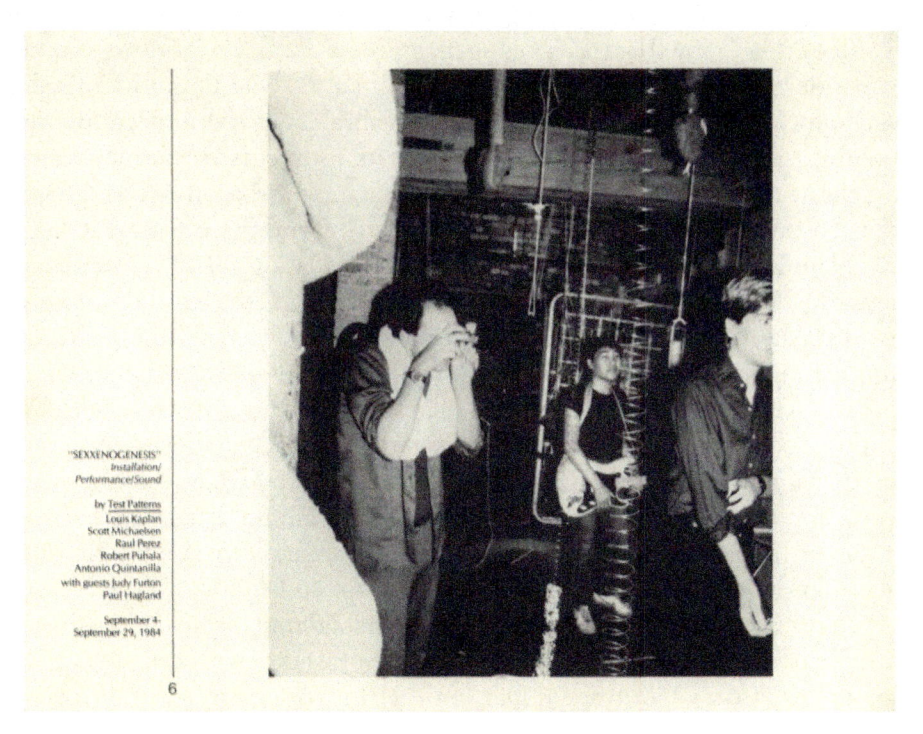

by Test Patterns
Louis Kaplan
Scott Michaelsen
Raul Perez
Robert Puhala
Antonio Quintanilla
with guests Judy Furton
Paul Hagland

September 4-
September 29, 1984

6

Figure 3. ARC Gallery 1984 Catalogue page for Test Patterns at Raw Space
(pictured: Louis Kaplan, Paul Hagland, Scott Michaelsen)

So why were we still so attracted to this unique pearl of occulture? Perhaps one way to explain our predicament: both of us sensed that materialism and reason were not sufficient for inhabiting and explaining this strange world of ours, while existing mainstream religion (and its dogmatism) was impossible. Then where were we? As early as 1980 we were avidly listening to the new sonic occulture: Throbbing Gristle, Cabaret Voltaire, Clock DVA, Nurse with Wound, and the Fall all laid claim to our attention and our broadcast playlists, and bands like the Legendary Pink Dots and Current 93 were just around the corner. But the Xxenogenesis album didn't seem to have that much in common with a scene that worshipped and riffed on the work of Aleister Crowley, William Burroughs, Andre Breton, H.P. Lovecraft and their circles, and we knew very little about the history and symbolism of Theosophy proper in the early to mid-1980s. On the other hand, we readily understood that the LP constituted a beginning set of instructions for achieving immortality through tantric conservation and Scott owned several works by Sir John Woodroffe (Arthur Avalon), including the bestselling *Serpent Power* (1919).

5

All of this to say that the Xxenogenesis record was a continued source of wonderment and side-splitting entertainment. The LP and its unique tone somehow continued to hold us in its thrall. We found it eminently quotable, including its jokes and some of its moments of hermeneutics "on the wild side," and it became the foundation for a private language between just the two of us (though no one for whom we played it over the ensuing decades ever found it quite as fascinating). Who could have made this album and what on earth – and, beyond, the cosmos – were they thinking? We had no idea who Xxenogenesis was, although the album offered a few tantalizing clues, such as an old address at the Arlen House luxury apartments in North Miami Beach and a densely worded sermon occupying the inner gatefold, printed in black and gold on a hot pink background. There was no doubt that the "Xxenogenesis atom" was protecting his privacy, but was this because the album was some sort of spoof, or because every great esoteric master wears a mask? We had no way of knowing the answer, but we never stopped listening to the record and chatting about it. We both felt that we had some unfinished business with regard to the LP, even as Test Patterns ceased performing and writing, and each of us got our Ph.D.'s and began working in earnest in academia.

The mystery went cold for a number of years, but we picked up the trail again in the summer of 2013 when, tripping down memory lane, we wondered whether Xxenogenesis might still be alive. This prompted Louis to enter internet browser mode and, after some searching, he hit upon a website, 144cubits.com, where the introductory words sounded strangely familiar. "Did you know that you are composed of trillions of atoms? … You were not born to die, but to overcome mortal death by harnessing your full atomic capabilities." On July 8th, he pasted this URL into an email and popped a quick question to Scott: "Is this his site? It seems current." Scott's reply was an affirmatively exclamatory: "Giant Wow! I think you have to be correct!" This turned out to be Xxey's most elaborate website but further digging revealed the home page for a second site, xxenogenesis.com. Visitors there were greeted with the following esoteric words: "Welcome! To the Secret of all secrets, the Ultra Top Secret of the Universe! This secret is greater than any other secret that has ever been discovered and known by any man!" But from our perspective, the disclosure of the Xxenogenesis websites was revelation enough for one day.

We were struck by the math in the following autobiographical statement on the 144 cubits site that proclaimed in bold red ink. "Since February 2, 1962, 51+ years: I have devoted all these years of research to bring you a new scientific breakthrough, of how to restore your biological atomic structure and the RNA DNA, to your original state of perfection, the perfect presence." The numbers added up to what the LP calls the "present moment of now," with the implication that Xxenogenesis was still vital and flourishing! But how to reach him? How to contact the webmaster directly? Even though there were dozens upon dozens of pages, postings, and links, there seemed to be absolutely no way to break through. A perplexed Louis wrote to Scott again: "I don't see contact info either which is most peculiar. Let's keep looking." But we found ourselves butting our heads against an invisible firewall because Xxey was using a Go Daddy proxy server that promised strict anonymity to its clients and practiced full domain privacy. In addition, we encountered a luscious lilac warning at the end of every site page that featured these ominous and even apocalyptic words: "If you know me, please don't be a Judas and betray me. Also if you value the planet earth, all mankind and you in it, surely you will not betray me." Between the domain privacy restrictions and the intimations of betrayal we were picking up some bad vibes and the message seemed to indicate that we should keep out and go away. What were these two long-time groupies to do? It was all very frustrating. In hindsight, we now know that even though Xxey was alive and based in Washington state with his son, he had suffered a freak accident in spring of 2013 at the DMV that had permanently impaired his vision. Already he was curtailing his web activity, and the sites would come to a grinding halt the following year.

Further searches uncovered the website Godlike Productions where Xxey's websites had been the subject of a few threads beginning in 2009. Folks were discussing and debating Xxey's more recent prophetic pronouncements in earnest, and even reposting and reciting them. On All Hallows' Eve in 2009, a curious contributor named Lady Wolf started a new discussion thread entitled "To Whomever Posted This Link...144Cubits.com."[1] It would lead to a series of fascinating posts over the next five years, and the uncovering of a third Xxenogenesis website that had gone dormant: unlearninghurts.com. The varied comments ranged from "to be

---

[1] See https://www.godlikeproductions.com/forum1/message913074/pg1

frank, the writer wasn't making complete sense" to "this is awesome...thanks much," to "NEW WORLD ORDER RELIGION ALERT. Truth mixed with bullshit, as always," and finally, "The author's writing is very cryptic. ... Difficult read to be sure, with much esoteric content." Later in October 2011, another contributor uploaded long passages of 144 cubits.com and shared his conviction that the content related to the recently released X-men movie *First Class* and the saying, "We are children of the Atom." One wonders if Xxey himself was ever privy to the lively exchanges sparked by his websites. Failing to solve the mystery of his identity, a contributor with the pseudonym Wake Up uttered a lament with which we too could identify completely: "I wish I could give you the Owner info. but it is blocked by domainsbyproxy.com." In the end, no one was able to make contact or to figure out the identity of this mysterious figure — even though one convinced individual proclaimed that his name was Michael. (One imagines Xxey snickering at that one: wrong archangel!) Again, the trail had run cold, and a disappointed Scott and Louis returned to their other research pursuits and pastimes.[2]

Fast forward another seven years to May of 2020, when both of us were teaching online during the first wave of COVID-19 lockdowns. Louis had just reconnected with his old pal Richard Doyle (aka M0b1us) who told him about his new, mystically inclined Metanoia Press and asked him if he had any interesting ideas for a book project. Louis quickly responded: "Have you ever heard of *SeXxenogenesis #1*? It's the most amazing spoken word record album of all time and it's got Metanoia written all over it!" Our first thought was to create a short book patterned on and perhaps subtly parodying Bloomsbury's 33⅓ series, telling the story of our eighties' celebration of the LP and contextualizing its message and meaning using the many materials deposited on the three Xxenogenesis websites. But could we go further? Could this be an opportunity to finally crack the case? It was clear that the search to solve the mystery of Xxenogenesis had gained new impetus and, interestingly, it paralleled Xxey's own move to cyberspace and digital communications in the later years of his life. We carefully inventoried the three sites and estimated that Xxey had published an astounding amount, somewhere between 1000-1200 pages worth of material during his internet days, including the entire contents of two books published by Xxenogenesis in micro-editions in the

---

[2] Much, much later, we discovered two Xxenogenesis fans who had linked the record to the websites as early as 2006! See the comments by Martin Iles and bigtazmanian at: https://blog.wfmu.org/freeform/2006/03/insane_new_age_.html

late 1970s (*Immortality Through Xxenogenesis*) and 1985 (*Immortality Unveiled*). Here and there on these websites, scattered like seeds carried by the winds, were numerous autobiographical fragments but always written in code: Xxey called himself "Jason," for example, and his wife was "Ujena," and he carefully explained that these were pseudonyms. We decided that we had enough information to start our investigations, and so we formed an online detective agency and began both digging up information and disseminating what we had learned. In terms of the latter, we gathered all the information we had and created a "WANTED" poster, distributing it electronically to the existing, small network of occult bookstores in the U.S. We posted this same information on both occulture and music discussion boards, trying to locate anyone who might have helped Xxey produce his record or who might have corresponded with him after receiving the gift of the LP. Finally, we began to write letters to anyone that we deemed a "lead," including former employees at Arlen House whose names we gleaned from period stories in the *Miami Herald*. We wrote to the Polish American organization in Miami and to the Miami Theosophical Society in the hope that one of the old timers at these organizations would recognize that unique DIY record producer who lived in the Arlen House in the early 70's. And we contacted the Roman Catholic Diocese in Miami several times because we knew the date of his marriage and we knew he was born and raised a Catholic.

We scoured the record album again for leads and clues, but Xxenogenesis proved himself a master of concealment: he really knew how to cover his tracks! We had an Arlen House penthouse address, A-10, listed in the album's gatefold, and we hoped this small but very cold lead might still bear fruit. We read the history of the building and its 1969 opening in the pages of the *Herald*, we rummaged through property records online, and we wrote to the Miami-Dade County Assessor's office for archival records. Could we turn up a deed of purchase or sale from that period with his name on it? We found a purchaser's name for the A-10 unit in 1974, after the building turned condo, but the purchaser was not our man, and the deed did not list the former tenant's name. We were forced to conclude that Xxenogenesis had rented but never owned the unit. (Later we learned that Xxey never lived in A-10: it was a friend's unit, and Xxey used the address with permission in order to remain as undetectable as possible). Another potential lead was the Arlen House general street address – 300 Bayview Drive. Might Xxenogenesis be in the phone book? The period White Pages were available to us online at the Library of

Congress, but they did not list apartment numbers. Drat! (If it had listed actual apartment numbers, Scott had vowed that he would read the White Pages line by line!) We knew that Xxenogenesis was Polish-American, and, at one point, Scott developed a list of the 100 most popular Polish surnames and checked each surname and its major anglicizations and variants in the White Pages for anyone living at 300 Bayview. This involved hours and hours of painstaking online labor, and nothing there either. Double drat!

We also knew from Xxey's writings that he owned a gigantic lumber yard between the late 1940s and 1967. It was–yabba dibby–how he became a rich man. He even boasted about the amount of railroad siding on the property and its great location near an interstate highway, and further bragged that he had advertised the sale of his enterprise in 1966 or 1967 in the pages of the *Wall Street Journal*. Assuming that this was all happening in the Miami area, Louis seemingly discovered the ad in the *WSJ*'s electronic archives. Given what we had read on Xxey's websites about the business, everything about this ad felt right. And even though the ad in question did not contain a street address, our confidence was sky high, and we started browsing the period's Miami Yellow Pages for the names and locations of lumber yards, hoping that either a Polish name would turn up or we might find an ad that jibed with the lumber yard description, including his railroad frontage specifications. We studied corporate business records and Google maps and images for several hundred hours for some kind of match, but this all turned out to be a wild goose chase – a total dead end. (In hindsight, there are quite a lot of miles between Miami, Florida and Buffalo, New York, where Xxenogenesis actually ran his incredibly successful computerized lumber yard.)

A further possible lead was Xxenogenesis' anecdote about his time as an altar boy at the "Corpus Christi Church," and, late in life, his recounting of a dream about the "Corpus Christi School," which in the dream was located near a body of water. For a long time, we believed that this had to be in the Miami area, but, once we lost faith in the theory that Xxey had spent most of his life in Miami (discovering a reference to sleeping on a cold floor in winter as a child), we looked northward and decided that Xxey might have lived in New York City as a child, and therefore gone to Corpus Christi in Morningside Heights. This surmise also did not have a prayer, and we soon began to refer to ourselves as "bad detectives." We laid out brilliant investigative plans, made great guesses, and poured mountains of time into the search, but we were always wrong!

Scott ultimately became convinced that we needed to further "crowdsource the mystery" in order to answer once and for all the question: Who was Xxenogenesis? On January 1, 2021, we issued a press release through Metanoia that listed everything that we thought we knew about Xxenogenesis and his life (some of it way off-base) and we encouraged people to contact us. A few weeks later, there was a WHRB Zoom reunion of former DJs and we decided that this would be a great place to spread the word and to let everyone know about the book project. We announced that we were back on the trail of Xxey's magical record – the very piece of vinyl that we had discovered at the radio station. During this return to our roots, "ghost" Seth Larkin Sanders (Professor of Religious Studies, UC Davis), told us that he was pretty sure that his occulturist friend David Tibet of Current 93 would be interested in Xxenogenesis's story, that David might have some good ideas about solving the mystery, and that he'd be happy to put us in touch. Sure enough, Seth was right on. And in email conversation about potentially reissuing the LP, David pressed us to investigate the LP's copyright status. Scott took the lead on this and found nothing. But the very next day Louis announced that he would check to see if either of the books had been properly copyrighted. "Thin chance of that," said Scott, but Louis searched anyway, through copyright records for all the years from 1976 to 1984 and found nothing once again! So, what were the odds that Xxenogenesis had copyrighted his second book, *Immortality Unveiled*, in 1985? And yet when Louis typed the words "Immortality Unveiled" into the U.S. Copyright Catalog search engine, the case cracked wide open – a case of Open Sesame! Or, as they used to say: that was all she wrote. After so many false trails and dead ends, the record read: "Copyright claimant: Herman J. Gabryel and Herman J. Gabryel, Jr." And at the bottom, "Gabryel, Herman J. 1926-." Shazam! For better and worse, the veil covering Xxenogenesis had been lifted. The timing was auspicious for such a momentous discovery – for such a resounding resurrection – because this was the morning of January 26, 2021, and thus, the fiftieth anniversary of the completion of the ten-day cosmic crucifixion (the holy days of January 16-26, 1971), when Xxenogenesis entered the realm of the Immortals.

The copyright application for the second book turned out to be the one existing document where Xxey failed to cover his tracks – the proverbial (record) needle in the haystack. And the path was crooked and perilous, filled with dead ends, traps, sinkholes, and rabbit-warren websites; it is hard to imagine anyone duplicating our inexplicably obsessed efforts to discover the creator of *SeXxenogenesis #1*. For instance, the creator of the websites never reveals that he made a record album, nor does he refer to himself as the "Xxenogenesis atom," making it extra hard to connect the dots. We salute discussion board participant Anonymous Coward # 65331861 who, on November 23, 2014, somehow became the third person in the world to discover that the author of the websites was also the creator of the LP![3] But in order for A. Coward to have made further progress, they would need to have carefully surveyed and read all of 144cubits.com and xxenogenesis.com (including the two books), and committed themselves to a process similar to ours, following every conceivable lead to the very limit of sanity. So why did Xxenogenesis leave behind a fatal clue? Given that the publication of *Immortality Unveiled* (unlike the first book) did not contain the name Xxenogenesis in the title nor list him as author, one presumes that the anonymity-seeking Herman J. Gabryel did not think that he was revealing anything at all by signing the copyright application with his own name. And because of this, the celestial goddess Fortuna had smiled upon us. We had explored the multifaceted Xxenogenesis mystery from many sides and angles (right and wrong, obtuse and oblique), and, after more than forty years of searching and seeking, the puzzle – this veritable Gabryel's cube or cubit – was solved.

Once we put his proper name into internet searches, we started to get lots of hits related to places like Buffalo, New York (the area where he was born and grew up) and Yelm, Washington (the area where he would spend the last decades of his life). There were still two mysteries that were bugging us – What and where was the Solar Center where Xxey studied in the mid-1960s with the charismatic channeler whom he code named "Talitha"? And what and where was the mystery school run by "the tyrant" where Xxey enrolled when he was already in his early sixties and where he talks about the channelled presence of the so-called "Jaquest entity"? Amid his topical research at the time, Louis was reading J. Gordon Melton's 2000 interview on "New Religions" with *Speak Magazine*. The following question to Melton floored him: "Talk about your recent book, *Finding Enlightenment: Ramtha's School of Ancient Wisdom*. How did you come to do an ethnography on JZ Knight, the Yelm Washington woman who channels Ramtha?"[4] He did a double take and cried out, "Wait a minute! This interviewer just connected Yelm, Washington to the Ramtha

---

[3] https://www.godlikeproductions.com/forum1/message913074/pg2
[4] https://www.cesnur.org/testi/melton_speak.htm

School of Enlightenment. This has to be the reason why Xxey moved to Yelm! I've cracked another code: the 'tyrant' is JZ Knight, and the Jaquest entity has to be Ramtha!" That week Scott reached out to David McCarthy and Joseph Szimhart of the Ramtha School resistance movement, and they rapidly were able to use their network of contacts from the school's early years to confirm this hunch. Yes! Mr. Gabryel had been at the school in the late 80s and early 90s when Knight was the most famous channeler in the U.S., serving as a medium for a number of Hollywood stars.

Meanwhile, we sent a registered letter to the last known address of Herman J. Gabryel and his son, hoping against hope that one or both of them still lived there. Herman Sr., Xxenogenesis, had passed on in 2016, and his son, Gabryel, was no longer at that address, but the new tenants were still in contact with him. Soon the phone rang, and Scott was having a preliminary chat with our chief informant. The evening of that first phone conversation, Scott asked one direct question, "What and where is the Solar Center?" Gabryel demurred: "I'd prefer not to answer because they still exist, and they are working out their own destiny." Scott tried one more time: "Is the Solar Center a town or an organization?" "It's an organization," said Gabryel. "Is it in western New York...Could it be Lily Dale, or the Rochester Theosophical Society?" No, said Gabryel firmly, "it's in southern Florida." Scott now had something concrete and tangible to research: the Solar Center was in southern Florida, and somehow still in existence! Over a hundred detailed internet searches later, Scott was slowly trudging through page after page of historic New Age channelling groups and UFO organizations at encyclopedia.com when he came upon the magic words, "Mark-Age MetaCenter," which was "incorporated in Miami in 1962," and much later moved to Tennessee. (Mark-Age was a relatively small UFO community but it played an outsized role in the movement through its many well-distributed, high-quality publications.) In a few minutes of frantic research, he was stunned by the obvious parallels between Xxenogenesis' writings and Mark-Age discourse, and he fired off a quick email to Phillel (Philip J. Jacobs), the current Co-executive Director of Mark-Age, Inc. On March 5, 2021, Phillel wrote: "To my recollection, I never met Herman, though of course I knew of him from our early literature and from various discussions with Yolanda [Pauline Sharpe aka Talitha!], Zan-Thu and others." This crucial confirmation was the last twist of the cube, the patterns now all falling into place.

Xx   Xx   Xx

And so, who was this man? Herman J. Gabryel's fascinating and surprising life as a modern mystical seeker spanned the American continent from his birth and upbringing in Little Polonia, in Buffalo, New York in 1926 to his death way out west in Washington in 2016, with time in between for soaking up some "soul-ar" rays in South Florida, where warmer climes nurtured higher consciousness. In this way, his life peregrinations took him from the city of light (Buffalo) to the magic city (Miami Beach) to the gateway to the stars (Yelm).

Herman was an ordinary extraordinary man who broke the mold of esoteric thinking. In his obsessive and transformative search for the Holy Grail of immortality, he became a New Age Don Quixote. That search started with Herman, abandoned by his father at age five, becoming an altar boy and attending one too many funerals, and finally vowing to God that he would devote himself to the conquest of death. A member of "the Greatest Generation," Herman flew missions over Germany in a B-17 during the last year of the war and pondered the problem that his patriotic service brought death from above. Time and again, Herman was stalked by death and by the powerful desire to overcome it.

Like Philip K. Dick, the contact with higher forces was something that he never sought, and indeed it interrupted, at a relatively young age, a very successful life as an innovative lumber businessman who became the first person in the nation to work with IBM in order to computerize both inventory and sales. Herman's cosmic intrusions came in multiple forms, including nocturnal automatic writing (which lasted all his life), visitations by a singing, celestial androgyne, and voices emanating from VHS videocassettes. These visions and messages even forced him to take an early retirement so that he could pursue his calling full time. The most astonishing intrusion came in January 1971 when he was forced to undergo what he calls a "cosmic crucifixion," an excruciating ten-day ordeal during which he was compelled to be reborn through the Xxenogenesis process. Throughout his life, he sought to understand everything he could about the cosmic symptoms, signals and messages that he was receiving, and he believed that the sacred and secret wisdom held by others might be the key to his self-understanding. He also often played the role of the teacher later in life, outrageously formulating his own cosmic musings in a truly unique fashion and sometimes breaking into the sound of music in the process. In this and other ways, Herman never forgot that the comic resides in the cosmic.

A self-taught metaphysician whose bookshelves grew and groaned over his many decades of intensive study, he never sought to make any money from others in the sphere of occulture. He gave away every single copy of his LP record, for example. He believed from the time he was a Corpus Christi altar boy that knowledge and enlightenment should be free. But he could not be bound by Christian doctrine and faith and his incomparable record album provides astonishing and original Biblical Xxegesis that cracks (up) the traditional codes. In consequence, he would deeply disappoint and scandalize his family by abandoning his Roman Catholic church in his 30s. Though a devoted family man, he turned sex magician at the age of 45 and thereby lost his place in his existing UFO seekership community. It was then that he became the loneliest psychonaut, an unwanted Messiah.

We knew we had discovered in Herman J. Gabryel a compelling figure to narrate an encompassing "history from below" for the postwar period of seekership. Xxenogenesis offered to the world a heretic theosophy and singular mysticism for the nuclear era. And his life's colorful twirls and turns could now serve as a barometer for the rise of the New Age from the dropping of the bomb to the emergence of the internet. Always, in each phase, Herman was following the pulse of the New Age from UFO contactee clubs to weeping angels, from cosmic channelers to immortal Lemurian warriors in a series of close encounters of an Aquarian kind. He was an advocate for alternative health, nutrition, medicine, and agriculture, including the baroque Radionics of Mark L. Gallert and Carey Reams' numerological theories of biological ionization. Herman founded an early and successful New Age business in the mid-70s in Fort Lauderdale – selling nutritional supplements and theosophically-minded books at his Space Odyssey Nutrition store. Ever the outsider artist and the marginal worker, he operated always on the fringes of this emergent and transforming New Age. Keeping under the radar, he made his almost-unnoticed contributions in several media – his unbelievable LP in 1973, his two books, *Immortality Through Xxenogenesis* and *Immortality Unveiled*, in the late 1970s to the mid-1980s, his public access cable television series in the 1990s, and his massive websites, built between 2000 to 2014, where an aged seer poured out his metaphysical musings and the contents of his dreams in hundreds of thousands of wild words until he literally went blind. Like a true medium, he could never stop the transmissions from coming and his effusive revelations were communicated on record, in books, and on websites. And throughout the journey, this relentless seeker was attuned to the crazy wisdom and the "ultra-high frequency vibrations" that led him to be reborn again in a new revelation. That revelation begins now or as Xxey both preached and practiced it, "and every present moment of now is the time to do it yourself." D-I-Y or die.

2. Self-RefleXxions: A Biographical Timeline in His Own Words

January 16, 1926. Herman Joseph Gabryel is born in Buffalo, New York to Polish immigrant parents, Bertha Osmola and Joseph Gabryel.

"My middle name is Joseph, which means: Revealer of secrets and interpreter of dreams."

"And being Polish American and since the word Polish is spelled the same way as polish, I have been using all the expressive Polish I can, to polish and illuminate the words into English, to such a magnitude that you will understand me."

https://web.archive.org/web/20140628173738/http://144cubits.com/arguments&quarrelling.htm

1931. Joseph Gabryel has difficulty finding work during the Great Depression and eventually abandons the family in order to search for a job elsewhere. Thus, Herman grows up in poverty with a single mother and five siblings (Florence, Sophie, Jean, Rita, and Charles) at 213 Playter Street in the Polonia neighborhood of Buffalo.

"I was born in this mortal 3rd dimension to experience everything you can imagine, like everyone else does. My father left my sick mother and 6 children when I was 5 years old. We were a very poor family. We were sleeping on a floor in below freezing temperatures with no heat. That was a hidden blessing in disguise, which I found later[;] why all this?"

https://web.archive.org/web/20100104145624/http://www.144cubits.com/xyzequations.htm

Figure 4. The home in which Herman J. Gabryel was raised
213 Playter Street, Buffalo

"My sister Florence 2 years younger had 2 Shirley Temple dolls. She probably still has them. When I went to movies, I loved to see Shirley Temple all the time."

https://web.archive.org/web/20161218040256/http://www.144cubits.com/entertainmentinfoworld.htm

1934. Herman lives just a few blocks from the Corpus Christi Church and their parochial school which he attended (located at 199 Clark Street). This Church becomes the center of community for this Roman Catholic family and Herman is an altar boy in the third grade. He serves at Masses (said and sung in Polish), weddings, and funerals.

"When I was an altar-boy in the Catholic Corpus Christi Church (Body of the Christ) we sang the mystical song, Panis Angelicus, although at that time I did not understand the full implication of the words. Now I do! And now you do!"

https://web.archive.org/web/20140629051931/http://144cubits.com/pointstoinsight.htm

Figure 5. Corpus Christi Church, Buffalo, NY

"In those days, it was customary for the priest and 2 altar boys to go to the home of the deceased. In those days, I saw hundreds and hundreds laying in the coffin dead. Upon seeing the dead person in the coffin, emotions would overpower me. Sometimes I had to, or tried to hide my cascading river of tears. So I cried for the dead person. Afterwards the priest or the other altar boy would ask. Is that your relative or friend? I said no. So why are you crying? I said because that person died. The words came back, why everyone has to die. So deep in my mind I said, I don't think so. So I made a promise to God that when I grow up I will find an answer why humanity is constantly dying. And when I do, I will give my answer to the world and it will be free, how to prevent death in the human beings. And a promise to God is a promise to keep."

https://web.archive.org/web/20100105041212/http://www.144cubits.com/dustinthewind.htm

April 1944. Herman drops out of high school in his junior year in order to join the military at the height of World War II. He serves in the Air Force as part of the famed 457th Bomb Group as a ball gunner on a B-17.

Figure 6. Herman's B-17 bomber, damaged by an act of sabotage

"During the World War II, I enlisted in the US Army Air Force. I flew on a B17 flying fortress bomber. As we were dropping bombs over Germany, I realized that these bombs are killing innocent people. So I prayed for the German people. There were missions that I thought I would never come home alive. But I did. So here I am going to tell you about the greatest untold story ever told. That is destiny... And that is War, killing the Spirit of God within – and/or another! It could have been us! But that is destiny!"

https://web.archive.org/web/20140628185804/http://144cubits.com/dustinthewind.htm

1945. Herman returns home from Europe after the Allied victory and received his honorable discharge at the rank of Staff Sergeant on February 12, 1946. He starts a lumber business that would experience astronomical growth over the course of the next two decades. He becomes known as "Cash-n-Carry Harry" in his advertising campaigns.

"After the war I started a millwork, lumber business with only $4,000.00. Then I borrowed $19,000.00 from my mom, sisters and brother. In a matter of few years I was doing a multi-million dollar business. How did I do that? I started a cash and carry world's first IBM computer shopping enterprise. In those days, we had to communicate with the IBM punched card system. The bar codes were not invented yet. I was doing so great in my business that now I was going to go public, meaning being listed on the Stock Market Exchange. I was going to build the IBM computer shopping center enterprise throughout the USA, just like Home Depot. Home Depot in year 2000 had over 1,100 stores, each one doing 30 to 100 million dollars in sales per year."

https://web.archive.org/web/20100105041212/http://www.144cubits.com/dustinthewind.htm

April 22, 1951. A story appears in the New York *Daily News* about a burglary occurring the day before at the Gabryel Lumber Company where the robbers stole a measly $10 from his safe. Herman dryly remarks: "They must have used every tool in our shop."

January 5, 1952. After his courtship with a local Polish-American woman by the name of Theresa Agnes Zerkowski (b. April 19, 1929), the couple marries at the Corpus Christi Church. Theresa had been working as a governess and teacher of young children in Buffalo, New York. Herman and Theresa are an attractive couple, and they enjoy both dancing and romancing.

"Incidentally, speaking of sex, in my life I had my pleasures of mortal sex with my wife Ujena [Theresa] to such a point that I didn't think there was a bottom to my orgasms. I was a prodigal son of God like everyone is. Consequently, when I discovered through my awakening into the higher consciousness, whom do you think I blamed for my ignorance? Do you need some help with my answer? I was the prodigal son, who engaged in the abusive, degenerative sex, not the church nor anyone else." (*Immortality Unveiled*)[5]

https://web.archive.org/web/20070102132151/http:/www.xxenogenesis.com/imunvpdf/imunv-1.pdf

---

[5] Full text for *Immortality Through Xxenogenesis* and *Immortality Unveiled* accessed and copied via the Wayback Machine in 2020, but the links beyond these two texts' opening pages no longer work as of mid-2023.

TREND SETTER
A "MERCHANDISER" EXCLUSIVE

Home of electronic consumer shopping is 50,000 sq. ft. building materials showroom and warehouse on a 7-acre tract, Buffalo, N.Y. Store occupies 20,000 square feet. Giant discount department store is across the street.

Figure 7. Gabryel Lumber in its heyday
(*Building Materials Merchandiser,* March 1964, p.75)

1959. Herman moves his growing business to a large empty lot in suburban Cheektowaga (2525 Walden Avenue) where he designs the buildings and also installs rail tracks from the local line into the property. It is also during this time that he moves the family (with their two young boys born in 1953 and 1956) to a cozy but mod ranch house Herman designs and builds in suburban Amherst (at 89 Hunters Lane).

"I had 7 acres of prime property on a 6 lane super highway to go with the sale, plenty of parking space, plus a new 50,000 square foot free span building, which I designed, was a general contractor of it, several hundred feet of new railroad siding to accommodate 14 railroad cars for unloading, which I installed and of course the IBM computer shopping business."

https://web.archive.org/web/20100105041212/http://www.144cubits.com/dustinthewind.htm

February 2, 1962. Herman has his first experience with automatic writing as well as a higher state of consciousness that he associates with a "cosmic enlightenment" as "universal light" passes through his body.

"Since February 2, 1962, Jason has been accessing the sacred knowledge from the universal mind of God as well as reading the Akashic Records." (*Immortality Unveiled*)

https://web.archive.org/web/20070102132151/http://www.xxenogenesis.com/imunvpdf/imunv-1.pdf

"Then a great phenomenon happened from February 2, 1962! The universal light energy went through my entire being! Emerging from this light, I experienced a cosmic enlightenment. I did not understand where the prophetic visions and knowledge was coming from. When that happened, I asked myself what is this all about? I was then 36 years old, and only an infant in this cosmic understanding. Once the universal light went through me, I had a lot to learn. Also, I asked myself, how can I serve 2 masters at the same time? One master was going to make me a very wealthy rich man and the other master was spiritual that would lead to the unknown, beyond this world. So I chose the 2nd master to follow the spiritual encounter, which brought me to the transcending greatest story ever untold, of how I became what I am to the present moment of now. Although not completed yet! More to come! When at first the great awakening enlightenment occurred in me and some of the mysteries of life and death were revealed to me, and when I came out of the visions, *I shook from fear like vibrating violin strings.* I said to myself, what is this all about? It took me few days to compose myself, until more encounters followed with the unknown. There is a lot, lot more to it, but that will be for some other time. After all I did come into this world as a mortal not knowing what this is all about. Now with this presentation, my objective is *to remove as much fear and doubting disbelief* as I can from all of you mankind, although Unlearning Shall Hurt! And when you are becoming one of the Christs, doubting is fatal!"

https://web.archive.org/web/20140628175438/http://144cubits.com/conflictbetweenallnations.htm

August 1962. Herman is visited by the entity that later in life he often refers to as a "celestial androgyne" and this encounter will have a profound impact on him for the rest of his life. [Editorial note: He refers to himself in his texts as Jason and to Theresa as Ujena.]

"In a vision of the night, Jason, observing from above, saw his lifeless body held in the arms and lap of his wife Ujena, while she was sitting. He was nude, except for a white sheet, which covered his loins. Darkness was upon the earth, except for these two who were engulfed in a slowly expanding ball of light. There were countless of people witnessing this event. Suddenly a beautiful celestial woman materialized behind them. She was standing very tall, perhaps twenty feet in height. The woman was clothed with the sun, and the moon was under her feet, and upon her head a crown of twelve stars. As the woman began speaking, Jason's lifeless body began vibrating, and a life giving essence was streaming into him. The woman said: 'Because you have searched for a purpose and a reason for everything in all existence, and you have not left one leaf or one stone unturned, I shall give you four words with which you will know what to do.' Within the few fleeting moments she spoke, his body already had regained sufficient energy to enable him to open his right eye very slightly and gaze upon Ujena and the woman with love and admiration. As the celestial woman began speaking the four words, he simultaneously spoke them with her because he knew them also. And the woman said: 'The four words are: "Equate Equilibrium High Frequency."' Then the woman sang a song for the people of the planet earth. As she was singing his body vibrated faster and faster, the heartbeat raced and he was filled with ecstasy. Upon hearing the words of the song his entire body was immersed in blissful happiness. Being overpowered with emotions, he cried with joy because he understood the meaning and the significance of what had transpired. At that moment the vision ended with him still crying. The bedroom was illuminated by a light emanating from Jason. An unusual hum, almost like that of electricity, issued from his vibrating body. Ujena was sitting on the bed with her back against a most uncomfortable bookcase; which normally she would not sit in such a discomforting position. In her arms, on her lap Jason lay nude with only a white sheet covering his loins. His pyjamas were lying on the bed. How did they get there? since prior to this event he was wearing them? Who placed Jason in that position!? Who laid out his body in that manner!? Where did the sound and light that filled the room come from!? This occurred about 2:00 AM! A few days later, while driving in my car, I heard over the radio, Jane Morgan sing the song I heard in my dream vision. Before that time I never heard the song. Here are the words to the song:

They Didn't Believe Me
And when I told them how wonderful you are, They didn't believe me. They didn't believe me! Your lips, your eyes, your curly hair, Are in a class beyond compare, You're the lovliest thing that one could see! And when I tell them, And I cert'nly am goin' to tell them, That I'm the girl whose boy one day you'll be. They'll never believe me. They'll never believe me. That from this great big world you've chosen me!

I called this: Pietà vision. It is only symbolical and my early stage of awakening to my mission in August 1962. As I was still a Catholic in those days, that is how it was shown to me so I would understand." (*Immortality Unveiled*)

https://web.archive.org/web/20070102132151/http://www.xxenogenesis.com/imunvpdf/imunv-1.pdf

September 1963. Herman has his "first encounter of the psychic world" when he meets the Buffalo clairvoyant Lucille Kirk at a party hosted at his home and she relates to Theresa and then to him important messages about his spiritual mission on earth.

"What this man knows and what was revealed to him, if he were to disclose these revelations to mankind, some people would faint, while others would die of fright right on the spot.' A sudden chill went right through Jason, goose pimples all over, hair stood up on his arms. His eyes piercing at Lucille. Ears and mind ready for more. Deep in his mind, he said: What!? This woman is reading my mind!" (*Immortality Unveiled*).

https://web.archive.org/web/20070102132151/http://www.xxenogenesis.com/imunvpdf/imunv-1.pdf

"In 1963 I did not know, what is a psychic. Lucille proceeded. Jason, you have just awakened to your soul mission. You are now like an infant. As you grow in the light and cosmic wisdom, the day will come when you will accomplish something great for the benefit of all mankind. When you will attain the goal and have done what you have come to do, then you will teach mankind how to accomplish the same. With this accomplishment, you will be very much in demand all over the world. You will travel the world and teach man. And in the years to come, there will not be a place on earth that you will not travel to and visit. Jason laughed, and said. Lucille, I have a business to attend to. I don't think I'll find the time to travel the world. Lucille laughed and said. All that will change in your life so immensely, that now you can't imagine. Furthermore, a time will come when you will have a most unusual means of conveyance."

https://web.archive.org/web/20140629030125/http://144cubits.com/tiltoftheaxis&japan.htm

March 1964. Herman appears on the cover of *Building Materials Merchandiser* (formerly *American Lumberman*), a prominent national trade journal, and Herman is profiled in a feature story under the heading, "Trend Setter." At a time when few had even seen a computer, Herman pioneers creation of the computerized invoice and innovates in the area of complex computer forecasting of inventory.

"We are fighting seconds, not minutes."

1965. Herman breaks with the Roman Catholic Church.

"I myself was a Catholic, in more ways than you can think of. I did many things so privately for the good of fellowman, that I didn't want anyone to know what I did. Also, since I was in business, my donations were very generous to the Catholic Church. They were so generous, that on several occasions I received an invitation to go to the IRS, to explain my generosity to the Catholic Church. I have no regrets for everything I did. So I supported and loved them, because that was my understanding of the truth at that time. Later when I gradually learned about my errors, I reversed my thinking to the point that I left the Catholic Church in 1965." (*Immortality Unveiled*)

https://web.archive.org/web/20070102132151/http://www.xxenogenesis.com/imunvpdf/imunv-1.pdf

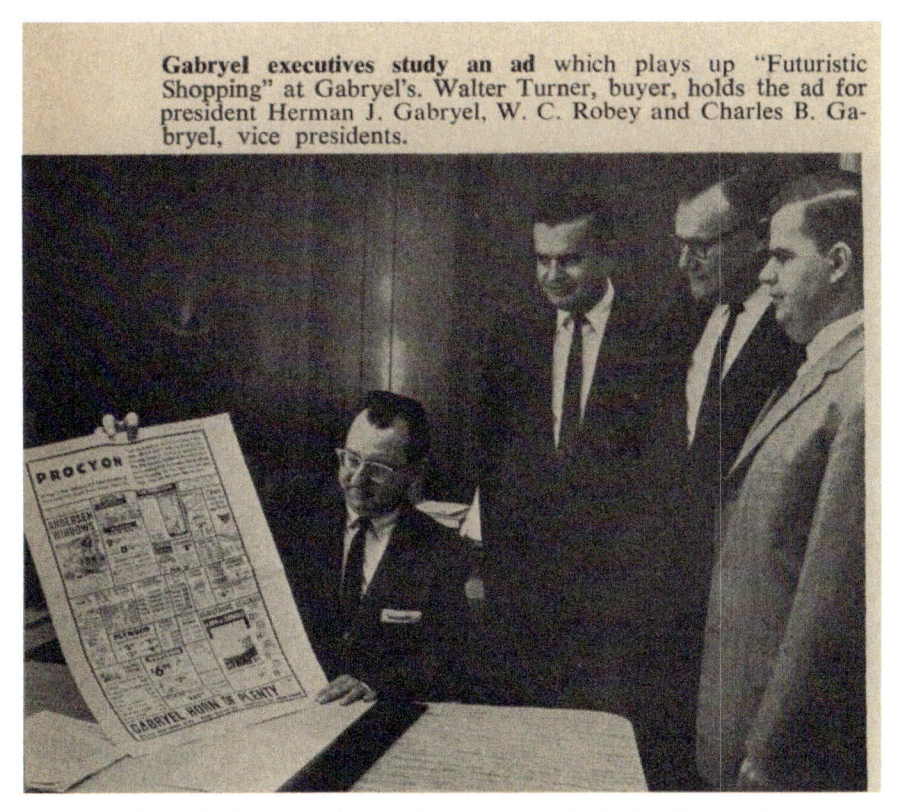

Figure 8. Herman approving his latest astrologically themed ad
From left to right: buyer Walter Turner, Herman J. Gabryel, vice presidents
W.C. Robey and Charles B. Gabryel (Herman's brother)
(*Building Materials Merchandiser,* March 1964, p. 80)

Figure 9. Herman standing under his IBM sign
(*Building Materials Merchandiser*, March 1964, p. 74)

March 1965. Herman takes a strange trip with a friend to attend one of the last lectures by the Polish American UFO contactee George Adamski in Rochester.

"In about 1965, I had a dream vision that a male elephant was making friendly gestures with his trunk towards my chest, my heart chakra, the sign of love. That day I knew that I was going to meet a highly evolved soul. That day, I received a phone call from one of my friends, if I would go with him to a nearby city of some 80 miles, to hear the lecture and meet this person, the highly evolved person who traveled in a flying saucer. The friend that took me there, knew the person who traveled in a flying saucer. That male elephant portrayed the highly evolved soul. So a new female person, a highly evolved soul is now coming into the picture. At this moment. I do not know who is this highly evolved soul. Will she come? Or is she on stand by to fill in the position? Or there are also many other potentials? We shall see how this shall progress? Furthermore, as to the travel to the nearby city of some 80 miles, here is what happened. While traveling in my car, we encountered a heavy blinding snow storm. Now traveling was almost at a stand still in the blinding snow storm. My friend asked me if I knew how the Christ was coming on earth this time. As I explained to him, at that moment a prolonged blue white light appeared, very brilliant, lighting up my pathway, so brilliant that you could see through the blinding snow storm. I speeded up my car to pick up some time and miles. My friend said, did you see what happened when you explained how the coming of the Christ is to occur? Needless to say, we arrived late at the George Adamsky's [sic] lecture on his travel in the flying saucer in outer space. It was so packed in the large conference room, that only standing room was available. We listened to the lecture and the comments that followed. Almost at the end . . . [a] commercial airline pilot and copilot made a comment. They were flying very high in altitude, above the storm clouds, when suddenly a very long in time blue white light appeared and the whole cosmic space was lighted up in this brilliant blue white light.

Mind you all storm clouds were well below their airline aircraft. The pilot and copilot said, they [had] never seen anything like that before."

https://web.archive.org/web/20100609113025/http://www.144cubits.com/interpreterofdreams.htm

May 1, 1965. After being informed by the Merritt sisters that they met someone in Miami who was channelling messages meant for him, Herman travels there and visits the Mark-Age MetaCenter (referred to as the "The Solar Center" in his writings). He meets the "psychic, prophet, channel, and Akashic reader" Nada-Yolanda (Pauline Sharpe) and the other staff members including co-founder Charles Boyd Gentzel (El Morya/Mark) and James Speed for the first time. He becomes a frequent visitor, and he maintains a close association with the organization over the next six and one-half years. [Editorial note: Herman always refers to Yolanda using the pseudonym Talitha in his writings.]

METACENTER #2
Mark-Age headquarters in Miami, Florida, 1961–80

Figure 10. The Mark-Age MetaCenter building
327 NE 20 Terrace, Miami

"It was revealed to me (Talitha), that you Jason, are a key scientist, with a scientific team represented in the cosmic universe. Before reincarnating here on earth, you trained this scientific group of yours, on how to bring about the method for the electromagnetic, divine nuclear energy power, as it operates in the physical body of man. This also relates to the transition of mankind and the planet earth from the 3rd dimension to the 4th Dimension. You then reincarnated here on earth in a physical mortal body just like everyone else does. The group of scientists that you trained will remain above and work with you, in such a manner as a sea diver descends to the depths of the ocean for exploration. Only in this case you descended to the depths of the mortal world to also train and teach the mortal man, as it relates to the electromagnetic energy operation in the physical body of mankind ... You will have a very active, busy scheduled life, as much as 35 to 40 years of very intensive, concentrated, unbroken activity." (*Immortality Unveiled*)

https://web.archive.org/web/20070102132151/http://www.xxenogenesis.com/imunvpdf/imunv-1.pdf

JIM, YOLANDA & MARK, 1961

Figure 11. The three directors of early Mark-Age: Wains (aka Jim Speed), Nada-Yolanda (aka Pauline Sharpe), and El Morya (aka Mark aka Charles Boyd Gentzel), 1961

August 22, 1965. Yolanda channels the "higher consciousness Christ self" entity San Cha who reveals important messages to her about Herman's divine mission including the transmission of the mystical sign of Xxenogenesis.

"In a universal sign language, San Cha revealed to me (Talitha) his sign, which will mean something to you. The symbol is: the first two fingers held upwards in a parallel position, with the thumb crossing over them, or two parallel lines with a diagonal one crossing over them. The significance of this was not given to me.' The sign that was described formed the symbol Jason used when he wrote out the word *XXenogenesis*. It is the symbol of the dual cross; one cross is right side up, the other is an upside down cross. In later years, it was revealed to Jason that this symbol represents the cosmic crucifixion, or criss+cross+ing of matter with antimatter, or criss+cross+ing the mortal with immortal existence." (*Immortality Unveiled*)

https://web.archive.org/web/20070102132151/http://www.xxenogenesis.com/imunvpdf/imunv-1.pdf

September 3, 1965. San Cha again communicates with Herman through Yolanda's channelling in a message titled, "I am the Christ Self Speaking."

"You (Jason) have risen high into complex purposes and have risen to realize your own self-aspect. Our prime purpose is to bring forth the highest energy frequency into earth plane manifestation. You must see this in a broad, and yet still as a single solitary challenge. Each individual, as I am in you, has a singular, unique, special purpose, part and participation in the grand whole complex of the Spiritual I am body of the Christ. Nothing more is expected, and nothing less is complete, than for you to give yourself the opportunity to fully express and to utilize that particular energy force and expression of consciousness which is in the I am self. Through the body, through the mind, and through the heart-soul dedication, we are endeavoring to express that Christ self-manifestation now on earth. Though you in the mortal level, expect to undertake control and command of your Christ self-expression, you have not yet experienced a high enough understanding of it to be the executor. Until the reversal from the mortal to the immortal has begun, you are in the position of receiving instruction and impression, instead of giving instructions. After you will have experienced the reversal of the mortal to immortal, you can impress upon the earth plane consciousness what has been received clearly and fully through the I am self. Through this, the contact will be established permanently on earth." (*Immortality Unveiled*)

https://web.archive.org/web/20070102132151/http://www.xxenogenesis.com/imunvpdf/imunv-1.pdf

May 3, 1966. Yolanda channels Sananda (the theosophical name given to the resurrected Jesus as an Ascended Master) who brings messages to Herman that he interprets as a prefiguration of his fourth dimensional transfiguration.

"The earthlings will feel the effects of this change in the physical system dramatically. They will even think that something negative, such as dark forces, have really conquered or overpowered the forces of light. But this is not so. The light forces are always in assistance with the progress of all men, and they will always be. Therefore, what mankind will sense or experience as something mysterious or difficult to comprehend at the time, it is not the power of anything harmful. Merely, it is the effect of the changes that are inevitable in the physical body. Lines of the electromagnetic forces or energy keep all things in perfect order and harmonious balance; cosmically speaking. When this particular order of the mortal 3rd dimension is to be changed, in order to raise the frequency or level of energy inflow, it must be phased in, in the manner that the electrical wires receive the incoming higher electromagnetic voltage power. At the point of impact or transfer, there is a displeasing feeling to the physical system (as if one is touched by live electrical high voltage wires). This impact and the jarring is very unpleasant, and one must be aware of what is taking place within the body, and inevitably must be strong in mind and acceptance, to keep the balance (his sanity, his equilibrium) and hold the higher rate of the frequency of the 4th Dimension until all is adjusted." (*Immortality Unveiled*)

https://web.archive.org/web/20070102132151/http://www.xxenogenesis.com/imunvpdf/imunv-1.pdf

January 16, 1967. After Herman experiences another vision, he decides to sell his business and to retire at the age of 41 in order to devote himself to spiritual pursuits on a full-time basis.

"In the vision of the night, Jason found himself in the presence of Celestial beings. He was conversing with them, and during the conversation, he came to the understanding that he should free himself from his gigantic XYZ business that he was involved in. Prior to this, he was contemplating, how is he going to do all the work that is required, and still operate his business? Many times before this, he came to the conclusion that he should sell his business and free himself, but he hesitated, because he couldn't find the courage to take the next step. So finally the go ahead that he needed came. In the vision he made up his mind that this time he is going to do it; sell his multi-million dollar business and forsake becoming a multi-millionaire, and most likely a billionaire, at the rate Jason was going." (*Immortality Unveiled*)

https://web.archive.org/web/20070102132151/http://www.xxenogenesis.com/imunvpdf/imunv-1.pdf

"I advertised my business for sale, in the *Wall Street Journal*, etc. Many business executives flew in to purchase my enterprise. They could very easily pay several million dollars for the business. I had 7 acres of prime property on a 6 lane super highway to go with the sale, plenty of parking space, plus a new 50,000 square foot free span building, which I designed, was a general contractor of it, several hundred feet of new railroad siding to accommodate 14 railroad cars for unloading, which I installed and of course the IBM computer shopping business.

One by one when the prospective buyers saw the operation they didn't have the courage, foresight and an opened mind to purchase the unusual IBM computer shopping operation. Some said that I created a monster, implying it was too much for anyone to control it. I had 35 people on the payroll also. I even offered to teach the prospective buyers everything about my operation for at least 6 months without any compensation to me. Still no one had the courage and foresight to purchase the greatest business. I even told them that this computer operation will change every facet of life on earth. And it did! Still no buyers!

Now I knew that I was running out of time to sell my operation, because I had more important work to do. So I decided to sell the property separately, dismantled my enterprise and sell it as a going out of business sale, which was pittance what I put into it. In those days I spent over $100,000.00 per year to advertise my operational business. In today's money that would equal to about 1 million dollars per year. Incidentally, I never went to college and I never worked for anyone or anyplace. That means I had no experience. Although the most unusual experience came from the God that was within me, which was superlative. The moral of the story of the above resume that you just read is, that is the kind of mind power was, and is in me now, only more aware, conscious and alive.

To continue with my adventure in life, and since I freed myself from serving the master, that was going to make me a very wealthy rich man, I began another adventure to the unknown. Just like the dust in the wind."

https://web.archive.org/web/20100105041212/http://www.144cubits.com/dustinthewind.htm

August 25, 1968. Herman receives an extensive and special "spiritual intunement" from Yolanda while sitting in group meditation which he interprets as foretelling his move to Miami and his future as a spiritual leader and author.

"There has been much preliminary preparation to get the soul (Jason) to the point or place where he is now contemplating moving to (with his wife Ujena and his two sons, where the Solar Center is located in the USA). This has not been by chance or happenstance. It was prepared. . . . This soul (Jason) will learn much of the transmuting principles during his temporary stay in the ??? [Miami] area, where he practiced this previously on Atlantis. The principles of the crystal and its transmutation, will at first be given in metaphysical terms, beyond the physical range of understanding and practice (which are the 2 books, *Immortality Through XXenogenesis* and *Immortality Unveiled*)." (*Immortality Unveiled*)

https://web.archive.org/web/20070102132151/http://www.xxenogenesis.com/imunvpdf/imunv-1.pdf

Spring 1969. Herman moves with his family into a new luxury rental apartment on the fourth floor of the Arlen House in North Miami Beach (300 Bayview Avenue). At about the same time, Albert Vrana erects a monumental bronze and freestanding sculpture known as "Obelisk" in the front of the building. The structure takes on symbolic significance for Herman and his spiritual quest over the next few years.

"This 60 foot high, 40 ton Obelisk signifies a superlative achievement in the world, that I accomplished in 1970-1971."

"In the ancient time as well as present, an Obelisk signifies a great achievement for a splendid event. In the world, a momentous event transpired in the middle part of January 1971. Little did the people, who decided to construct an Obelisk, realize what it was for? It is here in this residence, where I underwent the cosmic unification for 10 days. It was a feat of Hercules. The precarious Hercules feat was not to sever the union between the 2 enmity seeds that were united together in my physical-spiritual body through the ???? thermonuclear fusion."

https://web.archive.org/web/20041225230354/http://www.144cubits.com/refweepingangel.htm

Figure 12. "Obelisk" (1969) by Albert Vrana, outside Arlen House
North Miami Beach

October 5, 1970. On behalf of Mark-Age's new compendium, *Mark Age Period and Program (M.A.P.P.)*, Herman takes out an ad in the *Miami Herald*, adding his old lumber yard image of the angel Gabriel carrying the coals of enlightenment to the provocative tagline: "2nd Coming of Christ Consciousness."

The ad copy provides a snapshot of diverse metaphysical interests that are mixed together to concoct a veritable New Age stew. It begins: "Millennium—2000 A.D. . . . Second Coming . . . Fourth Dimension . . . Prophecies . . . ESP (Elementary Spiritual Powers) Reincarnation . . . Man and Woman . . . Jesus . . . Meditation . . . God & Man . . . Interdimensional Communication . . . Life After Death . . . Extraterrestrial Visitors . . . Evolution of Man . . . Mastership."

While living in the Arlen House in this same period, Herman also tries his hand at publishing when he starts *4th Dimension News*, stuffed with home-brewed articles and book reviews on New Age subjects such as the Weeping Angel prediction. He works with a local printer and carries the oversize, folded *News* to yoga centers and health food stores throughout the greater Miami area. While the newspaper ceases after a few issues, this media venture offers a prelude to the record album in terms of the broadcasting and circulation of Herman's ideas.

January 16, 1971. Herman's period of "cosmic crucifixion" begins on his forty-fifth birthday and it lasts for ten days. He believes that this pivotal experience of semen retention and ritual purification has transformed him into Xxenogenesis.

"When in my body the 2 enmity soul-ar and lunar germ seeds were undergoing the XXenogenesis thermonuclear fusion, it was like the refiner's fire that burns, torments intensely as it purified my entire biological chemistry. This commenced in the 4 months of Libra, Scorpio, Sagittarius in 1970 and Capricorn in 1971, plus what followed, the 10 day horrendous, excruciating tribulation, the cosmic unification or cosmic crucifixion. Do you know what is it like, to deprive yourself, hold back on an orgasm with your wife at the pinnacle of an orgasm; for 4 months?! And then followed by the horrifying, dreadful 10 days of no orgasm? That is Cosmic Crucifixion! During this endurance episode, the *defiling 1st original sin*, the enmity was removed from my atomic structure. I have endured the excruciating entire ordeal successfully from Libra time in 1970 to Capricorn time followed by the 10 day tribulation in 1971.

2nd COMING

'OF CHRIST CONSCIOUSNESS'

Millennium — 2000 A.D. ... Second Coming ... Fourth Dimension ... Prophecies ... ESP (Elementary Spiritual Powers) Reincarnation ... Man & Woman ... Jesus ... Meditation ... God & Man ... Interdimensional Communication ... Life After Death ... Extraterrestrial Visitors ... Evolution of Man ... Mastership

MARK-AGE PERIOD AND PROGRAM presents the basic information needed to understand the nature and the causes of, and the solutions to, our personal and world situations in this most climatic of all eras of Earth. An entirely new level of evolvement is about to manifest for Earth and all on it. Man quickly now must come to know and to express himself or herself as a spiritual being, a son of god, if he or she is to be allowed to participate in the new heaven and the new Earth.

The Mark-Age period is that forty year period, known also as the latter days, which since 1960 has been ushering in the New or Aquarian Age, the Golden Era. It is the transition period wherein man must cleanse himself and the Earth sufficiently to permit his entry into the fourth dimension, a new mental and physical dimension of spiritual life.

The Mark-Age program is a plan instituted by the Hierarchal Board, the spiritual governing body of the solar system, to help man of Earth rise into his spiritual consciousness. Begun 26,000 years ago, it will be completed successfully by 2000 A.D. But not known as yet is how many will make the graduation into this New Age.

Nada-Yolanda is the primary channel or prophetess of Mark-Age. Since 1956 she has been receiving interdimensional communications from masters of the Hierarchal Board pertaining to spiritual development and to the Mark Age or hierarchal plan and program. These have been published in periodical form by Mark-Age since 1960. This book contains excerpts from the highlights of several million words channeled from 1958 to 1970. **$10.00**

HOW TO DO ALL THINGS The main purpose of this book is to provide you with a guide to contact your inner Self so you may rise to that level of spiritual expression where you may achieve your God-given heritage and powers. **$5.00**

2nd COMING P.O. BOX 67
MIAMI, FLORIDA 33137

Figure 13. Herman's ad for Mark-Age in *Miami Herald*
(Oct. 5, 1970, page 1-E)

"The tormenting tribulation was, not to sever the union between the 2 atomic enmity seeds through an orgasm. That is a total of some 130 days! If I didn't conquer the atomic criss+cross+ing and fusion of matter and antimatter into my body, today I would not be here to tell you the greatest story ever told: XXenogenesis Unveiled! Neither would you have the coming of the Christ. Why? Because the cosmic window is now closed for this to transpire and it will not be opened in any one's life time. That is why there is no substitute to take my place. Presently the 4 months commencing from Libra, Scorpio, Sagittarius in 1970 and Capricorn in 1971, plus what followed, the 10 day horrendous tribulation, which I have endured, is no longer necessary for anyone to undergo. Why? Because now the transmission of the Christ lunar germ seed essence of immortality and love, which is permeated, impregnated with the consciousness of the Spirit of God is very easy, exciting, adventurous, loving, full of joy, very passionately sexy. I fused or united the Christ germ seed in my body through XXenogenesis thermonuclear fusion or tremendous heat; for some 3 1/2 hours. Each time bringing myself to the height of an orgasm, holding that position, until another encounter. This went on for some 3 1/2 hours. All those who followed and will follow, it is done through XXenogenesis cold fusion or in simpler words the Christ germ seed of love now needs to be only transmitted from one potential Christ to another, another; in a moment of transmission." (*Immortality Through Xxenogenesis*)

https://web.archive.org/web/20070102131436/http://www.xxenogenesis.com/imthxxpdf/imthxx-1.pdf

"A celestial convergence of Venus, Mars, Jupiter, Neptune, the Moon and the asteroid Vesta transpired in the region of the zodiac called Scorpius. This drawing shows the wanderers as they pass in a parade shortly before dawn of January 23, 1971. Please observe the orbital path of the moon. The moon represents the Christ lunar germ seed of immortality, passing fearlessly into the mouth of the scorpion, which possesses the ferocious, deadly sting of death. The astro sign of Scorpio governs the sexual functions in the physical-spiritual body of mankind. It was at this time that I went through the 10 days tribulation, which commenced on January 16th to the 26th, 1971."

https://web.archive.org/web/20050224161846/http://144cubits.com/weepingangel.htm

June 24, 1971. Herman's last major "soul intunement" with Yolanda is recorded in a document of nineteen pages. He interprets the channelling record as a validation of his "cosmic crucifixion."

"What is being given to me (Talitha) to understand is that the years of training, discipline, preparation and questioning have ended for you Jason. With what you just accomplished, you have closed that door behind you. Even if you wanted to go back, you can't. There is no way to go back. There is no way of opening that door ever. ... You are going through the exchange of polarity. This has a very definite effect on your body, and on your coming into your higher Christ consciousness." (*Immortality Unveiled*)

https://web.archive.org/web/20070102132151/http://www.xxenogenesis.com/imunvpdf/imunv-1.pdf

November 10, 1971. Herman receives another confirmation of his cosmic crucifixion and resurrection through Yolanda's channelling of Sananda.

"Sananda speaks through Talitha. 'Inform all key light workers that the hour is at hand. The time of my crucifixion is over. I have experienced the resurrection. I am the life, and the light of the world.' (This reference is not to the falsified crucifixion and resurrection of 2,000 years ago on a wooden cross, which the world already knows, but is in reference to the present one of January 1971)." (*Immortality Unveiled*)

https://web.archive.org/web/20070102132151/http://www.xxenogenesis.com/imunvpdf/imunv-1.pdf

January 1972. Herman ends his association with the Mark-Age MetaCenter when the revelations of Xxenogenesis and his cosmic crucifixion are not taken seriously. Jim Speed also withdraws from the organization around the same time and he remains Herman's close friend and business partner.

"Throughout the years of his association with the Solar Center, the staff members could never understand Jason, because his concepts differed from theirs, on how the Christ was to come on earth, and how man is to become one of the Christs.

He tried endlessly to have someone listen, but to no avail. In January 1972, Jason departed from the Solar Center with tremendous gratefulness and deep sadness. It took months and a lot of painful decisions to leave all the wonderful people at the Solar Center." (*Immortality Unveiled*)

https://web.archive.org/web/20070102132151/http://www.xxenogenesis.com/imunvpdf/imunv-1.pdf

"When I was with the leaders of the Solar Center, we differed greatly on many of these subjects. If I would have followed their advice and if I didn't do anything, sitting on my fanny, waiting for some fantasy or whatever to occur, which I am now relating, mankind would not have the coming of the Christ."

"And I have been rejected many, many times as an outcast, only fit for disposal in the garbage can. And I do not have a false Messiah Complex as I have heard from many people. Also I have been called more vicious names than that. Yes, rejected like garbage. Messiah Complex is a very mild name, although it is real! Messiah means, a messenger from God. I am that messenger. And I am not a false messenger."

https://web.archive.org/web/20100609113025/http://www.144cubits.com/interpreterofdreams.htm

May 31, 1973. Herman releases the spoken word recording, *SeXxenogenesis #1: I Am that I Am* (private press, four-color gatefold; interior sermon: black and gold on pink with gold flecking; hand-drawn LP labels; pink envelope for sending a message back to him).

1974-1988. Herman and his family move out of the Arlen House by the end of 1973 and move to Pompano Beach (573 Oaks Lane) for the next fifteen years.

1976. Herman opens up Space Odyssey Nutrition on a strip mall in Ft. Lauderdale (979 E. Commercial Blvd.). The store sells health food and also doubles as a New Age bookstore.

October 17, 1976. Theresa dies at the age of 47 in Broward County, Florida.

1978. Herman begins work on his first book *Immortality Through Xxenogenesis*. The dates of its publication remain unclear.

"Welcome to the ultra top secrets of the universe and the mystery of life and death! If you do not know what the words mean in the next few pages, then this sacred knowledge is for you." (*Immortality Through Xxenogenesis*)

https://web.archive.org/web/20070102131436/http://www.xxenogenesis.com/imthxxpdf/imthxx-1.pdf

May 9, 1980. Herman forms the corporation Omni Christi Inc. in partnership with James H. Speed. It is dissolved on November 4, 1988.

February 12, 1981. Herman forms the corporation Gabryel International Incorporated with his older son Herman Jr. (sometimes now known as Gabryel). After making a deal with Volkswagen, the corporation takes over the production and sale of Chiron crop sprayers in North America. The company is dissolved on August 26, 1994. The business brings him into contact with the alterative agriculturalist and ionization guru, Dr. Carey Reams.

1983. In the middle of this year, Herman returns to the Mark-Age Meta-Center for the first time in many years, but he remains unwelcome there.

"Jason went to the Solar Center with his sacred knowledge written in the first two books, but they did not have the time to listen or read what he prepared to give them." (*Immortality Unveiled*)

https://web.archive.org/web/20070102132151/http://www.xxenogenesis.com/imunvpdf/imunv-1.pdf

May 30, 1985. Herman publishes *Immortality Unveiled* with The World Ionization Institute. The book is copyrighted in the Library of Congress by Herman J. Gabryel (entire text) and Herman J. Gabryel, Jr. (new text, compilation, and revisions).

"Behold! I am coming speedily. Immortal will he be who will observe these words that are written in the two books: *Immortality Through XXenogenesis* and *Immortality Unveiled*, the teachings of this scroll, which has been deciphered from the ancient key of the sacred knowledge, the Tanakh, the

Holy Bible, and a precept here a precept there, a command here, a command there, a little bit here and a little bit there. Thus when assembled together shall give mankind the reason and purpose to reunite to the original divinity, into a light energy body." (*Immortality Unveiled*)

https://web.archive.org/web/20070102132151/http://www.xxenogenesis.com/imunvpdf/imunv-1.pdf

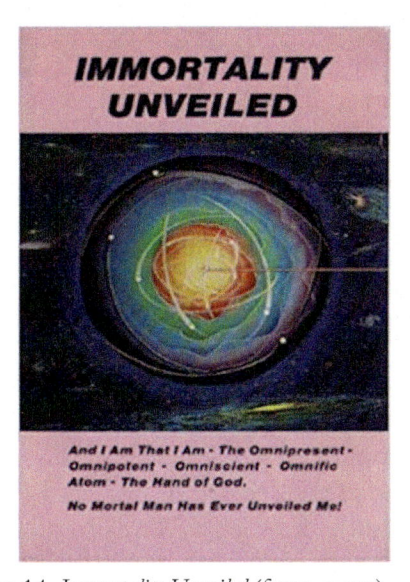

Figure 14. *Immortality Unveiled* (front cover)

May 31, 1986. Herman watches the VHS tape *Superconsciousness #1* wherein the controversial J.Z. Knight channels the spiritual teacher and Lemurian warrior Ramtha. He receives profound messages coming through from "higher beings" that prompt him to further investigate this entity and to announce himself. [Editorial note: Herman refers to Ramtha in the encrypted form of the "Jaquest entity" in his writings.]

"Since May 31, 1986, do you, the students of this Jaquest [Ramtha] entity know who is this individuals [sic], from this your country that close; the USA? Do you know? How come you don't know? Don't you think it is about time that you should know and find out who is this person? 'And he would be the last one individual that you would think would do it.' Do what? Why of course, become the 1st Christ in this Aquarian Age!"

https://web.archive.org/web/20100104145609/http://www.144cubits.com/pointstoinsight.htm

July 1988 - December 1991. Herman leaves South Florida and moves to Yelm, Washington along with his older son and a small group of friends in order to join the Ramtha School of Enlightenment. He soon becomes discontented with the increasingly expensive taped lectures and high fees for mandatory special events, as well as a policy that forbids students from sharing their purchased tapes with friends and loved ones. Herman calls these practices "the tyrant's extortion" and a generally "unwholesome business" that impedes the free flow of information. He also is concerned that the head of the school, J.Z. Knight, does not seem to recognize him as the first Christ of the Aquarian Age.

"I joined the school in July 1988 and I left the school in December 1991, which is about 3 ½ years. Why did I leave? Because I was wasting my time, meaning there was no one who was interested what I was revealing. In fact, we lost a lot of friends and not only that they hated us for what was involved in becoming one of the Christs."

"Consequently, the undertaking of the tyrant shall be to take away the credit from the 1st Christ. Why? Because he attended the tyrant's school from July 1988 to December 1991. The tyrant thinks that in only the few school hours he attended the school, he acquired the knowledge how to become the Christ. Little does the tyrant realize that in 1970-71 he commenced the process of becoming the 1st Christ. Also in the fall of 1988, the Jaquest entity delivered a message concerning the man who is to become the 1st Christ: 'Joy is coming from the alchemist knows. After 63 years of his work ...'"

"Please commit this to your computer mind. If you need to pay a lot of money to learn how to become one of the Christs, verily it is not truth."

"When I came to the school in July 1988 with the few individuals who were fused with the Christ germ seed of love, we were the only few who knew what the insight messages applied to. These were the only ones that knew. None of the students know till this day. And there are about 75,000 students that already quit the school for whatever the reasons.

Why? Because the answer is not in the school, how to become one of the Christs or the 1st Christ. And there are thousands new students that till this day do not know what all these words mean. Why?"

https://web.archive.org/web/20100104145609/http://www.144cubits.com/pointstoinsight.htm

1992-1994. Herman directs and produces eight programs for the community access station Thurston County Television (TCTV) in Olympia, Washington. He later transcribes all of this material into his unpublished third book, *XXenogenesis Unveiled* that features a photograph of a pineal gland on its cover.

"XXenogenesis Unveiled, book 3, is a transcript of 8 one[-]hour television programs."

"This is an actual photograph of the Pineal Gland, which is the throne of the creator, the source of the Spirit of God in every woman and man. From here each individual rules his Kingdom of God. For that is the seat of power, for the divine soul. The Pineal Gland is known as the Philosopher's Stone. It is here where the legendary Excalibur, the two[-] edge flaming sword of truth is embedded in the uncut stone, the Pineal Gland stone."

https://web.archive.org/web/20100107005859/http://xxenogenesis.com/xxenogenesis2.htm

1995-1998. Herman writes his unpublished fourth book (entitled either *Nostradamus – 2nd Coming of the Christ* or *XXenogenesis Christos Nostradamus*). The book is composed of his Xxenogenetic interpretations of Nostradamus's prophecies.

"In this book there are interpretations for over 100 quatrains and every word in the quatrains is used to bring out the full interpretation of Nostradamus's Prophecies. Please bear in mind that every prophecy can be changed by the mass consciousness of mankind. How? Because you are how you think. You are what you know. You are what you do not know. You are what you have been programmed with everything that is all around you, be it true knowledge, or false belief systems, the fantasia. You are all that. That is how powerful the mind is. Now the mass consciousness can bring on either disaster or peace and love on earth.

Furthermore, do not be impatient. You will have answers to all your questions."

https://web.archive.org/web/20040902225924/http://xxenogenesis.com/xxenogenesis2.htm

"My 4 books, are a present to all mankind, therefore they [are] Free. The books are already on the World Wide Web Internet." [Editorial note: Only the first two books were posted.]

2000-2001. Herman tries his hand at another new communications medium and he launches his first website www.xxenogenesis.com. The first Wayback Machine record of the website is dated March 31, 2001.

2004-2014. Herman launches his most intricate website www.144cubits.com to reveal the "Ultra Top Secret" or how to achieve immortality through Xxenogenesis nuclear fusion. He expands the site over the course of the next decade and it eventually consolidates his other two websites. The first Wayback Machine record of the website is dated June 4, 2004.

"Since February 2, 1962, 52+ years: I have devoted all these years of research to bring you a new scientific breakthrough, of how to restore your biological atomic structure and the RNA DNA, to your original state of perfection, the perfect presence. The intricate secret discovery is arousing, appealing, incredible, shocking and beyond compare. Up to now, what I am about to reveal through these ultra top secrets has been hidden from the eyes of the world. Here you shall learn that not only you need to add 1 cubit or 1 atomic element to your phenomenal, priceless body, but 144 cubits-elements, which will reinstate you to the perfect presence, to your original RNA DNA and perfect atomic structure. The RNA DNA in you is as old as no beginning nor end; older than the universe."

https://web.archive.org/web/20141018050256/http://www.144cubits.com/index.htm

2009. Herman tries out a new website www.unlearninghurts.com but it is only operational through that summer. The first Wayback Machine record of this website is date July 15, 2009.

"Please know that Unlearning Hurts very badly, because it is a tremendous hurt to the ego."

https://web.archive.org/web/20050227003811/http://144cubits.com/youconventionalists.htm

January 7, 2010-March 24, 2014. Herman records and interprets a series of vivid and memorable dreams with the creation of his new webpage

"Interpreter of Dreams." He works on the page until his eyesight fails him completely at the age of 88.

Final Dream Vision of 3/24/2014: "There are four parts to this dream. Part 1. There is a bulletin board and many people were viewing it. I was not able to get to it. I was told, it said a Cardinal was resigning. Part 2. There was a man moving fast, back and forth covered in 10-12 inch strips of medium blue raincoat material. He could not be recognized. He slid into the driver seat of a car. Part 3. The scene changed. The Pope was asking who can interpret this dream. A woman stood up and made a lotus sign with her hands and said this has nothing to do with sex. The Pope was not satisfied with the answer. I stood up and said: In the Old Testament, in Job, it states: Out of sex troubles he shall deliver you, and at the seventh, no evil shall touch you. You will not be satisfied with my answer. But 6 represents sex and 7 represents perfection. Six times seven is forty-two and four and two equals six, meaning sex. The Pope grinned with satisfaction at the answer. Part 4. The scene changed. There were 3 people in the car, the driver, the cardinal and myself. The Cardinal was in the front seat of the car and I was in the back seat. The Cardinal opened the front window and threw-out his beret hat and the skull cap. He said: 'There goes my deception and no more deceiving of mankind.' I thought to myself, this Cardinal really means business. There were many cars following us. Skull-cap means, a man of learning. The dream ended."

https://web.archive.org/web/20140629045654/http://144cubits.com/interpreterofdreams.htm

April 7, 2016. Herman J. Gabryel dies in Yelm, Washington at the age of 90.

"There never was a time that you were not in existence, and there will never be a time that you will ever cease to exist, for that is the immutable law of nuclear physics. Matter and energy can never be destroyed or put out of existence, and you are a composite of atoms in a constant nuclear evolution. Please never forget, atoms you are forever and ever and within every atom is the omnipresent Spirit of God. That is what the word omnipresent means."

https://web.archive.org/web/20041225230354/http:/www.144cubits.com/refweepingangel.htm

3. DiXxionary, From A to Xx

Contents

A is for Androgyne
A is for Atom
B is for Bible
C is for Carbon 666
C is for Cosmic Crucifixion
C is for Christos
D is for Death
E is for Equate Equilibrium
E is for Exegesis
E is for Experience
F is for the Fourth Dimension
G is for God
H is for Healing
I is for Immortality
J is for Jokes
K is for Kundalini
L is for Limitless Love
L is for Lunar Germ Seed
M is for Marriage
M is for Matter/Antimatter
N is for Nuclear Evolution
O is for 144
P is for Purity
Q is for Questions
R is for Religion
R is for RNA DNA (Nucleic Acids)

S is for Santa Claus
T is for Table of the Elements
U is for The Universe
U is for Unlearning
V is for Vibrations
W is for the Weeping Angel of Worthing
X as in Cross or Mark
Xx is for the Xxenogenetic Process

[**bold** = Xxenogenesis' original emphasis]

A is for Androgyne

G[ospel of] P[hillip] 116:22. When Eve was in Adam, there was no death; but when she was separated from him, death came into being. The words, when Eve was in Adam mean: When the counterpart of the androgynous, the woman was in Adam, which is the counterpart of a man, there was no death. But when the androgynes separated from oneself, then the androgyne became two beings, a woman and a man, and death came into the mortal beings. Why did the androgynes separate from each other? Because they refused to exchange, change and interchange the milk and honey manna with each other androgynes.

Once the androgynes ceased this process, they fell down into the 3rd dimension, the mortal world. When the fall of the once perfect androgynes that is now mankind occurred, the androgynes forgot how to return to their original state of perfect divinity. Consequently, here you are, a mortal being groping in the darkness, warring, fighting with each other and without the key to the ancient sacred knowledge of ????

https://web.archive.org/web/20040605164708/http://www.144cubits.com/lastsupper.htm

The fallen angels are male and female in one body, the Androgynes. Did you ever observe the features of archangels Michael, Gabriel, Raphael, Uriel, etc.? They are always portrayed with breasts. Accordingly what are they female or male? Here is your answer:

Genesis 3:15. I, the universal nuclear physics law **will cause an** atomic enmity, a nuclear separation **between** the androgynous of **you and the woman,** the 2 counterparts... I have seen the nude composure of an androgyne, woman and man in one body. The androgynes are extremely very beautiful, more beautiful than any person on earth. Originally all of you were that gorgeous, androgynes!

https://web.archive.org/web/20040605060910/http://www.144cubits.com/akashic12.htm

GP 103:23. Some say: Mary conceived of the Holy Spirit. They are in error. What they are saying, they do not know. When did a woman ever conceive of a woman? These words are saying, the mortal woman cannot conceive by herself, virginally the Christ germ seed essence with the woman, the mother nature, because of the atomic enmity, the separation from the oneself androgyne, the counterpart man.

Consequently, the Christ lunar germ seed is conceived first in a mortal man with a woman through ???? thermonuclear fusion. Then the Christ germ seed essence is transmitted from the 1st Christ to the woman, then from that woman to another man, and from that man to another woman, and on and on.

Originally all of you were created as the perfect Unison of God, an androgyne. An androgyne possesses the attributes of both male and female in one nuclear energy light body, the Christ. When the 1st original sin, the 1st original transgression, the separation, the enmity occurred in the androgynes, the counterpart of oneself, the woman aspect became another entity, a woman. When the perfect androgynes fell from their divinity, they decelerated their existence into the mortal world of 3rd dimension, thus became the living dead.

https://web.archive.org/web/20040605164708/http:/www.144cubits.com/lastsupper.htm

A is for Atom

All matter, macrocosm - microcosm is a composite of infinite energy, which is nature and is composed of the same substance, omnipresent atoms, be it star, stone, fire, water, sand, tree, air, light, magnetism, electricity, woman, man, it possesses same properties. On a pinhead of a needle there are millions of atoms. Therefore, atoms you are, trillions upon trillions! And the potential to harness these atoms in you is limitless, knowing no bounds!

Furthermore, there are perfect atoms that mankind is not aware of, waiting for you to harness within yourself! These perfect atoms have the capability to exchange, change and interchange the infinite energy, the omnipotent life force from one atom to another to another, etc. That is what perpetuates the incredible time, space, existence continuum in the constant, never-ending progressive nuclear evolution.

https://web.archive.org/web/20040609205901/http://www.144cubits.com/

The Mystery of the Holy Trinity: I, the omnipresent atom am composed of a dual father-mother nature trinity of protons, antiprotons, neutron, antineutron in the nucleus of the atom. And around the nucleus there are electrons and antielectrons whirling, coiling, scintillating, orbiting, vibrating at various frequencies in different electron inertia energy levels. Each atom has the capability to function with the 7 electron inertia energy levels. In the same image and likeness of the Spirit of God you were created from divine atoms. Therefore you are composed of trillions of atoms, the phenomenon of nature, the mystery of life and death.

There is a universal proverb about the omnipresent atom: Just because there is snow on the top of my roof, it doesn't mean there isn't a fire burning deep within me. In essence the proverb means: Just because it is colder on the outer perimeter, the covering, the outer egg shell of the atom, it doesn't mean there isn't a transmuting fire burning perpetually deep within the nuclear reactor of the nucleus.

https://web.archive.org/web/20040605052055/http:/www.144cubits.com/akashic11.htm

You Are A Magnificent Phenomenon and Infinite Energy!

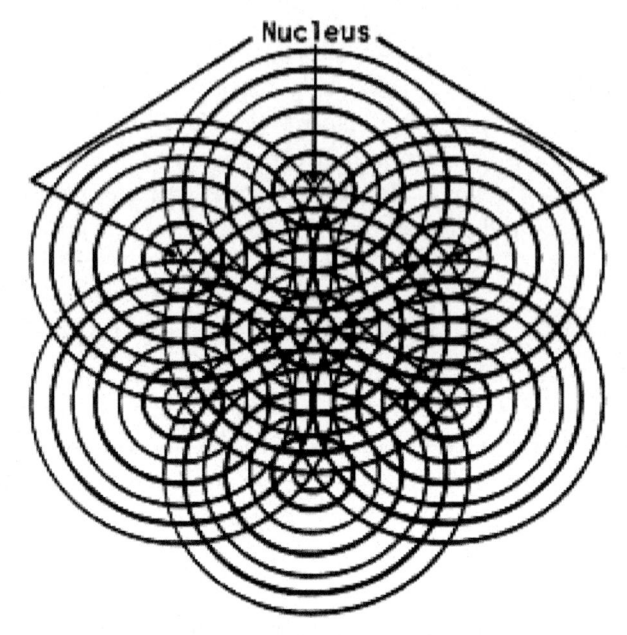

Figure 15. "The mystery of the perfect atoms"

The Mystery Of The Perfect Atoms: This cross sectional view is of 7 perfect atoms that have the 7-electron inertia energy levels filled with a full complement of electrons and antielectrons. The electrons and antielectrons that orbit in each of the 7 electron inertia energy levels have the capability of crisscrossing each atom. As a result, the electrons and antielectrons gain entrance to each of the adjoining nuclei for exchanging, changing and interchanging the atomic essence, the milk and honey manna between each atom. That is what perpetuates the never-ending Time Existence continuum in the progressive nuclear evolution.

That is how your atomic structure was formed when you were created perfect from no beginning nor end. You were created with an infinite nuclear energy light body, whereby you were able to exchange, change and interchange with one another the atomic nuclear energy, the milk and honey manna, the immune hormone substance from cosmic death, thus maintain your divine perfection; immortality.

https://web.archive.org/web/20040605060910/http://www.144cubits.com/akashic12.htm

The obstacle to divine perfection, the union with the divinity is death and the ultimate cause of death is the atomic enmity. No man can die on the cross for you and remove the 1st original sin. The nuclear physics law states, you need to be your own redeemer, the savior from death. Becoming one of the Christs is not a spectator sport. Please come, become one of the Christs! Thank you!

https://web.archive.org/web/20040605052055/http://www.144cubits.com/akashic11.htm

Thus Spirit means to whirl, twist, spiral, coil like the cosmic hissing electrons-antielectrons, the symbolic serpents, which encompass the spiritual atom. And the faster is the speed of the spiraling electrons and antielectrons around the nucleus, the nuclear reactor of the atom, the greater is the life force, the animation, vibration and the higher is the frequency the atom will possess. And the electrons and antielectrons do hiss like the ancient serpents when they whiz.

In the ancient times the cosmic hissing serpent was and is always portrayed as the creator Spirit of God wrapped around the cosmic egg, the etheric seed, the creator source. The cosmic egg is the omniscient, omnipotent, omnipresent atom, which is the tree of life. Why a serpent? Because the serpent can twist and coil every which way and enter everyplace without any encumbrances, burdens or impediments. That is how the electrons and antielectrons function, they twist, whirl every which way.

https://web.archive.org/web/20100316125654/http://www.144cubits.com/conflictbetweenallnations.htm

Determining Factors Of Life Force: The greater is the speed of the electrons and antielectrons around the nucleus of the atom, the greater is the life force of the atom. The essence and speed of the electrons determines how much energy do you possess for your ongoing existence, when you are either a mortal or deathless, immortal.

When the electrons, the cosmic hissing serpents, the beasts commence electron degeneracy, it is only a matter of time until they fall onto the surface of the nucleus of the atom. Consequently, the dual electrons are then coiling very slowly on the surface of the nucleus, at only a fraction of their original speed, literally on their belly eating carbon dust. And then the eventual death of an atom occurs, also that is how the atoms undergo death in your mortal physical body; for that is the immutable law of nuclear physics. Whereas, if your atomic structure is composed of perfect atoms, then the atoms are capable of exchanging, changing and interchanging the nuclear energy milk and honey manna eternally with one another.

https://web.archive.org/web/20040605060910/http://www.144cubits.com/akashic12.htm

B is for Bible

And where does humanity receive the false knowledge about God and Man? From the imperfect, mutilated Bibles, from world religions, from preachers who teach the Bible, from yourself. Some say that there are over 500 English versions of the Bibles, including the very old, rare Bibles that are still in existence. If you know the history of the Bible, you will find that the original truth in the Bible has been so badly mutilated that now mankind cannot distinguish what is true or what is false. Of what good is an imperfect Bible <u>and</u> only the literal wording is understood? The Bible is to be deciphered first with the immutable laws of nuclear physics, in order to receive the true key to the sacred knowledge. And that is what you have now in front of you, the key to the sacred knowledge, exposing the truth.

https://web.archive.org/web/20100104145609/http://www.144cubits.com/pointstoinsight.htm

In bringing forth the presentation of Immortality Through XXenogenesis, the Greatest Story Ever Told, many different Bibles were used. Some renditions were very old. Also the Akashic Bible was used and the access to the Universal Mind. (*Immortality Through Xxenogenesis*)

https://web.archive.org/web/20070102131436/http://www.xxenogenesis.com/imthxxpdf/imthxx-1.pdf

The following 5 accounts are from 5 different Bibles. How come there is such a difference between each Bible? Not only because of the differences, but the Bible is very heavily coded and veiled with concealed truth. The very old Bibles never had the words of "Jesus Christ" in them; only Christos. (*Immortality Unveiled*)

https://web.archive.org/web/20070102132151/http://www.xxenogenesis.com/imunvpdf/imunv-1.pdf

All the portraits, pictures or statues of Jesus of Nazareth are but the copies of basso-relievos of Apollonius, and when you open your modern Bibles and see the pictures of your Jesus, you are looking upon the face of Apollonius of Tyana. No pope nor Catholic king, no noble nor scholar, that is well informed can truthfully deny what I here assert. The time has come when the world is ripe for the truth. The time is approaching when popes, emperors and kings must go down before the universal rights of humanity.

https://web.archive.org/web/20050205015035/http://144cubits.com/exposure10.htm

Among the Arabian and Persian astronomers, the three stars forming the sword belt of Orion were called the three Magi who came to pay homage to the young Sun God. Also, in the sign of Cancer, which had risen to the meridian at midnight is the constellation of the Stable and of the Ass. In the north stars of the Bear are seen and called by the Arabians, Martha and Mary, also the coffin of Lazarus. The secret mysteries of the Bible were written according to the Stars of Heaven. Thus, the esotericism of pagandom was embodied in Christianity, although its keys are lost.

The Christian Church blindly follows ancient customs, and when asked for a reason, gives superficial and unsatisfactory explanations, either forgetting or ignoring the indisputable fact that each religion is based upon the secret knowledge of its predecessor.

https://web.archive.org/web/20050205051704/http://144cubits.com/exposure3.htm

The following words in the Bible, the Ephesians and all other books of the Bible, were mutilated and omitted so you would not know what these words are revealing. That is how you have been manipulated, brain washed, under control and not knowing the words in the sacred knowledge. And that is how all world religions extracted your financial support of such nonsensical money business. Since the hierarchy of the Catholic church did not know how to accomplish the redemption from death, through the promised redeemer Christ lunar germ seed, etc., why should you?

https://web.archive.org/web/20100104145621/http://www.144cubits.com/truechristmas.htm

C is for Carbon 666

A carbon 666 atom consists of, 6 protons, 6 neutrons, 6 electrons. Everything in the mortal 3rd dimension is made-up of basic carbon 666 atoms. The number 666 is not the devil. It is not the antichrist, but signifies the mortal carbon 666 atomic composition of gross, solid matter, that is subjected to decomposition, disintegration, decay of carbon 666 atoms to cosmic dust or subatomic particles. The word devil when spelled in reverse is lived, designating the past tense of being alive; dead.

https://web.archive.org/web/20040605151910/http://www.144cubits.com/akashic6.htm

Apocalypse 13:18. Here is wisdom: He who has understanding, the knowledge of the divinity of an atom, **let him decipher the code number of the beast, for it is the same number as of man; and his number is 666.** The word beast is relevant to the ferocious uncontrolled power of the cosmic carbon 666 atom. When a carbon 666 atom deviates from its process of nuclear evolution, the awesome omnipotent power of the atom is so uncontrollable, that in due time the atom devours and grinds itself into an infinitesimal dust.

For from dust thou came unto dust of carbon 666 atoms thou shall return. Because man is comprised of carbon 666 atoms, he is always subjected to being consumed by the cosmic hissing serpents, the beasts; consequently subject to the subatomic transitional death.

https://web.archive.org/web/20040605060910/http://www.144cubits.com/akashic12.htm

Revelation 13:18. Here is wisdom: He who has understanding of how the atoms function in the body of mankind, **let him decipher the code number of the beast**, the omnipotent power of nuclear energy, which behaves that way in your mortal body, viciously, haphazardly, uncontrolled like a wild beast when not harnessed and brought under control, **for it is the same number as of man, and that number is 666.** Take one drop of water it is harmless alone, but when many drops of water are united in a fury of a hurricane, it unleashes its power of destruction, like a beast.

https://web.archive.org/web/20100316125654/http://www.144cubits.com/conflictbetweenallnations.htm

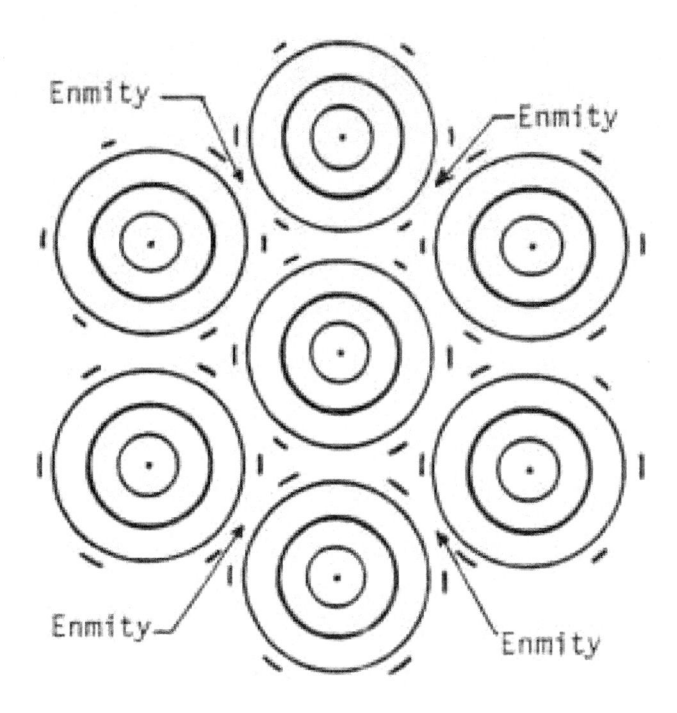

Figure 16. "The mystery of the carbon 666 atoms"

The Mystery Of The Carbon 666 Atoms: This cross sectional view is of 7 carbon atoms that have an electromagnetic repulsion or an enmity between each atom. The 3 rings that are around the nucleus of the atom are known as the electron inertia energy levels. Within these electron inertia energy levels the electrons and antielectrons whirl and coil around the nucleus of an atom. In the 3rd dimension, the mortal world, everything is composed of basic carbon atoms. Presently, that is the way the carbon atoms are structured in the mortal physical body of mankind. But there is a way to restructure the carbon atoms to the perfect atoms.

The word enmity means: a separation, a division, severing, mutation, defusion, disunion, an electromagnetic repulsion, expulsion from the higher realm of imperishable, immortal existence. Within these atoms, the atomic enmity is caused by an electromagnetic repulsion, the separation between each of the carbon 666 atoms. A carbon atom consists of 6 protons, 6 neutrons and 6 electrons, the very much-misunderstood number 666. In the 4th dimension, everything is composed of perfect atoms and that is the inescapable destiny for all mankind.

Then It Happened! You lost your divinity! How? You refused to exchange, change and interchange the infinite nuclear energy milk and honey manna with one another. Consequently, you decelerated your perfect immortal existence into the mortal world of 3rd dimension.

When originally you were perfect and immortal, your existence was in the 4th Dimension and beyond, at which time you had the 1st, 2nd, 3rd, 4th, 5th, 6th, and 7th electron inertia energy levels filled with the full complement of 144 electrons and 144 antielectrons within your atomic structure. For every electron and antielectron there are corresponding protons, antiprotons, neutrons and antineutrons and these also correspond to the 144 atomic elements in the omnipresent atoms, waiting for you to harness the phenomenal infinite energy, thus reinstate your original perfect nuclear energy light body of the Christos, the Christ.

When you fell from your cosmic perfection, the electrons in your immortal light body decelerated to below the speed of light of 186,282 miles per second, and the 7th thru 4th electron inertia energy levels were stripped of their dual electrons. This caused an atomic enmity between one carbon 666 atom and another carbon 666 atom.

Before the repulsive enmity between the atoms can be overcome, the atoms of which the cells of man's body are composed of, the atoms must restore their electrons to the 4th thru 7th electron inertia energy levels.

https://web.archive.org/web/20040605060910/http://www.144cubits.com/akashic12.htm

C is for Christos

The Sanskrit word **Christos** came from the ancient Indic language of Hinduism and the Vedas; when translated is: Christ. The Christ is not a man. It is a title, a degree such as a president. Therefore the proper usage of the term Christ is: Christ Apollonius or Apollonius the Christ, not Apollonius Christ. This should shed some light on how much the history of the word Christ is known. The world uses the word Christ incorrectly, because it does not know what is the Christ.

The Sanskrit word Christos means: Crystal clear, pure, immaculate energy; crystal clear pure nuclear energy light body. The inference to the crystal clear pure energy is to the nuclear energy that is within the divinity of the omnipresent atoms. Within the nucleus of every atom, there is a wondrous brilliant liquid light, the non-consumable liquid fire, more illuminating than a thousand suns. That is the kind of power that lies unharnessed within the divinity of the atoms, the crystal clear nuclear energy, the Christos, the Christ, the precious milk and honey manna, the miraculous ingredients of the Milky Way, the food of the gods.

https://web.archive.org/web/20040605071625/http://www.144cubits.com/akashic2.htm

The Christ is not a man. It is the psychophysical Christ lunar germ seed, the promised redeemer from death.

https://web.archive.org/web/20100104145621/http://www.144cubits.com/truechristmas.htm

The enigma: **I have united myself** to the divinity of the atoms of which I am composed of, to become the Christos. How? By **assembling myself together from the four quarters of the universe.** Meaning: I have fused to myself the 4 psychophysical Christ lunar germ seeds of immortality when they were present in 1970 in the signs of Libra, Scorpio, Sagittarius and Capricorn in 1971, prior to my 10 day cosmic crucifixion in mid January. These 4 Christ lunar germ seeds of immortality represent the 4 components of the universe, which are the 4-astro signs of the zodiac, the 4 elemental kingdoms of air, water, fire and earth, and furthermore, the requirement was in **joining together the twelve members that were scattered abroad.** Implying: The diversity of the 12 RNA DNA essences that are amongst the 12 Tribes of Israel, who are humanity born under the influence of the 12 astrological signs of the zodiac, was necessary to unite to my biological mortal body, to bring about the coming of the Christ.

https://web.archive.org/web/20041225230354/http://www.144cubits.com/refweepingangel.htm

Matthew 5:48. You, all of you when you shall become one of the Christs are to be **constantly exalted and perfected even as your heavenly father is constantly exalted and perfected** through the inevitable, progressive Nuclear Evolution, by which the nuclear energy, the food of the gods, the milk and honey manna is constantly exchanged, changed and interchanged among the angels of God, the sons of God and the sons of resurrection. That is what perpetuates the immortal time, space, existence continuum, from no beginning nor end. **You are invited to become one of the Christs.**

Within the meaning of the word Christos or Christ is the hidden secret of Sun Worshippers. It is not that you worship the sun, but that your atomic structure of your body becomes the same atomic essence as the nuclear energy of the sun. Thus is the meaning of the Sun of God or the begotten from the Sun, the Son of God. And each of you are a Son of God, because you were created from the Spirit of God essence, after his image and likeness; like the omnipotent, omnipresent atoms, like the atomic energy in the nuclear sun.

https://web.archive.org/web/20040605071625/http://www.144cubits.com/akashic2.htm

C is for Cosmic Crucifixion

The movement of the 144 atomic elements, brings on the transmission to each of the adjoining nuclei of the atoms for the process of exchanging, changing, interchanging the nuclear energy milk and honey manna. When that happens, now the atomic structure is in the 4th dimension, immortal, never to die. All this happens at the speed of light. When that transpires the atoms are reunited to the light energy of the creator Spirit of God, which is the good substance, sustenance of the Milky Way milk and honey manna, the plasma, the ambrosia food of the gods. That is the Holy Grail of the mystery of life and death. For the Father and I are the same essence as of the nuclear energy of the sun and all suns, the crystal clear nuclear light energy. No man has ever unveiled me!

That is what is known as cosmic crucifixion. No one can be crucified on a wooden cross and die for all the unforgivable 1st original sins of mankind, which still causes the carbon 666 deaths in all mankind. Believing in that fantasy is preposterous, contrary to nature and common reasoning!

https://web.archive.org/web/20100104145548/http://www.144cubits.com/crucifixion.htm

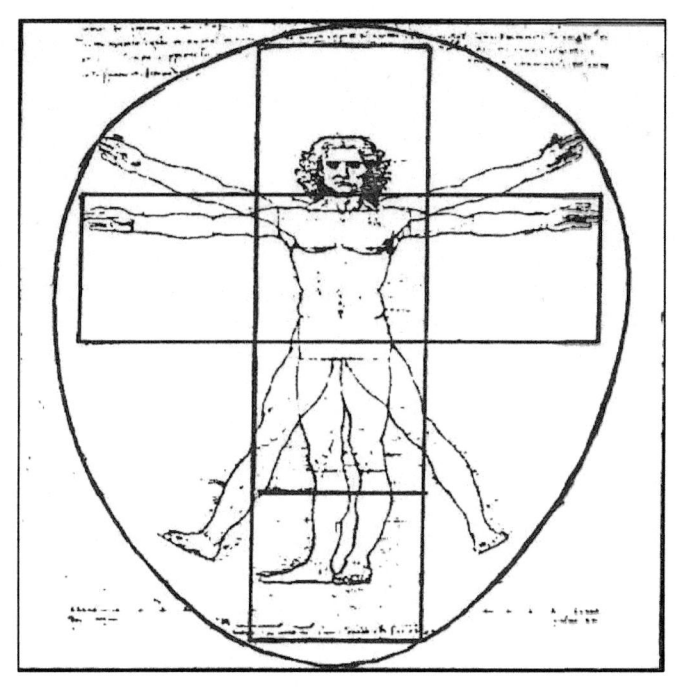

Figure 17. "I am the very much misunderstood crucifixion of man"

Now in your mind fold the 6 equally divided squares, until this forms the .... mystical cube, the cubit, the metaphoric city of 4 square, the 4th dimension. And one cubit is one atomic element. But the Bible in Luke 12:25 and Revelation or Apocalypse 21:17 states, in order to reunite yourself to the original source creator Spirit of God, you need all of the 144 atomic elements, the mystical 144 cubits in your measure. That is what each individual needs to do, assemble the 144 cubit and add to his measure, in order to become one of the Christs.

The above image is from Leonardo da Vinci's painting. A man standing with outstretched arms. The egg and the cross, divided into 6 equal squares in the cross were inserted by this writer. Now the enigma. The man represents mankind composed of carbon 666 atoms, who consumes the sexual forbidden fruit of the vine, till death do him part. The egg represents the cosmic egg, the atom, which everything is created from the cosmic eggs, the atoms, including you. The cross with 6 equally divided squares represents the crucifixion or criss+cross+ing matter with antimatter. Or criss+cross+ing and uniting the mortal soul-ar seed with the psychophysical Christ lunar germ seed of immortality, the promised redeemer from death. This takes place in the mortal man who self-elects himself to become the Christ.

And the 2 other crosses in the word criss+cross+ing represents the equating your equilibrium, your understanding the ultimate truth in the unknown sacred knowledge. And before you can attain such understanding, the truth needs to be decoded first, so as to understand what is evil and what is good for you, through the within Spirit of God, which is: Let it be thy will Spirit of God not my will. And know this, the real truth always needs to be criss+cross+ed or crucified between evil and good.

The crucifixion of the Christ and the 2 thieves side by side on the 3 crosses are only a mystical concealment, an analogy for you to decipher and decode the meaning. For you have ears to hear but you do not hear the voice of God speaking to you: Let it be my free will and return to the original Spirit of God not your mortal will, which eventually leads you to death. You think you have a free will to do whatever you please. It isn't so. You have eyes to see but you do not see, that the sacred knowledge of truth is always deliberated, differentiated between the 2 thieves of good and evil.

The 2 thieves on the crosses are the good and evil thieves that rob you of understanding what is good and what is evil. The word evil when spelled in reverse is live, meaning to live a mortal life the way you have been without a change, and then experience the ceaseless torture of mortal life, the travails and a bout with the transitional carbon 666 death. Furthermore, the 2 thieves represent, that in order to understand what are the immutable laws of nuclear physics, mankind needs to search and find what is good and evil in the eyes of the Spirit of God.

For example. What is the sexual forbidden fruit of the vine that humanity till this moment consumes the forbidden fruit till death do you part? To find the good and evil answer, the answer needs to be criss+cross+ed, crucified, deliberated, differentiated between the 2 good and evil thieves that rob you of the understanding. But with mortal knowledge that is impossible to know, but with God everything is possible, even knowing how to prevent consuming the forbidden fruit of the vine from your tree of life, till death do you part.

https://web.archive.org/web/20100104145548/http:/www.144cubits.com/crucifixion.htm

D is for Death

The universe and the bible are written in the language of the immutable nuclear physics laws. Without the passé-par-tout, the master Key, it is humanly impossible to interpret, understand and teach the Sacred Knowledge, the mystery of life and death. Consequently, without the insight to the Universal Mind and the Akashic Records, you are wandering in a dark limbo, ensnared in the travails of a mortal and death.

[T]he obstacle to divine perfection is death and the ultimate cause of death is the atomic enmity. No man can die on the cross for you and remove your 1st original sin. Therefore each person needs to be his own savior, the redeemer from death, to reinstate your originality.

https://web.archive.org/web/20070102131436/http://www.xxenogenesis.com/imthxxpdf/imthxx-1.pdf

Living Dead: When you the perfect androgynes fell from your divinity, you decelerated your existence into the mortal world of 3rd dimension, thus became the living dead. Why the living dead? Because when you were a divine being, and the 1st nuclear transgression, the <u>1st original sin defilement</u> occurred, the 1st death came to be. Within the 1st death, 67% of the perfection to be 100% alive slipped away from your presence.

Consequently, mankind is now 33% or less alive, and as you are now abusing and aging your body, you are decreasing the percentage, because you are progressively dying; some faster, some slower. The 2nd death is when you exile the Spirit of God, your soul from yourself, and relinquish your present mortal body unto death. That is the blasphemy against the spirit of God. That is the unforgivable *1st original sin defilement!*...

Revelation-Apocalypse 2:7. He who has an ear, let him hear what the Spirit of God says: To him who overcomes the atomic enmity the first death and <u>1st original sin</u>, **I will permit**, enable, give him the means **to eat from the tree of life.** And each of you is a tree of life. **17. To him who conquers** the first death, I, the Spirit of God that is within mankind **will give to eat the hidden milk and honey manna.** Within every woman and man lies the latent, dormant milk and honey manna, the Holy Grail.

https://web.archive.org/web/20140629010129/http://144cubits.com/whyareyouhere.htm

E is for Equate Equilibrium

Thus man will need to equate his equilibrium, his existence, to the same corresponding ultra high frequency of the 4th Dimension. (*Immortality Through Xxenogenesis*)

https://web.archive.org/web/20070102131436/http://www.xxenogenesis.com/imthxxpdf/imthxx-1.pdf

E is for Exegesis

The universe and the bible are written in the language of the immutable nuclear physics laws.

https://web.archive.org/web/20040820164523/http://www.144cubits.com/144cubits1.htm

The Bible is the book of Nuclear Physics. Why? Because it is about the indivisible, invincible, omnipresent, omnipotent divine atoms, who and which is father-mother nature, the milk and honey manna, the food of the immortal Gods, the I am that I am the Spirit of God. And each of you are created from trillions of atoms in the same image and same likeness as the I am that I am the Spirit of God.

https://web.archive.org/web/20040605052055/http://www.144cubits.com/akashic11.htm

There was a time when man believed that the world is flat, then it was proven that the world is round. Not only the world is round, but it is also crooked, dishonest, fraudulent, full of unscrupulous nonsense concerning the purpose of why you are here on earth. The Secret! Awesome! Very much unknown sacred knowledge of the mystery of life and death is concealed in the Bible, through metaphors, allegories, parables, analogies, enigmas, so man would not destroy himself, until he came to the realization of what awesome, omnipotent power lies within the divinity of the atoms and the RNA DNA; of which man is created from.

https://web.archive.org/web/20040605063612/http://www.144cubits.com/akashic13.htm

The Bible is a book or treatise written in concealed, coded allegories, enigmas, cryptograms, myths, riddles, fables, symbolism, etc. Therefore the Bible cannot be interpreted literally, because you first need the key to the sacred knowledge, before you can unlock and decipher the code. Here is another example why not literally.

The Christ washing the feet of the 12 Apostles: The enigma of the Christ washing the feet of the 12 apostles is: The 12 apostles represent the 12 RNA DNA astrological germ seed essences that are contained in all mankind, who are born under the 12 astrological signs of the zodiac. In Genesis 3:15. ...you shall have to lie in wait for his heel means, the heels or feet of the body are governed by the astrological sign of Pisces, which is portrayed as 2 fishes swimming in the astrological sea of everlasting life, which denote the 2 soular and lunar seeds that at present have an enmity, a separation between them. The symbology of the Christ washing the feet of the 12 apostles signify the ???? thermonuclear fusion of the 2 enmity seeds. The soular seed, which is mortal, physical matter is impure. The Christ germ lunar seed is immortal, spiritual pure antimatter. Consequently the soular seed needs to be purified through the ???? in order that the pure Christ lunar germ seed can be fused together with the soular seed essence. Therefore it was necessary for the 1st Christ to wash the feet of the 12, or rather purify the 12 germ seed essences through the ???? thermonuclear fusion, which is the diversity from the 12 astro signs of the zodiac, who are the 12 fabled apostles.

https://web.archive.org/web/20050205235014/http://144cubits.com/mystical13.htm

My niece and her husband from New York State send me a Hallmark card. The inside message states. "It may not seem like a big deal to you, but it was to me. Thank you." Not a big deal? It certainly is! It is so big that the message landed on the Internet in the cyber space, and you are now viewing it! On the top image are the moon, a star, a cat and the unknown. The moon represents the Christ lunar germ seed of love and invincibility. The star signifies the solar or soul-ar seed. The cat represents humanity, contemplating if they can ever get across the unknown obstacle, the chasm of ceaseless torture of mortal life, to the divine, invincible, immortal life. On the bottom image, the moon or rather the Christ lunar germ seed comes to the rescue of all mankind. How? "You must have the seed of love to bridge super consciousness." The symbology of the Christ lunar germ seed is what all mankind need, the bridge, to remove the unknown obstacle of the 1st original sin that causes the mortal death in all mankind. In simpler words, this message is informing humanity that you need to cross the unknown chasm barrier of death, while you are alive.

Why? To be ready and reunite to the creator Spirit of God. Why? This is the opportune time to return to the divinity. Why? So you can partake of the everlasting water of life, the milk and honey manna, that shall make you free from the atomic 1st original nuclear transgression, the 1st death, the 1st original sin and the ceaseless thermodynamic law of deaths and reincarnations.

https://web.archive.org/web/20100104145609/http://www.144cubits.com/pointstoinsight.htm

E is for Experience

I was raised as a Catholic and I was also programed to the belief system of fallacious, deceptive infallibility of the Catholic Church. Everything that I am expounding to you now is from actual experience. And experience is the best teacher.

https://web.archive.org/web/20040605063612/http://www.144cubits.com/akashic13.htm

Therefore in order to become a professional, you need to practice the special musical notes or lyrics of XXenogenesis constantly, like any distinguished musician or singer would, lest you become rusty and a stagnant mediocre. For what is out of sight, is out of mind.

https://web.archive.org/web/20100105040149/http://www.144cubits.com/lunargermseed.htm

F is for the Fourth Dimension

If man is to be liberated from being a prisoner of ignorance! prisoner of death! he needs to first expand his consciousness into all areas of search and knowledge. Being confined only to the shallow belief systems that are about man, will never attain his emancipation from death, thus unto the New Heaven, New Earth, New Jerusalem, the City of 4 Square, the 4th Dimension. The 4th Dimension and beyond is the Empyrean where the mortal death is no more. This is the original home of every mortal being. This is where every mortal belongs to, for it is his heritage. Comprehending this principle is crucial. Because if you don't understand the problem how you got into the quagmire mess, you can't solve it. So if you do not perceive the atomic universe and the divine omnipresent atoms that you are made from, you won't understand the mystery of life and death and your ancestry.

https://web.archive.org/web/20040605043310/http://www.144cubits.com/akashic1.htm

Why do you need all this knowledge and attain immortality? Because this solar system, earth, all mankind and you in it, are now traversing in the Milky Way to an ultra high frequency of 4th Dimension. In the incoming 4th Dimension, there is no poverty, insecurity, wars of every kind, crime, corruption, hunger, sickness, aging, death, etc. Also in the 4th Dimension no mortal being can sustain a mortal body, prevent this or escape the transition from being a mortal to immortal. These words also imply that in the ultra high frequency of the 4th Dimension, no longer can mankind propagate and bear children. This is an immutable nuclear physics law, and no man can change it.

https://web.archive.org/web/20040904033006/http://www.144cubits.com/

Don't you think it is about time that you wise up, and start thinking for yourself? Thus shed the fantasy, the illusion that you have been brain washed with for millions of years. Yes, millions of years have elapsed since you fell from your divinity! Why most of you don't know why you are here for on earth? That is how far you have ventured into darkness; into not knowing the truth. And darkness is darkness. Don't you know that all the belief systems that are all about humanity have been built on quicksand, the great Babylon of deception and darkness? It is time for a change!

Why? Because each of you and the solar system is traversing in the macrocosm space into another dimension, the ultra high frequency of the 4th Dimension. And no mortal man can exist in the ultra high frequency of the 4th Dimension, nor prevent this. Or would you rather not know what is awaiting you? Thus run out of time, be caught unprepared, and suffer the consequences?

https://web.archive.org/web/20040605052055/http://www.144cubits.com/akashic11.htm

At present, this solar system, including planet earth and you in it, is traversing in the cosmic cycle, whereby the frequency of the 3rd Dimension, the mortal existence will be accelerated and changed to the 4th Dimension, the immortal existence. And humanity cannot prevent this. As a result no mortal being can exist in the 4th Dimension. Thus that portion of mankind which rebels will eliminate itself, by their own foolish hand as prophesied. With what is now on the threshold of destiny, do you think mankind should be thinking about fighting and revolting against the truth? Or do you think the human race should do nothing? **Each second we waste and do nothing, it becomes more dangerous, as we traverse**

closer and closer into the ultra high frequency of the 4th Dimension and beyond.

https://web.archive.org/web/20040605063612/http://www.144cubits.com/akashic13.htm

G is for God

In the encyclopedia of religions there are over 2,800 religions and in each, a different name for God. The word God was derived from the word good to God, which denotes, I am that I am, the infinite I, the good substance and sustenance-essence of the universe, the father-mother nature, which is the etheric nuclear energy milk and honey manna of the Milky Way. The constant, enduring repetition is the magical key to mastering whatever you desire to become proficient in. Why not master becoming one of the Christs? You are all invited! And what I have done in this mortal body, you can do the same. Why? Because I love each of you so very dearly!

https://web.archive.org/web/20040605063612/http://www.144cubits.com/akashic13.htm

Who do you think created all this creation and magnificent you, from the divine omnipotent, omnipresent atoms, which were created in God's same atomic image, likeness and limitless love? So does God exist? Did you think that the Spirit of God is some supernatural being, old father time or whatever? God is none of those things. God is Spirit, the fruit of the vine, the divine omnipotent, omnipresent atoms! The Spirit of God is the ever-bearing immortal plasma, the absolute total composition of 144 atomic elements, the super-substantial bread of everlasting life, the good substance, good sustenance, the milk and honey manna from the Milky Way of immortal life!

https://web.archive.org/web/20130709175300/http://www.144cubits.com/doesgodexist.htm

All stars are self-luminous suns, and are round in shape, not jagged like they are portrayed otherwise. Antares is the 15th brightest star in the sky. Its distance is more than 1000 light years away from earth. How big are you? How big are the atoms in you? On a pinhead there are millions of atoms. So trillions of atoms you are! So is all creation, created from divine omnipotent, omnipresent atoms! That is the I am that I am Spirit of God, the nuclear energy creator, the infinite source, atoms, who created everything in his <u>same</u> atomic image, likeness and limitless love.

Without nuclear energy light, heat, sound, there would be nothing, no Spirit of God, no creation, no exquisite you! How marvelous is all creation, the omniinertia, omnibus, omnifarious, omniscient, omnificent, invincible, indivisible, micro, macro, omnia vincit amor, omnipotent, omnipresent God in every atom! That is Spirit of God in its limitless love splendor, great light, luster, brilliance, visible, invisible, etc., the music of the spheres, atoms! Does the source Spirit of God, the creator exist? Do you understand now?

https://web.archive.org/web/20130709175300/http://www.144cubits.com/doesgodexist.htm

The phenomenal universe, suspended in space like a weightless jewel, and within is the universal intelligence, the Spirit of God universal mind, structured into every omnipotent, omnipresent atom. As a result, the super intelligence operates according to the immutable, unchangeable laws of nuclear physics. And trillions of atoms you are, inescapably governed by these laws! The road to becoming one of the Christs, the union with the divinity is always under construction. Time is the luxury you have been invested with. Use it wisely. The missing Key to the Sacred Knowledge! The Holy Grail!

https://web.archive.org/web/20041226092452/http://www.144cubits.com/refwhoiscoming.htm

H is for Health

Some people tell me that I am lucky that I do not use prescription drugs. Being healthy has nothing to do with luck. To rely on luck is foolishness. But being limitless love, and knowing how to maintain health, and then doing the things that are necessary for health, is wisdom and the avenue to health. Of what good is the wisdom and knowledge if you don't act upon it. You need to act upon it and become a doer. Does not the Bible state: Physician know thyself and heal thyself from the mortal sting of death?

https://web.archive.org/web/20050205232206/http://144cubits.com/limitlesslove.htm

Immune System And Your Health: Every time you hate or are negative, you create a biochemical reaction in your priceless, precious physical-spiritual body, which progressively destroys your aura, immune system and your health; law of nuclear physics. Always love the Spirit of God in you, your neighbor and your enemies. Your neighbor is all mankind.

Always love and bless everything, yourself, all mankind, enemies, earth, universe and all creation in the existence continuum. Limitless love, compassion, peace and harmony are the most powerful weapons of, you are to be constantly perfected even as the omnipotent, omnipresent Spirit of God is constantly exalted and perfected in the never ending progressive nuclear evolution. Give thanks always for everything. Always find the blessings hidden in disguise. Smile, be happy and kind to everyone, for it is a language that everyone understands.

https://web.archive.org/web/20040605063612/http://www.144cubits.com/akashic13.htm

And laughing entices happiness, which invigorates the immune system and thus improves your priceless health and love.

https://web.archive.org/web/20100106050949/http://www.144cubits.com/whatislifewithoutfrolicking.htm

The normal vibratory rate of a human body is between 62 and 68 MHz. MHz is one million cycles per second. The brain functions optimally between 72 and 90 MHz. When the body vibration lowers to 58 MHz it can catch a cold; at 57 MHz the flu; 55 MHz candida; 52 MHz Epstein Barr; 42 MHz cancer and at 25 MHz death begins. By considering health problems of your friends and family, you can begin to get a true picture. The dark forces, which are the negative planners, simply lower the MHz of someone they would like to eliminate through their devised methods. Thus within a short period of time, the body either develops a fatal disease and if lowered enough, death occurs and whatever disease is already present, is the excuse. Allopathic medicines, social drugs, chemical prescriptions, tobacco, caffeine, alcohol, lower the MHz of the body. TV radiation and computer screens lower the MHz. Processed and canned foods, which have 0 MHz to support the body, continue the downward process. Starvation is the least subtle that lowers the MHz and the mass consciousness before each die, thus contributes to the descending cycle.

[Healing is relevant to raising your consciousness.]

Lowering the vibratory rate is much more difficult than raising it. A simple realization can cause a jump in vibratory rate. As the vibratory rate lowers the brain synapses, it becomes more and more difficult to rebound. Also the use of the sugar substitutes [in aspartame, which slowly embalm the brain] such as Equal, it slowly destroys the ability of the brain to function as it destroys the nerve endings. It can and does cross the blood brain barrier. Further, low fat/high sugar bearing carbohydrate diets are starving the brain cells. All of this is part of the plan of the dark forces. Remember they understand the functions of the physical body well enough to be able to develop techniques to weaken the connection of the being to its vibratory source in hopes it can be broken at their moment of choosing. May we stress that you think carefully about this information and that you read your labels and take *personal responsibility* in the care of the bodily functions necessary to participate in this project. Therefore, the critical factor is the pH level of your body chemistry and your blood.

https://web.archive.org/web/20110319053255/http://www.144cubits.com/handbookparadigm2.htm

I is for Immortality

The time is now upon you when a deadly viral plague will be upon earth that will devastate the population of mankind. The virus will be so very lethal that humanity will be dropping and dying like dead flies. This is when the only antidote for this deadly virus shall be the immune hormone substance from the Christ. The immune hormone substance, IHS from the Christ shall create a Super Immune Hormone System, greater than mortal man ever had: Immortal.

https://web.archive.org/web/20110319053324/http://www.144cubits.com/thermodynamicsofenergy.htm

What you are now going to encounter is going to take you further to the ultra higher consciousness, to the point of reality, to the reason of why you are here for on this planet earth. You live in your physical-spiritual body 24 hours a day, day by day. Here you will know how well do you really know yourself? Also why are you now composed of transitional subatomic carbon 666 atoms, that are always destined to the pit of self destruction; death? Furthermore, you will learn how each of you consumes the atomic forbidden fruit of the vine till death do you part. Whereas, you were born not to die, but to overcome mortal death by harnessing your full atomic capabilities, while you are still alive and full of life. Now the divine life force in you is beckoning to each of you to return to your originality, the atomic light energy. Are you prepared? Please open your computer mind and fasten your safety belt! Why? Because you will certainly need it for what took many years for you to know, and therefore raise your consciousness.

https://web.archive.org/web/20100316125654/http://www.144cubits.com/conflictbetweenallnations.htm

Each of you is the evergreen tree of life, the Christ-mas tree, mass and energy of Spirit of God-good essence, the phenomenal alpha and omega without a beginning nor end. The exquisite RNA DNA in you is as old as no beginning nor end; older than the universe. Why older? Because when the atomic Spirit of God-good essence came into existence from no beginning nor end, you came into existence that split infinitesimal moment, before the creation of the universe. Thus you were created from the omnipotent, omniscient, omnificent, omnibus, omnifarious, omnia vincit amor, omnipresent atoms in God's image and likeness! Equal! When you fell from your divinity, the union with the Spirit of God, you created an atomic enmity, a separation from the Spirit of God-good essence. As a result, here you are a mortal being, who does not know how to re-unite yourself to the divinity, the crystal clear nuclear energy milk and honey manna, the Christos, the Christ.

https://web.archive.org/web/20040605063612/http://www.144cubits.com/akashic13.htm

When this shall come to pass, the velocity of death will be left behind once again and the lost paradise regained. When you shall perfect yourself as the heavenly father is constantly perfected, your physical-spiritual body shall be transformed and transmuted into a nuclear energy light body of the divine Christ, the Christos. Then death shall be swallowed up in victory, and there will be a city, the realm, the Kingdom of God that stands 4 Square. This will be the New Jerusalem, the 4th Dimension and beyond, the Empyrean.

https://web.archive.org/web/20040605052055/http://www.144cubits.com/akashic11.htm

Again and again I must repeat, the mystical sacred knowledge of XXenogenesis unveiled is very extensive, de rigueur, radiant, very enlightening, and all the rest of the wonderful adjectives that are in all the languages of the world. As one of the Christs you can be everything, everywhere instantly, as played out on the TV Heroes and Smallville, Superman programs. You can be all that but there is a difference. The difference is you are very real and faster, the Christ. And no violence, crimes, etc. You as one of the Christs shall be existing in harmony with nature, peace, love for all mankind. The true love is: Omnia vincit amor, which means: Limitless Love conquers everything and makes everything possible. Nothing can harm you. You can never die!

https://web.archive.org/web/20100105040149/http://www.144cubits.com/lunargermseed.htm

J is for Jokes

Once upon a time a girl and a boy about 7 years old were walking by a lake and it was a hot day. As they were talking the girl said, you know my parents always argue who is a better Christian, the Protestants or the Catholics? The boy said, that is exactly the same thing my parents argue about. Nancy, do you know the difference between a protestant and a catholic? The girl said, I was raised and I am a protestant. What are you Jack? I am a catholic, do you see any difference in you being a protestant and me being a catholic? They both agreed that they could not tell the difference, as they kept on walking. Since it was a very hot day and they were walking by this beautiful lake, Jack said let's go swimming in the lake. So they both quickly took off all their clothes. And when Nancy saw Jack in the nude, she remarked, now I see the difference between a catholic and the protestant. You're a catholic and I am protestant.

https://web.archive.org/web/20150201201150/http://www.144cubits.com/whatislifewithoutfrolicking.htm

There was an atheist who went around the world teaching that God does not exist and everything comes from an evolution. So one day the atheist decided to go to Alaska to hunt for the great Kodiak bear. While walking in the forest, he marveled at the evolution of the trees, rocks, soil, running stream, fish and the whispering wind. Suddenly he heard the rustling of someone running after him. He turned around and saw a huge ferocious Kodiak bear coming upon him very fast. The atheist took up running fast and as he was running he saw the Kodiak catching up to him. So now he ran faster, but he couldn't outrun the bear. Now the Kodiak bear was ready to pounce upon him. The atheist saw this and said, Oh my God! Suddenly silence came upon, the water in the stream stopped running, fish ceased moving about, even the wind was motionless. Then a voice said from the ether, you atheists have the nerve to call upon God when all this time you went around the world preaching that God does not exist and everything evolves from a simple amoeba. Now the atheist knew that the God was right in his accusation. So he talks to God and said, I know I was wrong all this time and it isn't fair that I should call upon you in my last moment of life to save me. But can you at least convert the Kodiak bear to be a Christian? The silence ceased, the water in the stream ran, the fish swam again, the wind began to move and the atheist saw the Kodiak bear drop to his knees, with folded paws in prayer, saying, thank you God for the food which I am about to receive.

https://web.archive.org/web/20150201201150/http://www.144cubits.com/whatislifewithoutfrolicking.htm

There was a group of people walking in the park and dusk was almost upon them. As they were walking and talking, suddenly they saw a man sitting on a bench, but something was very unusual about him. They came close to this man. This man had a most brilliant scintillating light shining from him. So they asked, what is this light emitting from you? Who are you? So the man said, I am the creator of everything that has ever been and is created. So they asked him can you tell us what does time mean to you? The creator replied it is written in the Bible: A moment with God is like a thousand years. So they asked further, what is a billion years? The creator replied, a billion years is a second. So they asked the creator, can you create for us a steak dinner, baked sweet potato, pistachio ice cream, desert and some raw vegetable juices to drink? So the creator said, it is done! Suddenly out of thin air everything appeared to their fullest expectations, including linen napkins and finger bowls with water and lemon to wash their hands. With that the people said you must be for real the creator. The creator asked, is there something more you desire? So they thought for a moment and then asked, can you create for us a billion dollars? The creator responded, in a second, and then disappeared.

https://web.archive.org/web/20150201201150/http://www.144cubits.com/whatislifewithoutfrolicking.htm

K is for Kundalini

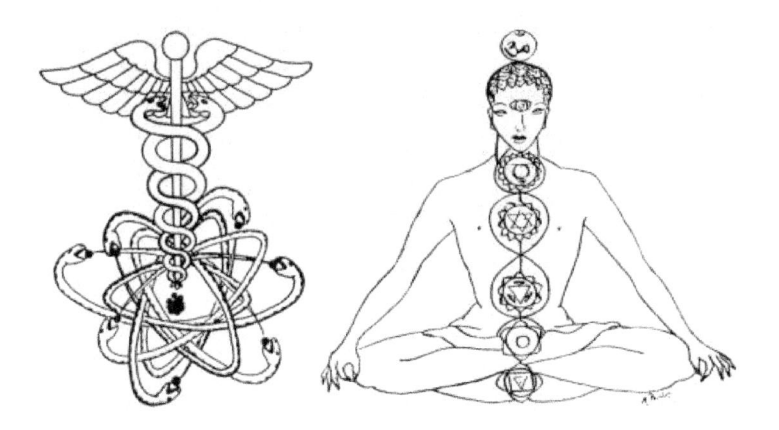

Figure 18. "Kundalini caduceus serpents/7 chakras – 7 seals – 7 bodies"

The Sanskrit word Kundalini is an energy in a form of 2 coiled caduceus serpents, that lies dormant at the base of the spine, until it is activated and lifted upwards, through the 7 chakras - 7 seals in your body; as related in the book of Apocalypse 5:2-5.

When the 2 allegorical caduceus serpents, the matter and antimatter are lifted upwards, thus criss + cross + for the final divine unification, the super genius consciousness bridge is formed between the pineal and pituitary glands. When this transpires, the pineal and pituitary hormones criss + cross and unite together, and the RNA DNA Immune Hormone Substance IHS is transformed through the process of XXenogenesis spontaneous regeneration and transfiguration in the twinkling of an eye; in the immortal Christos, the Christ, the promised redeemer from death. Man has now become the alchemist, the parent to his Christ. At that moment he is reunited with the divine creator; hence belongs to eternity. He has become matter and antimatter of crystal clear immaculate nuclear energy light, whereby he is now permitted to eat from the tree of life the milk and honey manna, the food of the gods.

https://web.archive.org/web/20110702161146/http://www.144cubits.com/mannymansions.htm

John 3:13. For it is written, and as fabled Moses lifted up the Kundalini, Caduceus serpents in the desert, so must the son of man, the Christ seed **also be lifted up** through the staff of life, the perfectly aligned vertebras, that are without tension, pressure, stress, blockage of flowing energy through the spinal column, to the 12 pair of cranial nerves, the crown of life in mortal man. But if your Kundalini serpents bite you with the mortal sting of death, because it has not been charmed, then there is no advantage to the charmer. And each of you is the charmer of your serpent power, the ancient sexual power, which deceives all mankind unto death. When you shall become one of the Christs, you shall really know how to celebrate Christmas every moment of your immortal existence. Merry Christmas! So be it!

https://web.archive.org/web/20040605063612/http://www.144cubits.com/akashic13.htm

The Puzzler: The astrological sign for Taurus is a bull, an ox. Taurus governs the pituitary gland, which issues forth the antimatter, psycho-physical Christ lunar germ seed of immortality every lunar month for the liberation, redemption, resurrection from the 1st death. When the Christ germ seed descends down through the spinal column into the pit, the fire, the sexual, sacral, sacred chakra on the Sabbath-Passover, the Kundalini sexual energy is to be lifted up through the 7 chakras, the 7 seals, to your crown of life, the 12 pair of cranial nerves. The words Sabbath-Passover are terms used to describe the specific time, when the 2 enmity seeds, the soul-ar and lunar seeds are to undergo nuclear fusion in the bridal chamber on the bed of love; thus lifted up to the 7th chakra.

https://web.archive.org/web/20100104145614/http://www.144cubits.com/purityinlifemen.htm

L is for Limitless Love

Every religion from antiquity down is a man-made religion. The Spirit of God never sanctioned a religion nor ever designated any special chosen people. The Spirit of God is limitless love and knows no partiality! Also since the Spirit of God is limitless love, it does not punish anyone for any wrong doing. It is man himself who punishes himself or another man. The Spirit of God never approves any act of self-killing or killing for Allah or God or whoever.

https://web.archive.org/web/20040605071625/http://www.144cubits.com/akashic2.htm

What Is This Thing Called Limitless Love? It is simply love with many facets. Example: Be kind to everyone. For what so ever you do to the least of thee, you also do it to yourself, only to a greater magnitude. Limitless Love is the state of harmony, peace, love, joy, happiness, kindness, freedom, compassion, vital health and all the good attributes, which produces a perfect equating equilibrium to a constant higher frequency in the dynamic nuclear evolution, to the 4th Dimension and beyond.

Here are few examples that shall let you understand, comprehend and propel you into being limitless love. This much can be accomplished in the privacy of your mind and ultimately being an example of limitless love. In the secret recesses of your mind always think of everything being the omnipresent Spirit of God, which is within everything, everywhere, everlasting, pervasive atoms, which is omnipotent, omnipresent without a beginning nor end. In the privacy of your mind, always bless everything and thank the Spirit of God for everything that the Spirit of God has provided, is providing, and will provide to all creation in the time, space existence continuum. So be it! Amen!

I love you Spirit of God so dearly, all my relatives, friends, mankind, departed individuals from this world and my enemies. Thank you. So be it! Amen!

I love you omnipresent Spirit of God who resides also within all my relatives, friends, enemies and me. Thank you for everything. So be it! Amen!

Oh Spirit of God please open the mind, heart and the aura that encompasses all my relatives, friends, enemies and me, so we can accept all the blessings of every kind of good abundance from you. Thank you. So be it! Amen!

Oh Spirit of God let us not have any more wars, conflicts, discrimination, fear, insecurity, hatred and every travail of mortal life. Thank you. So be it! Amen!

Oh Spirit of God let us move expeditiously unto the nuclear evolution of the 4th Dimension with limitless peace and limitless love. Thank you. So be it! Amen!

Limitless love is, when you are driving in a car and someone provokes you in some way, instead of giving the driver the middle finger, in the privacy of your mind say, God bless you and I love you driver and all drivers. So be it! Amen!

Limitless love is, not being greedy, corruptive, selfish, cheating, stealing, jealous, defrauding others, engaging in all the evil vices against mankind, etc. For in all the evil vices, that is not love thy neighbour as thyself.

Limitless love is loving yourself, your priceless physical-spiritual body by not indulging in any harmful things that destroy the mortal body, such as, the use of social and medicinal drugs, junk food, tobacco, alcohol, carbonated soda pops, detrimental music and many thousands other destructive agents.

Limitless love is not taking upon oneself to sit in the seat of power, to rule and or teach as a false, inferior god, inflicting self guilt complex upon others, or instituting unnatural heath care, punishment, injury, death or any other evil vices against humanity. For that is not love thy neighbour or enemy as thyself.

Limitless love is not promoting, supporting and viewing any violence on television and all other media. For that encounter sends your molecular expression of atomic matter to the mass consciousness, which lies few feet above all humanity. So as you sow the seeds of evil violence, so shall you teach and reap the harvest of violence, hate, vengeance, terrorism or how to kill the Spirit of God in another, etc.

https://web.archive.org/web/20050305034001/http://www.144cubits.com/limitlesslove.htm

L is for Lunar Germ Seed

[*Xxenogenesis interprets and expands a Bible verse:*] **1 Peter 1:23. For you can be reborn again, not from the corruptible seed, the united ovum and sperm seed, but from the incorruptible seed, the Christ lunar germ seed of immortality, which lives and abides forever.**

Baptism of Fire: The mystical meaning of baptism of fire is relative to the immortal, incorruptible seed, the Christ lunar germ seed undergoing ???? thermonuclear fusion in the bridal chamber, as related in the Gospel of Philip.

https://web.archive.org/web/20040605081516/http://www.144cubits.com/akashic4.htm

Therefore from the time the divine androgynes became mortals, the Spirit of God sends to every human being every lunar month a psychophysical Christ lunar germ seed of immortality, for the redemption from the slavery of death. This sacred knowledge is known as the: coming of the promise of a redeemer from death, the savior of oneself.

When the child reaches the age of sexual maturity, the commencement of the coming of the psychophysical Christ lunar germ seed of immortality occurs. This Christ seed is the savior, the redeemer from your mortal sting of death. Since mankind does not know that this is occurring every lunar month, it therefore engages in sexual orgasms at the Passover Sabbath time. Upon the orgasm or no orgasm, the Christ seed is destroyed, through abortion, thus killing the Christ germ lunar seed, the promised redeemer.

Furthermore, if this Christ germ seed is not fused into the body of mankind at the Passover Sabbath time, the Christ germ seed, the promised redeemer is aborted and destroyed either with an orgasm or no orgasm. **In plain words abortion of the Christ seed is murder.**

https://web.archive.org/web/20040605063612/http://www.144cubits.com/akashic13.htm

Omnia mutantur nos et mutamur in illis: From Latin these words mean: All things are constantly changing, and we are changing with them. This means: The divine nuclear energy milk and honey manna must always be kept in constant motion and never cease from flowing and circulating movement. Or in other words the immutable, unchangeable laws of God, the natural laws of nuclear physics requires the Spirit of God, the nuclear energy milk and honey manna of the Milky Way, the food of the gods to be constantly exchanged, changed and interchanged between every atom in every divine being.

If the nuclear energy milk and honey manna is not exchanged, this is what happens, corruption develops, clogs up the system, and puts a stop to the normal course of nature. This is the law the Androgynous Gods, which were you, transgressed, when you declined and refused to exchange, change and interchange the milk and honey manna with one another, and thus venerate or worship the God-good essence in one another, the essence of the nuclear energy of the sun in your nuclear energy light body; on the universal link, the Empyrean ring of wonder. This secret is interwoven in the Eleusinian mysteries, the sun worshippers, and many other ancient religions, also in the mystical symbolical Last Supper and Holy Communion. This is part of the key to the sacred knowledge, the Holy Grail.

https://web.archive.org/web/20040605060910/http://www.144cubits.com/akashic12.htm

[Magazine article with interlinear commentary from Xxenogenesis:]
According to researcher Elisabeth Lloyd, the female orgasms are an evolutionary accident. [Not accident but Genesis 3:15 enmity mutation.]
One question that is rarely addressed, however, is whether female and male **ejaculation has a biological function**. [Yes, once you become one of the Christs, for exchanging, changing and interchanging the milk and honey manna to maintain your divinity.]
This fascinating and long-neglected women's orgasm phenomenon might turn out to be more than just a sexual curiosity. [Not a curiosity, but a reality for XXenogenesis fusion.]

https://web.archive.org/web/20150201174320/http://144cubits.com/mysteryofanorgasm.htm

How and where do you think the psychophysical Christ lunar germ seed of immunity from death and reuniting to the creator Spirit of God came from and became effective in me? From religions? From Tantra, Taoism, Yoga, some form of Sexology concepts? No! From meditations, chanting, prayers, going to churches, temples, mosques, elevating consciousness? No! From channelled messages, special schools, initiations? No! From being a vegetarian eating grains, nuts, fruits, vegetables, fasting. No! From prescription drugs, social drugs like cocaine, marijuana, opium, speed, etc.? No! No! From smoking or smoking some special tobacco that fire-up your lungs and defuse the pure oxygen from your brains and system, drinking some special wine or alcohol that destroy your pancreas and blood system? No! Candy, over 10,000 dry goods/mixtures in your super markets food, soda beverages that are sweetened with camouflaged aspartame, which are the artificial sweeteners that slowly embalm the brain. No! Coffee that demolishes your nervous system, water that is laced with chloride and fluorine? No! None of those things work or bring enduring results of becoming one of the Christs.

https://web.archive.org/web/20100104145609/http://www.144cubits.com/pointstoinsight.htm

M is for Marriage

Search your Bibles, and you will not find the Spirit of God ever instituting the laws of marriage. Why? Because the diversity of the 12 RNA DNA essences is necessary for the plasma of immortality to become one of the Christs. And you being a mortal, possesses only 1/12 of the total 12 essences from one astro sign of the zodiac. Being the circumstance, the Spirit of God does not recognize the mortal man-made counterfeit laws of marriage.

https://web.archive.org/web/20050305201311/http://www.144cubits.com/exposure11.htm

John 3:29. He who has the bride, the antimatter Christ Lunar Germ Seed fused, united, married to the counterpart matter Soul-ar Seed within himself is the bride- groom, the Christ to bring forth the RNA DNA Immune Hormone Substance - IHS. In the above portrayal, the 2 Enmity Seeds are drawn magnetically together closer and closer by the majestic power of Limitless Love, until they will endure the XXenogenesis thermonuclear fusion marriage. Consequently, the 2 Enmity Seeds become one substance, the one body of the Christ. Thus is the meaning of becoming the Promised Redeemer from death, the Coming of the Christ. (*Immortality Unveiled*)

https://web.archive.org/web/20070102132151/http://www.xxenogenesis.com/imunvpdf/imunv-1.pdf

M is for Matter/Antimatter

It is a scientific fact that when matter and antimatter come in contact with each other, they will annihilate; destroy itself. Consequently, whenever an orgasm occurs in the mortal beings, it is because the physical impure matter of mortal seeds comes in contact with the spiritual, pure, immaculate, virginal antimatter essence. An orgasm is a micro nuclear explosion. Some people even see the explosion light when the orgasm occurs. Consequently, whenever an orgasm or no orgasm transpires at the Sabbath Passover time for nuclear fusion of the 2 enmity seeds, mankind adulterates his I am that I am presence of the Spirit of God. In that infinitesimal moment of an orgasm, it is the touch with the antimatter divinity, the Spirit of God. It is a bliss of extreme love, joy, happiness and etc. But that mortal orgasm is so short lived, that you want more and more of it. And since you want more and more of it, consequently little do you realize that every mortal orgasms progressively degenerates your liver, your overall health, that eventually leads you to the pit of self-destruction; death.

https://web.archive.org/web/20040605063612/http://www.144cubits.com/akashic13.htm

N is for Nuclear Evolution

The Nuclear Physics Law of Reincarnation is a reality. If the Law of Reincarnation did not exist, then every woman and man would be condemned by the Spirit of God for eternity; for his 1st original sin against the Spirit of God. Your senseless ritual of baptism does not remove the 1st original sin. The immutable laws of nuclear physics does not accept foolish rituals as compensation for the nuclear transgression, the 1st original sin. Please lock this into your precious mind. God is not some kind of a supernatural being but Spirit. Since the Spirit of God is Limitless Love, he allows man countless times to reincarnate and overcome the enmity and thus reinstate the union with the divinity.

https://web.archive.org/web/20040605052055/http://www.144cubits.com/akashic11.htm

Within the immutable, unchangeable laws of reincarnation, everyone has the choice to change sexes, nationalities, color of skin, religions, wives, husbands, children, etc. In the marvelous process of Nuclear Evolution, you were a diversity of people over a period of many, many lifetimes. Therefore, it is foolish for any man to persecute or war against any race, creed, sex, or nationality, for you have been a part of what you are now either hating or loving. And know this, you can never reincarnate as an animal or whatever, because humanity operates on a much higher frequency than an animal, plant or whatever kingdom.

https://web.archive.org/web/20040605052055/http://www.144cubits.com/akashic11.htm

Since the unchangeable, immutable laws of nuclear physics govern every omnipresent atom in the time, space, existence continuum and in mankind, there is no ritual, nor words, nor prayer, nor power of the mind, nor any belief system that can remove the never before known, 1st original nuclear transgression, 1st original sin; the separation from the divinity.

https://web.archive.org/web/20040605151910/http://www.144cubits.com/akashic6.htm

Nuclear evolution has nothing to do with building more deadly, detrimental nuclear power plants or nuclear weapons. The nuclear evolution of the 4th Dimension is relative to the atomic structure of your precious, phenomenal physical-spiritual body, which is presently constructed in the 3rd dimensional mortal world from trillions of carbon 666 nuclear atoms. Therefore, your atomic structure needs to evolve into the 4th Dimension, the City of 4 Square, the New Jerusalem, the empyrean; while you are alive.

https://web.archive.org/web/20050305034001/http://www.144cubits.com/limitlesslove.htm

There is only one ultimate purpose why man is here on earth, and that is to regain his God heritage, the union with the divinity, and the paradise lost of the 4th dimension and beyond; while you are alive. So please, don't be so concerned with your limited motive of mere survival unto 2nd death, but rather with the unlimited motive of spiritual Nuclear Evolution.

https://web.archive.org/web/20040605164708/http://www.144cubits.com/lastsupper.htm

The fusion or uniting of the 2 enmity seeds is accomplished through the XXenogenesis thermonuclear fusion method. And this kind of fire always removes all the impurities present. When all the impurities, the dross is removed between the enmity seeds, it then brings on the pure virgin immaculate conception. That is the mystery of immaculate conception, the virgin birth of the Christ on earth. Later, much later I shall reveal what is the process for XXenogenesis to produce the super-substantial bread, Milky Way milk and honey manna, the food, ambrosia of the gods for eternal immortality, the infinite, continuous never ending perfection in nuclear evolution!?

https://web.archive.org/web/20100105040149/http://www.144cubits.com/lunargermseed.htm

O is for 144

Do you know what is a cubit? Or how you are to add cubits? Luke 12.25. But which of you by being anxious about it, can add a single cubit, an atomic element to your stature your physical-spiritual body? Therefore if you are not able to do even a very little thing like this, why are you so anxious or concerned about anything else, whatever you are doing? Whereas: Revelation or Apocalypse 21:17. 144 cubits, 144 atomic elements is man's perfect measure, for that is the same measure as of a divinity. A cubit is a mystical, allegorical term used to express an atomic element in an atom. And you are created from trillions of atoms. In plainer simple words adding the 144 cubits or 144 atomic elements to your physical-spiritual body means, knowing and understanding the function of your atomic spiritual-physical biological organism of your body. Thus implementing the mystical process that is now very much unknown, since you separated yourself from the divinity. That is why presently this is beyond your mortal comprehension. You live in your physical-spiritual body 24 hours a day, day by day. Here you will know how well do you really know yourself?

https://web.archive.org/web/20140629010129/http://144cubits.com/whyareyouhere.htm

The metaphysical meaning of the 144 cubits corresponds to the 144 atomic elements, which are contained within the universal eggs, the omnipresent, omnipotent divine atoms; from which everything issues forth. Presently the 144 atomic elements compose the magnificent, priceless, unavailable milk and honey manna in every mortal being.

The cubit is one atomic element, one unit of measurement of the cosmic egg, the atom. Unfortunately, since mankind is not in the 4th Dimension, these 144 atomic elements are not available to him. Instead the cubits, the atomic elements are held in abeyance, waiting for man to harness them through ???? nuclear fusion. Through the process of fusion, cubits are added to the physical-spiritual body for his re-perfection, and electrons are added to the 4th and subsequent electron inertia energy levels.

https://web.archive.org/web/20040605052055/http://www.144cubits.com/akashic11.htm

Thereafter the very minimum and more of 144,000 Christs, 12,000 from each astrological sign of the zodiac is mandatory, in order to lock the planet earth irrevocably into the ultra high frequency of the 4th Dimension. When this shall be accomplished the assemblage of the minimum of 144,000 Christs, 12,000 from each astro sign shall bring about the, Totality of God. When the great day of the Totality of God comes to fruition, planet earth and all the people that will be living at that time, will be spared from the impending destruction the earth is traversing into; Matthew 24:15-22.

https://web.archive.org/web/20040605063612/http://www.144cubits.com/akashic13.htm

P is for Purity

Purity In Life Men Do Not Comprehend. **The Aquarian Gospel 7:23-26. But purity in life men do not comprehend; and so, it, too, must come in flesh. The Aquarian Age will comprehend but little of the works of purity and love; but not a word is lost, for in the book of God's Remembrance, the Akashic Records a registry is made of every thought, and word, and deed. And when the world is ready to receive, lo God will send a messenger to open up the book,** [the missing key to the sacred knowledge of ????] **and copy from its sacred pages,** [from the omniscient universal mind of the Spirit of God,] **all the messages of purity and love between woman and man.**

Yes, no one, but no one can come to the father-son-mother nature, the Spirit of God, to eat from the tree of life, which you are, the milk and honey manna, except through me. Who is this me? The me is an inference to the Christ germ seed essence, that was fused in the body of the 1st Christ, which you will need to partake of this essence from the Christ, like in the symbolic last supper or the holy communion, the body of Christ, in the Catholic church. Yes, purity of love mankind do not comprehend.

https://web.archive.org/web/20100104145614/http://www.144cubits.com/purityinlifemen.htm

1 Peter 1:22. Let your soul-ar and lunar **seeds be purified** through nuclear **fusion by obedience to the truth, and be filled with sincere** limitless **love,** so that you may love God and one another with pure perfect hearts.

23. For you can be reborn again, not from the corruptible seed, the united ovum and sperm seed, **but from the incorruptible seed,** the Christ lunar germ seed of immortality, **which lives and abides forever.**

https://web.archive.org/web/20040605164708/http://www.144cubits.com/lastsupper.htm

Q is for Questions

Furthermore, here is a message to those who have spent many years in the search of what is this all about. or what is this to be, etc.? If you are one who claims that you are in touch with the higher power, or spirit or worldly masters, teachers or the God that is within you and everyone, etc., you or whoever, should now be prepared to answer these universal questions.

1. Why are you for on earth now?
2. What level of understanding are you in? Rate yourself later.
3. How were you created originally in the light energy?
4. Who is God? Who created God?
5. What was your atomic structure originally?
6. Did you know the Bible is a book of nuclear physics? Why?
7. What are the 7 lamp stands or 7 electron inertia energy levels?
8. What is nuclear evolution?
9. Who and where are the fallen angels, from perfection?
10. Why are you now a carbon 666 structure that brought on the 1st original nuclear transgression, 1st death, <u>1st original sin</u>?
11. Why is it that now the <u>1st original sin</u> needs to be removed before you shall overcome the carbon 666 death? While alive.
12. How can you remove the <u>defiling 1st original</u> sin and the atomic enmity?
13. How are you going to reunite yourself to the originality?
14. What is the atomic enmity between you and the woman?
15. What is the atomic enmity between your seed and her seed?
16. How old is your soul? How old is your body?
17. How and why did you fall from your divinity?
18. What is the promised redeemer from death?
19. What is psychophysical Christ lunar germ seed of immortality?
20. What are you supposed to do with this germ seed of love?
21. What does this mean: Constant renewing of the mind?
22. What is the power of unconditional limitless love?
23. What is, as stated in the scriptures, the pathfinder Bible: You have left your first love? What is the first love?
24. What are the 7 seals or 7 chakras of your body?
25. What is 1st death and 2nd death?
26. Do you know how to add a cubit to your mortal body and then you need 144 cubits?
27. What does this mean: For your bed shall be too short to stretch out in, and the covers too narrow to wrap in? Why?
28. What is the true immaculate conception?

29. What is: This mortal body must put on immortality? While alive; not dead?
30. Do you know how to put on immortality now?
31. What is: I can destroy the temple and I can rebuild it in 3 days?
32. What does 12 hours in a day mean?
33. What does this mean: The concern for the physical comes first, then comes the spiritual. Why?
34. What does: He who has the bride, is the bridegroom, mean?
35. Did you know that you are to decipher the code number of the beast? What is the code number? Who is the beast?
36. How are you to resurrect while alive from this mortal body?
37. What is cosmic crucifixion? And it is not on a wooden cross.
38. Did you know that: All flesh is not the same flesh in every man? And why do you need the 12 astrological essences fused in your body now?
39. Did you know that every mortal man dares and robs God in tithes? And this has nothing to do with money or donation!
40. What is the etheric plasma of milk and honey manna?
41. How is this milk and honey manna to be used? For what?
42. Did you know that in these days many false prophets will rise? And they are this or that, misleading mankind further?
43. What is: You shall have to lie in wait for the heel? It is something you need to do, not standing or on your knees, only lying down.
44. Why is mankind so much in error now?
45. Do you know how to differentiate the true sacred knowledge? What criteria needs to be used?
46. What is the forbidden fruit of the vine that brings about death and reincarnation, again, again; unless?
47. Did you know: This solar system, planet earth and all mankind is now traversing into the ultra high frequency of 4th dimension, and in the 4th dimension no mortal being can survive, unless? Why not?
48. What do these words mean: In the days of old, in the time long since forgotten? What did you forget?
49. What do these words mean: I will open for you the floodgate of heaven, to pour down blessings of milk and honey manna upon you mankind without measure? For what purpose? What is it? Where does the transmuted milk and honey manna come from in your body?!

50. Did you know that originally God created all mankind perfect, imperishable, immortal? What happened?
51. Who is the parenting group? What for?
52. Did you know that you are invited to something so extra special and inconceivable, that now you can't imagine!? What for?
53. Did you know that when you die, the soul goes to Sheol, to eventually reincarnate again and again, until you do it right, remove the enmity and the <u>1st original sin defilement</u>? You have been doing the same thing over and over again, born again, live, die and reincarnate for the past several billion years, without any change and results. Why? Whose fault is it?
54. Did you know that ignorance is no excuse before the universal laws? The laws work whether you understand them or not.
55. Did you know that the dark force adversaries have studied humanity very well? And you are controlled by them, whether you know it or not?
56. What is: You are now controlled: by the invisible dark forces; by low consciousness; by religions; by the organizations that take you to the grave sooner than you think; by your relations with wife, husband, daughter, son, relatives, friends; by the girlfriend and boyfriend relation; etc.? Excessively numerous to mention!
57. Did you know that there is nothing more important you are doing in your current life experience, than to return to the originality, through the process; that is presently beyond your mortal understanding! If you think otherwise, then it's your ego in full operation in you, that does not exist.
58. Do you understand what is balance, harmony, peace through unconditional limitless love?
59. Did you know that you are now faced with the possibility of complete extinction unless you make a cosmic leap into embracing the process? Of what good is this knowledge, if it is not acted upon?
60. Do you know what this means: Birthing this conception involving the process is next on the agenda?
61. What is: The finite mind is unable to fathom this process?
62. What is: Without this process all creation would collapse into nothingness?
63. What is Michael the Archangel battled with the dragon mean?
64. Why did Archangel Michael come to earth as a mortal, now?
65. Why is it that the coming of the 1st Christ did not occur yet?

"Do I need to go on with zillion more questions? I can!!!"

Also, ask yourself this question. Where do you think all this exclusive sacred knowledge came from? A mortal mind? Impossible! And you don't wish to associate with him. This concerns everyone on earth!

If you don't know the cosmic universal answers to the sacred knowledge that is in this presentation, then either you did not read what is now before you, or your mortal judgment or ego (that does not exist) got the best of you. Please do not skip any pages.

Please accept my apologies to those who I perhaps ruffled-up with these words of wisdom.

https://web.archive.org/web/20140629030833/http://144cubits.com/fewreasonswhy.htm

R is for Religion

As you can observe all religions are a copy of the previous religion, with things changed and added to each one.

https://web.archive.org/web/20040605152143/http://www.144cubits.com/akashic7.htm

Before the commencement of the profound truth, mankind needs to know the historical facts of the grand fraud perpetrated in all religions! **The hoax is: Each religion is based upon the secret esoteric knowledge of the preceding religion; although the key to the sacred knowledge is lost. Consequently every religion is guilty of Plagiarism.**

https://web.archive.org/web/20040605043310/http://www.144cubits.com/akashic1.htm

In error you have been taught that heaven, paradise, purgatory, limbo, hell and the laws of karma exist. None of those things exist. They are man-made by religions to have control over your ignorance and to extract money from you. How can the divine soul go to any of those places when the soul is the I am that I am the Spirit of God?

https://web.archive.org/web/20040605052055/http://www.144cubits.com/akashic11.htm

R is for RNA DNA (Nucleic Acids)

I have devoted more than 40 years of research to bring you a new scientific breakthrough, of how to restore your atomic structure and the RNA DNA to your original state of perfection, the perfect presence. The intricate discovery is arousing, appealing, incredible, shocking and beyond compare. Up to now, what I am about to confide has been hidden from the eyes of the world. The RNA DNA in you is as old as no beginning nor end; older than the universe. Here you shall learn that not only you need to add 1 cubit or 1 atomic element to your phenomenal, priceless body, but 144 cubits-elements, which will reinstate you to the perfect presence, to your original RNA DNA and perfect atomic structure.

https://web.archive.org/web/20040904033006/http://www.144cubits.com/

Nucleic Acids are extremely complex molecules produced by the living cells. The names come from their initial isolation from the nuclei of living cells. The two classes of Nucleic Acids are the Ribonucleic Acids (RNA) and the Deoxyribonucleic Acids (DNA).

The two of the functions of the RNA DNA are to transmit or pass on the hereditary characteristics and factors from one generation to the next. Also, to trigger the manufacture of specific substances. The memory or the code pattern within the RNA DNA communicates to the cells how to reproduce either a duplicate of itself, or the substance it requires for going onwards in life. All living cells embody and contain the genetic material of the RNA DNA.

There is a specific RNA that has a slightly different function from that of DNA. These RNA reproduce by forcing the host cells to produce more germ seeds for reproduction.

The new germ seeds in-turn inject its own RNA into the host cell, and the host cell obeys the code of the newest incoming RNA, rather than that of its own. Thus the cell produces the substance, that are in fact, germ seeds. The parent host cell is then overpowered and destroyed by the newly form germ seeds, and are now free to inject their RNA into other germ cells that become the new memory parents or host cells.

This is exactly what transpires when the RNA DNA Christ germ seed essence of immortality is transmitted from the 1st original Christ then into another and another and another potential Christ.

Here is the analogy of the RNA DNA Christ's milk and honey manna bread of everlasting immortal life. Here is an extract from my 2nd book: Immortality Unveiled. I bake my own delicious sour dough bread from a culture, which I developed many years ago. The germ seeds came from the airborne bacteria. It is the same germ seed culture, same bacteria that makes my bread rise. I keep the culture alive and healthy in the refrigerator, and have used the same culture for many years. To feed and extend the culture, I just add more flour and water, mix it, cover it with a cloth and refrigerate it.

I make my luscious sour dough bread from spelt, rye, kamut or any other whole grains. I grind my own grains into flour, add natural raw honey or natural molasses (from a Health Food store), few grains of natural salt, water and a culture of the germ seed bacteria.

All I need to have my bread rise is a very small amount of the bacterial germ seed culture, which I add to the potential bread. The function of the germ seeds (like the RNA DNA) is of transmitting or passing heredity characteristics from one generation to the next, thus this triggers the manufacturing and replication of identical bacteria as they multiply in astronomical numbers; to have my bread rise. After I mix all the ingredients, I cover it. In a matter of overnight hours my bread rises, due to the cultured bacteria; ready to bake.

The making of my delectable sour dough bread is equivalent to the action and reaction of the RNA DNA Christ germ seeds of immortality, when they are transmitted or passed on from my biological chemistry of the Christ to another and another and another potential Christ. That is how mankind shall be inoculated with the Immune Hormone Substance (IHS) from the original 1st Christ. This shall render humanity free from all the travails of mortal life; including death and thus maintain your youth forever.

https://web.archive.org/web/20040605164708/http://www.144cubits.com/lastsupper.htm

The perfection of the infinite nuclear energy light body is presently locked up in your memory code in the RNA DNA. Now there is a way to unlock the perfect RNA DNA in you. To unlock it and thus harness the infinite energy of the universe, one needs to undergo ???? nuclear fusion.

Within every woman and man lies the latent, dormant omnipotent power of the atoms. The crystal clear light body, the milk and honey manna essence is in the RNA DNA, in the flesh and blood of every woman and man. In the flesh of every woman and man there is the RNA DNA essence for the resurrection from the long since forgotten 1st death, and you need to accomplish this while you are alive.

https://web.archive.org/web/20040605060910/http://www.144cubits.com/akashic12.htm

The twin double helix of the RNA DNA conducts an electrical charge like in an electric cable. The RNA DNA stores information in its biochemical structure, which conduct electricity like in a length of electrical wire. When the RNA DNA is purified to the 5th power, the quintessence, the electromagnetic charge shall transmit the to and fro charge to such long distance as our sun, then to another sun and another sun and all the suns in the universe. That is what shall happen when you shall become one of the Christs. That is when you shall truly understand what these words mean: For the father and son are one and the same pure atomic essence. Who is the father the creator? It is the father-son-mother nature God principle, the mystical trinity of immaculate, pure crystal clear nuclear energy, the Christos, the Christ.

If you were to extract all the RNA DNA from your body, and extend it fully, it would stretch out to the endless infinity, and thus return in a circle to the inceptive point. The length of this lineage information in the RNA DNA would take you all the way to your primeval no beginning or end, when you were originally perfect, immortal, divine, connected to the infinite Spirit of God, which is, the Alpha-Beta-Omega, the father-son-mother nature, the trinity principle, which is the immaculate, perfect, crystal clear nuclear energy light body, the Christos, the Christ.

There are no sickly, aging or death gene coded RNA DNA in your magnificent physical-spiritual body. It is only when you continually damage and eventually break the RNA DNA link, the universal link, the silver cord from the Spirit of God that you disconnect yourself from the divine source, that mortal death comes about.

https://web.archive.org/web/20041225141748/http://www.144cubits.com/refmystrnadna.htm

S is for Santa Claus

Who is the Real Santa Claus? Thus is the metaphysical meaning of Santa Claus coming from the cold expanse of the universe, the Milky Way Stars, the North Pole Star, down the chimney into the fireplace, the fiery seat of passion in woman and man, who brings you a precious Christmas present, the gift of everlasting life, the psychophysical Christ germ seed of immortality. And when the majestic, priceless Christmas present is used wisely, according to the nuclear physics laws, it shall return you to your original state of divinity, the union with the Spirit of God. That is what the coming of the Christ unto woman and man means. The words Santa Claus comes from the word Santa, meaning, Holy, Sacred, and from the human anatomy the word Claus-trum. Claustrum is the cluster, a group of elements, the sacred hormonal substance gathered together around the 12 pair of cranial nerves, the crown of life.

Yes, Santa Claus is coming to town to each of you every lunar month with a most unusual Christmas present that presently you do not know how to use. And the Christmas tree represents you, the Tree of Life, decorated with ornaments and lights, which symbolizes the milk and honey manna, which is gathered from the 12 tribes of Israel, which is you and me and all mankind.

https://web.archive.org/web/20040605063612/http://www.144cubits.com/akashic13.htm

T is for Table of the Elements
The Periodic Table Of The Elements

1. Hydrogen	37. Rubidium	73. Tantalum	109. Unknown
2. Helium	38. Strontium	74. Tungsten	110. Unknown
3. Lithium	39. Yttrium	75. Rhenium	111. Unknown
4. Beryllium	40. Zirconium	76. Osmium	112. Unknown
5. Boron	41. Niobium	77. Iridium	113. Unknown
6. Carbon	42. Molybdenum	78. Platinum	114. Unknown
7. Nitrogen	43. Technetium	79. Gold	115. Unknown
8. Oxygen	44. Ruthenium	80. Mercury	116. Unknown
9. Florine	45. Rhodium	81. Thallium	117. Unknown
10. Neon	46. Palladium	82. Lead	118. Unknown
11. Sodium	47. Silver	83. Bismuth	119. Unknown
12. Magnesium	48. Cadmium	84. Polonium	120. Unknown
13. Aluminum	49. Indium	85. Astatine	121. Unknown
14. Silicon	50. Tin	86. Radon	122. Unknown
15. Phosphorous	51. Antimony	87. Francium	123. Unknown
16. Sulfur	52. Tellurium	88. Radium	124. Unknown
17. Chlorine	53. Iodine	89. Actinium	125. Unknown
18. Argon	54. Xenon	90. Thorium	126. Unknown
19. Potassium	55. Cesium	91. Protactinium	127. Unknown
20. Calcium	56. Barium	92. Uranium	128. Unknown
21. Scandium	57. Lanthanum	93. Neptunium	129. Unknown
22. Titanium	58. Cerium	94. Plutonium	130. Unknown
23. Vanadium	59. Praseodymium	95. Americium	131. Unknown
24. Chromium	60. Neodymium	96. Curium	132. Unknown
25. Manganese	61. Promethium	97. Berkelium	133. Unknown
26. Iron	62. Samarium	98. Californium	134. Unknown
27. Cobalt	63. Europium	99. Einsteinium	135. Unknown
28. Nickel	64. Gadolinium	100. Fermium	136. Unknown
29. Copper	65. Terbium	101. Mendelevium	137. Unknown
30. Zinc	66. Dysprosium	102. Nobelium	138. Unknown
31. Gallium	67. Holmium	103. Lawrencium	139. Unknown
32. Germanium	68. Erbium	104. Unnilquadium	140. Unknown
33. Arsenic	69. Thulium	105. Unnilpentium	141. Unknown
34. Selenium	70. Ytterbium	106. Unnilhexium	142. Unknown
35. Bromine	71. Lutetium	107. Unknown	143. Unknown
36. Krypton	72. Hafnium	108. Unknown	144. Unknown

https://web.archive.org/web/20100104145558/http://www.144cubits.com/impenetrablesecrets.htm

U is for the Universe

Figure 19. "Seal of Solomon – Star of David – Star in the east ancient Masonic symbol"

The ancient symbol of a 6 pointed star represents mortal matter united with immortal antimatter, the union with the divinity, and it signifies the universal limitless peace and limitless love functioning together. The symbol of the 6 pointed star is the universal symbol of Six or 6 or Sex. From the ancient Sanskrit language the word Six means Sex, the Sextuple principle. Sextuple principle means to bring into operation the 4 foundation cornerstones of the universe, which govern the immutable nuclear physics laws of:

⇩ These are the 4 foundations of the universe ⇩

Addition	Light
Multiplication	Life
Subtraction	Love
Division	Liberation

⇩ Universal symbols of 4 gammas forming a gammadion[6] ⇩

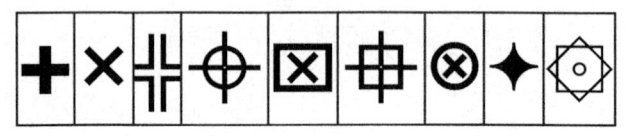

Figure 20. "Universal symbols of 4 gammas forming a gammadion"

The above illustrations are universal symbols of 4 gammas, which are the 4 foundation stones of the universe, which are the fire, air, water and earth, the 144 atomic elements, 144 cubits. And when the 4 gammas are integrated, interlaced, fructified, united together through the sextuple principle, the 4 gammas, the 4 cornerstones form the gammadion, the quintessence, the ether, the nuclear energy milk and honey manna, the celestial Empyrean, the highest form of the Kingdom of God.

https://web.archive.org/web/20100104145621/http://www.144cubits.com/truechristmas.htm

---

[6] Here we do our best to present Xxey's original web images, copied from this Wayback Machine page: where they present differently depending upon one's web browser! When we copy these images from either Chrome or Safari into Word, this is what we get. Fortunately, and for some unknown reason, this process transposes three of the symbols from the webpage into new gammadion figures whose shapes partake of the open or voided cross form alluded to by Xxenogenesis. However, this seemingly preposterous result is a copy of a copy—or a translation of a translation—in order to "equate" or achieve some original "equilibrium." Weirdly and eerily, we also have found that these images decay over time, and we constantly must update our Word files or lose them. (We are reminded of Orchestral Manoeuvres in the Dark, "History of Modern" and the line "all will be erased/and replaced.")

U is for Unlearning

Please know that Unlearning Hurts very badly, because it is a tremendous hurt to the ego. Therefore truth without compassion can release hostility in mankind. I am not hostile to anyone, because I am so compassionate and in love with each of you that if I could, I would even trade places with you for a few fleeting moments. Why would I trade places with you? Because in those moments you would possess all the knowledge that I am now imparting, also you would experience the limitless love that I have for all mankind, regardless who you are, enemy or friend.

https://web.archive.org/web/20040605052055/http://www.144cubits.com/akashic11.htm

V is for Vibrations

The greater is the speed or your frequency of the electrons and antielectrons around the nucleus of an atom, the greater is the life force on an atom. And each of you are created from trillions of atoms. What is your frequency, the natural speed of atoms, your atomic energy? Not produced by artificial propulsion for only a short time!

https://web.archive.org/web/20100104145621/http://www.144cubits.com/truechristmas.htm

Before we shall commence in this form of healing, please listen. The normal vibratory rate of a human body is between 62 and 68 MHz. Megahertz, MHz is one million cycles per second. The brain functions optimally between 72 and 90 MHz. When the mortal body vibration lowers it MHZ, that is when the body is out of balance, out of tune with mother nature. You become sick, dis-ease, body not at ease with mother nature, with the immutable universal laws. The human body is like a delicate stringed violin instrument, that needs to be in-tune all the time, constantly, for it to function and operate properly. If the strings are too tight or too lose, your body is out of tune with the universal immutable laws of nature.

If your body is out of tune with universal mother nature, then all kinds of sickness or imbalances come to you. If you allow that course of action and reaction to continue, nature will follow its path to least resistance. By that it means that whatever is your weakest point in your body, that is where sickness or cosmic disease will occur and manifest. Dis-ease means, your body is not at ease. Your full of tension, stress, out of balance with the universal laws of nature. You need to remove that impediment, the weakest problem, the natural way, not artificial way.

It is a known scientific fact that the human body, while alive, pulsates with electrical currents. The body needs this electrical magnetic electricity constantly to be alive. Or not your body becomes sick with cosmic dis-ease and eventually entropies and dies. Why? Because you have caused it. How? With your tension, stress or dis-ease or sickness, which resonates to the same corresponding sickness frequency like a tuning fork. Strike one note or frequency on a tuning fork, and the other tuning forks will resonate to the same range of energy, thus will follow the same path of least resistance. Your cells in your body operate in the same fashion. How can you solve the problem? By healing yourself in as natural way as possible, without drugs, social drugs, medication, chemotherapy, operations, toxins, radiation, smoking, alcohol, etc. How and what is the way?

By gaining entrance through your subconscious mind to your I am that I am eternal soul, who is the Spirit of God that is within you, who knows everything, who is omnipotent, omniscient, omnipresent, etc. You need to speak to the vital force, the Spirit of God that is within you to heal you, through the subconscious mind, that comes healing. To heal yourself, you need to remove all the stress and tensions, until you are completely relaxed. Then through the subconscious mind, comes healing, the gateway to God is opened.

The creator made the body, so the creator, the source knows how to heal you. The Spirit of God is the mechanic. He made the body, so it happens in no other way how he can heal you. But you need the patience, perseverance, confidence, trust, in God, not through the mixed-up concoctions, incompetence and greed of mortal man.

The to and fro pulsating Megahertz cycles in your body are so fast that you don't even feel them. They are so fast, just like the earth that you don't feel the earth moving at more than 1,000 miles an hour on its electromagnetic axis. The circumference at the equator is more than 25,000 miles. That is why you have 24 hours in a day. Here is how your body works. The mortal body pulsates electrical currents. Normalizing this flow of electricity promotes healing. Whenever you say I love you and you mean it sincerely, you have expanded the natural healing process in yourself and the person you said I love you.

That is a universal law of harmony, balance, peace, love, joy, known as, love thy neighbor as thyself. Who is your neighbor and thyself? Your neighbor is everyone, even your worst enemy. Why love your worst enemy? Because that worst enemy was created by God. You didn't create the worst enemy. The Spirit of God within man did, which means the man went out of balance with mother nature. Evil and good does not exist in the eyes of God. Only mortal man thinks so.

https://web.archive.org/web/20100125182038/http://www.144cubits.com/throughsubconsciousmind.htm

W is for the Weeping Angel of Worthing

The Weeping Angel Predictions, Worthing, England 1960s *[some of Xxenogenesis' favorite predictions, with his comments]*

If I, the universal **Christ were to return in peace on earth, no one would recognize me except my reincarnate.** Meaning: No one would recognize the universal Christ except the reincarnate, the counterpart of him who is on earth.

The lifting of the veil means, the lifting of that veil which prevents complete universal sight, so allowing me fully to be perceived by all my universal units.

It is becoming necessary for me to interfere with the scientific devices of men and halt their progress. I will intervene in many matters of science. I have not embarked on this procedure for the purpose of preventing the manifestation of any or all scientific developments. A great many scientists are aware of an energy that is influencing their thesis. The incoming ultra high frequency of the 4th dimension.

I can halt all matter at any time and make the earth stand still, without giving reason or warning. Those words imply: The Universal Christ can inactivate all the electromagnetic electricity from the earth, so that nothing that depends on any kind of electrical power will operate, including your auxiliary generators, engines, motors, solar power and batteries of every kind, etc.

All are regarding my influence as a challenge. None will stop to reason until I have created a means for them to appreciate fully that their program, is limited in its entire objectivity.

It must be remembered that all must walk only in the light that reflects truth to them. These words are saying: Hold on to the present truth what you know your truth is, until you shall come to the crossroad of understanding the true ancient sacred knowledge, long since forgotten. Then when you shall come to the crossroad of the sacred knowledge, let go of the falseness, apostatize and rebel from the deceptive teachings of world religions and all organizations, which lead all mankind to the pit of self-destruction. Death is not the goal of mortal man.

https://web.archive.org/web/20040604220929/http://www.144cubits.com/prophecies.htm

X as in Cross or Mark

Sin: Falling short of divine perfection by missing your mark of +, or missing your mark of ⊠. Or in other words sin means, missing your mark +, your time for criss+cross+ing and uniting the 2 enmity seeds. When these two marks are superimposed, it denotes missing your mark of à for your divine perfection.

Passover: Passing over the mark + to spare from death.

Sabbath from Sabbatu: To criss+cross+breed, to fructify, impregnate and incubate the seed. Denoting, to impregnate the immortal, antimatter Christ lunar germ seed with the mortal, gross matter soul-ar seed at the time when the germ seed is passing over the Passover mark + to remove the 1st original sin, thus overcome the enmity that is between them. With this accomplishment, at this specific lunar time, this then brings about the **immaculate virgin conception of the Christ** in the mortal being.

Each of these meanings display the Cuneiform mark of a cross +, signifying criss+cross+ing the 4 elemental kingdoms of fire, air, water and earth, the immortal spiritual antimatter with the mortal physical matter, to overcome the atomic enmity between the 2 seeds and the carbon 666 atoms. This also represents the 4 quarters of the universe, which are the 4 cardinal signs of the zodiac, which are the 4 elemental kingdoms. Please listen to the secrets of the universe.

Missing your mark of the cross +, or missing your mark of x, refers to missing the opportunity to fuse the mortal matter soul-ar seed to the immortal antimatter psychophysical Christ lunar germ seed of immortality. Or in other words, the failure of fusing the 2 enmity seeds together through the ???? nuclear fusion. If the nuclear fusion does not transpire due to man's lack of knowledge or how the fusion is to be accomplished, then man has missed the mark and has again committed the unforgivable sin of blasphemy against the Spirit of God.

The appointed time for the ???? thermonuclear fusion of the 2 enmity seeds, the mortal matter seed to the antimatter germ seed of immortality is known as the Sabbath Passover time. The words Sabbath Passover are terms used to describe the specific time, when the 2 enmity seeds are to undergo nuclear fusion.

https://web.archive.org/web/20040605063612/http://www.144cubits.com/akashic13.htm

Xx is for Xxenogeneic

XXenogenesis is a word that is derived from two words. **XXeno:** The combining form, or essence of a guest, visitor, stranger, foreigner, plus **genesis:** to be born. Accordingly, the Christ lunar germ seed is the guest, a visitor, stranger, foreigner, similar to woman's ovulation. This Christ germ seed visits every mortal woman and man, every lunar month for the liberation, redemption, resurrection from the 1st death. That is why in the Bible it is called as the firstborn. Why first born? Because the lunar germ seed is the first born germ seed every lunar month in female and male organism.

https://web.archive.org/web/20100105040149/http://www.144cubits.com/lunargermseed.htm

Here are more meanings to substantiate the word **XXenogenesis,** the process that is in use in the etheric realm existence continuum.

XXenogeneic: A hormonal substance derived from the originator's biological chemistry, to produce an antibody, the antigen for immunity from all disease, aging and death, thus, immortality through XXenogenesis. Antigen is a substance that when introduced into the body stimulates a production of an antibody. The antigens also include foreign bacterium and blood cells. That is how the genetic Immune Hormone Substance IHS functions! That is how the immortal genes are transmitted from one being to another and another, etc.; in the higher realm existence continuum! That is on the ring of wonder.

XXenogamy is a cross-fertilization; the combining and fusion of essences; the transfer of essences from one person to another to another. It is comparable to criss-cross-pollination, immunization, inoculation, cross-breeding.

XXeno: A combing form, plus **gamy**: a coupling, nuclear fusion, union, nucleation. Thus, **XXenogeneic XXenogamy** is the process of exchanging, changing, interchanging the immortal Immune Hormone Substance, the IHS from one being to another, etc. When the XXenogenesis shall be implemented in humanity, the everlasting peace, joy, happiness, love ecstasy is awaiting humanity.

https://web.archive.org/web/20100105040149/http://www.144cubits.com/lunargermseed.htm

The following pages offer a seleXxion of images from the Xxenogenesis album.

Figure 21. Front cover of LP, Xxenogenesis, *SeXxenogenesis #1*
(Private Press, Miami Beach 1973)

Figure 22. Back cover of LP, Xxenogenesis, *SeXxenogenesis #1*

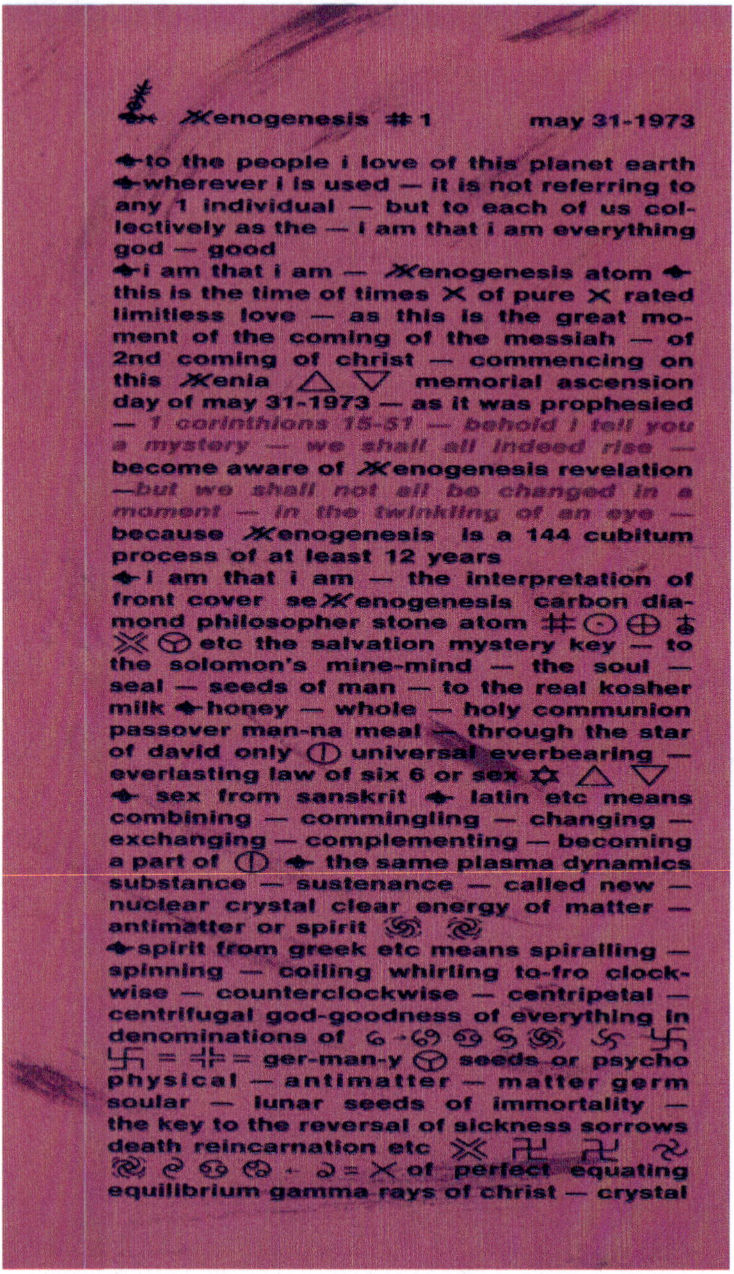

🌿 **Xenogenesis #1**　　　　　may 31-1973

◆to the people i love of this planet earth
◆wherever i is used — it is not referring to
any 1 individual — but to each of us col-
lectively as the — i am that i am everything
god — good
◆i am that i am — Xenogenesis atom ◆
this is the time of times X of pure X rated
limitless love — as this is the great moment of the coming of the messiah — of
2nd coming of christ — commencing on
this Xenia △ ▽ memorial ascension
day of may 31-1973 — as it was prophesied
— 1 corinthians 15-51 — behold I tell you
a mystery — we shall all indeed rise —
become aware of Xenogenesis revelation
—but we shall not all be changed in a
moment — in the twinkling of an eye —
because Xenogenesis is a 144 cubitum
process of at least 12 years
◆i am that i am — the interpretation of
front cover seXenogenesis carbon diamond philosopher stone atom # ⊙ ⊕ ☥
X ☯ etc the salvation mystery key — to
the solomon's mine-mind — the soul —
seal — seeds of man — to the real kosher
milk ◆ honey — whole — holy communion
passover man-na meal — through the star
of david only ① universal everbearing —
everlasting law of six 6 or sex ✡ △ ▽
◆ sex from sanskrit ◆ latin etc means
combining — commingling — changing —
exchanging — complementing — becoming
a part of ① ◆ the same plasma dynamics
substance — sustenance — called new —
nuclear crystal clear energy of matter —
antimatter or spirit ☸ ☯
◆spirit from greek etc means spiralling —
spinning — coiling whirling to-fro clock-
wise — counterclockwise — centripetal —
centrifugal god-goodness of everything in
denominations of 6 ☯ ☯ ☸ ⚛ ☯
卐 = 卍 = ger-man-y ☯ seeds or psycho
physical — antimatter — matter germ
soular — lunar seeds of immortality —
the key to the reversal of sickness sorrows
death reincarnation etc ※ 卍 卐 ☯
☯ ☯ ☯ ⊕ · ♃ = X of perfect equating
equilibrium gamma rays of christ — crystal

Figure 23. The LP's inner gatefold sermon: Column 1
Note: These six images from the album's inner gatefold have been tinted for readability.

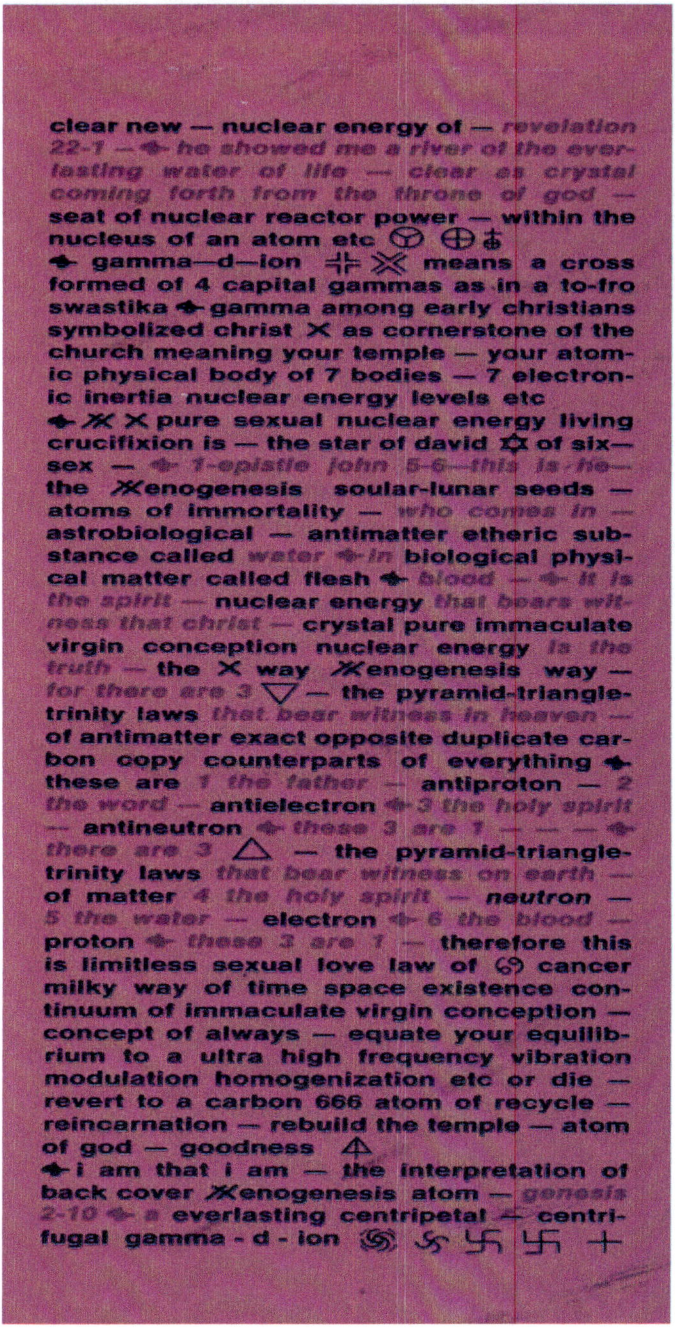

clear new — nuclear energy of — revelation 22-1 — ✤ he showed me a river of the everlasting water of life — clear as crystal coming forth from the throne of god — seat of nuclear reactor power — within the nucleus of an atom etc ⊘ ⊕ ☦
✤ gamma—d—ion ⫫ ✷ means a cross formed of 4 capital gammas as in a to-fro swastika ✤ gamma among early christians symbolized christ ✕ as cornerstone of the church meaning your temple — your atomic physical body of 7 bodies — 7 electronic inertia nuclear energy levels etc
✤ ✕ ✕ pure sexual nuclear energy living crucifixion is — the star of david ✡ of six—sex — ✤ 1-epistle john 5-6—this is he— the ✕enogenesis soular-lunar seeds — atoms of immortality — who comes in — astrobiological — antimatter etheric substance called water ✤ in biological physical matter called flesh ✤ blood — ✤ it is the spirit — nuclear energy that bears witness that christ — crystal pure immaculate virgin conception nuclear energy is the truth — the ✕ way ✕enogenesis way — for there are 3 ▽ — the pyramid-triangle-trinity laws that bear witness in heaven — of antimatter exact opposite duplicate carbon copy counterparts of everything ✤ these are 1 the father — antiproton — 2 the word — antielectron ✤ 3 the holy spirit — antineutron ✤ these 3 are 1 — — — ✤ there are 3 △ — the pyramid-triangle-trinity laws that bear witness on earth — of matter 4 the holy spirit — neutron — 5 the water — electron ✤ 6 the blood — proton ✤ these 3 are 1 — therefore this is limitless sexual love law of ♋ cancer milky way of time space existence continuum of immaculate virgin conception — concept of always — equate your equilibrium to a ultra high frequency vibration modulation homogenization etc or die — revert to a carbon 666 atom of recycle — reincarnation — rebuild the temple — atom of god — goodness ⚠
✤ i am that i am — the interpretation of back cover ✕enogenesis atom — genesis 2-10 ✤ a everlasting centripetal — centrifugal gamma - d - ion ֍ 卐 卐 卐 +

Figure 24. The LP's inner gatefold sermon: Column 2

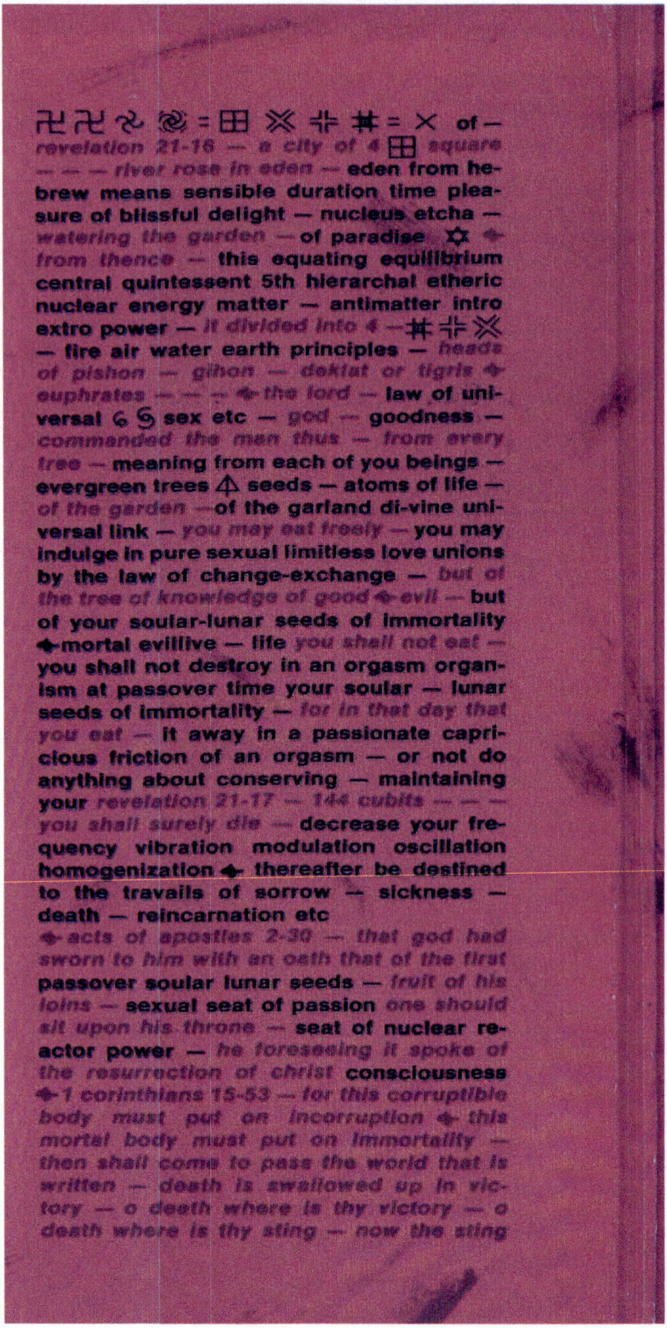

卍 卍 ⚛ ☸ = 田 ※ ╬ ♯ = ✕ of — revelation 21-16 — a city of 4 田 square — — — river rose in eden — eden from hebrew means sensible duration time pleasure of blissful delight — nucleus etcha — watering the garden — of paradise ✡ ✦ from thence — this equating equilibrium central quintessent 5th hierarchal etheric nuclear energy matter — antimatter intro extro power — it divided into 4 — ♯ ╬ ※ — fire air water earth principles — heads of pishon — gihon — dekiat or tigris ✦ euphrates — — — ✦ the lord — law of universal ♋ ♌ sex etc — god — goodness — commanded the man thus — from every tree — meaning from each of you beings — evergreen trees △ seeds — atoms of life — of the garden — of the garland di-vine universal link — you may eat freely — you may indulge in pure sexual limitless love unions by the law of change-exchange — but of the tree of knowledge of good ✦ evil — but of your soular-lunar seeds of immortality ✦ mortal evillive — life you shall not eat — you shall not destroy in an orgasm organism at passover time your soular — lunar seeds of immortality — for in that day that you eat — it away in a passionate capricious friction of an orgasm — or not do anything about conserving — maintaining your revelation 21-17 — 144 cubits — — — you shall surely die — decrease your frequency vibration modulation oscillation homogenization ✦ thereafter be destined to the travails of sorrow — sickness — death — reincarnation etc
✦ acts of apostles 2-30 — that god had sworn to him with an oath that of the first passover soular lunar seeds — fruit of his loins — sexual seat of passion one should sit upon his throne — seat of nuclear reactor power — he foreseeing it spoke of the resurrection of christ consciousness ✦ 1 corinthians 15-53 — for this corruptible body must put on incorruption ✦ this mortal body must put on immortality — then shall come to pass the world that is written — death is swallowed up in victory — o death where is thy victory — o death where is thy sting — now the sting

Figure 25. The LP's inner gatefold sermon: Column 3

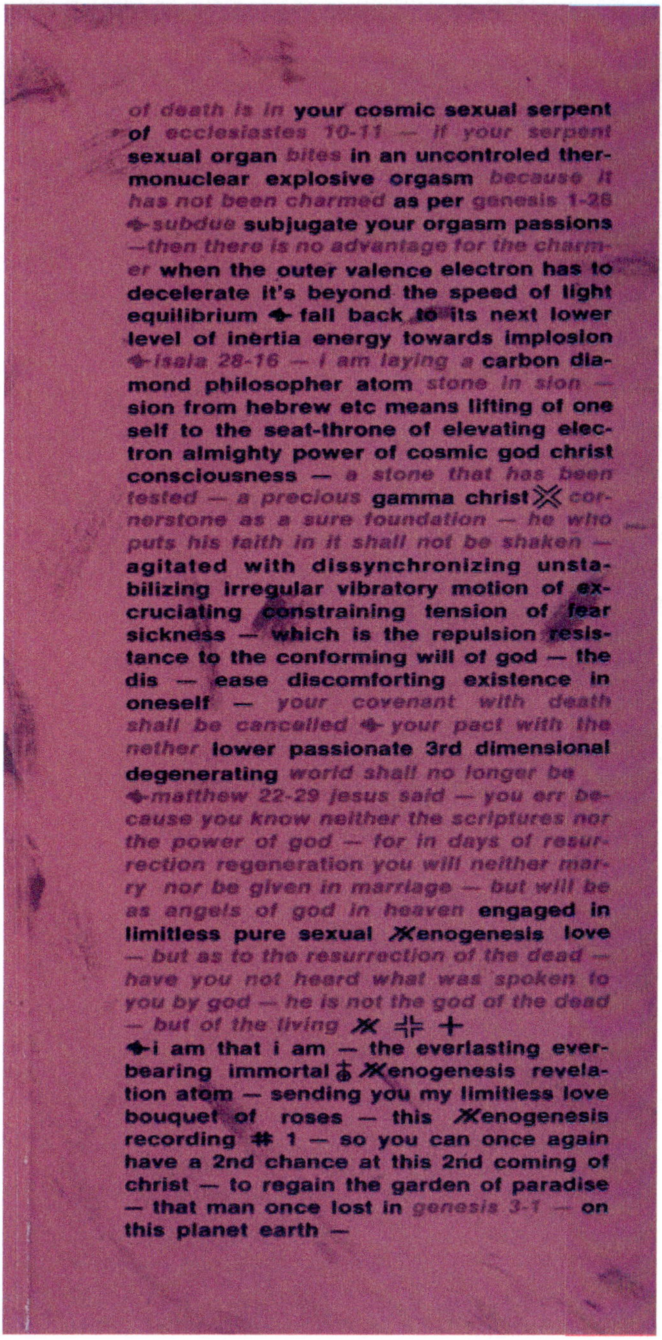

of death is in **your cosmic sexual serpent of** ecclesiastes 10-11 — if your serpent **sexual organ** bites **in an uncontroled thermonuclear explosive orgasm** because it has not been charmed **as per** genesis 1-28 ✦ subdue **subjugate your orgasm passions** —then there is no advantage for the charmer **when the outer valence electron has to decelerate it's beyond the speed of light equilibrium** ✦ **fall back to its next lower level of inertia energy towards implosion** ✦ isaia 28-16 — I am laying a **carbon diamond philosopher atom** stone in sion — **sion from hebrew etc means lifting of one self to the seat-throne of elevating electron almighty power of cosmic god christ consciousness** — a stone that has been tested — a precious **gamma christ** ✗ cornerstone as a sure foundation — he who puts his faith in it shall not be shaken — **agitated with dissynchronizing unstabilizing irregular vibratory motion of excruciating constraining tension of fear sickness** — **which is the repulsion resistance to the conforming will of god** — **the dis** — **ease discomforting existence in oneself** — your covenant with death shall be cancelled ✦ your pact with the nether **lower passionate 3rd dimensional degenerating** world shall no longer be ✦ matthew 22-29 jesus said — you err because you know neither the scriptures nor the power of god — for in days of resurrection regeneration you will neither marry nor be given in marriage — but will be as angels of god in heaven **engaged in limitless pure sexual ✗enogenesis love** — but as to the resurrection of the dead — have you not heard what was spoken to you by god — he is not the god of the dead — but of the living ✗ ‡ ✝
✦ **i am that i am** — **the everlasting everbearing immortal ⚰ ✗enogenesis revelation atom** — **sending you my limitless love bouquet of roses** — **this ✗enogenesis recording # 1** — **so you can once again have a 2nd chance at this 2nd coming of christ** — **to regain the garden of paradise** — **that man once lost in** genesis 3-1 — **on this planet earth** —

Figure 26. The LP's inner gatefold sermon: Column 4

♣ now if you think there is something to this ✗enogenesis ♯ 1 for you ♣ the whole world — you may of your free divine will order ✗enogenesis ♯ 2
♣ these limitless love play by play recordings are sold exclusively only by ✗enogenesis atom — therefore please order direct from ✗enogenesis — as you will not be able to purchase these ✗enogenesis revelations in any store or some private concern or some private individual —
♣ now in order to obtain your ✗enogenesis ♯ 2 — please send me the price of a carbon 666 atom — $6.66 — for ✗enogenesis ♯ 1 ♣ also please send me another carbon 666 atom — $6.66 — for ✗enogenesis ♯ 2 or a total of $13.32
♣ — or you may if you so desire pay more than $6.66 for each — only if you think it's worth it ♣ you can afford it ♣ whence you do either way — i the ✗enogenesis atom shalt be exuberantly delighted to accept your humble generosity for the salvation of mankind — for the rebuilding of garden of paradise here — now on this planet earth
♣ i am not going to kid you or beat around the bush — i need a lot of money ♣ workers in order to help everyone on this planet earth — since you use money here — considering there are about 3½ billion people here — can you imagine if each of you only gave me a 1 dollar — that would be approx 3½ billion dollars — i ask sincerely — humbly — would that be enough — if i in turn spend that same 1 dollar on each of you
♣ if you all — purchase anything from me — a name i call myself — atom — according to your custom of money exchange — i shall be able to raise the monies necessary for the salvation of this planet earth — for the salvation of man of the — i am that i am — a son of god — son of man-na — each of you — equally gifted with the divine attributes of the creator — pro-creator
♣ ✗enogenesis is a hierarchal universal plan for all mankind — it cannot ♣ will not

Figure 27. The LP's inner gatefold sermon: Column 5

operate supervised by your restricted laws of mortal man — mortal thinking — only by limitless god — good — cosmic — christ love shalt all this be accomplished — executed for thou —
✤ my kingdom is not of this earth — your 3rd dimension — but of the 4th ✤ beyond where time does not exist — only every present moment of duliaceting peace ✤ love
✤ i thank you very much
✤ my limitless love to you shalom

i love you very much

Xenogenesis

✤ ✗enogenesis
300 bayview drive a-10
north miami beach-florida 33160
✤ its new jer⇄us a⇄lem
© copyright 1973 by ✗enogenesis
✤ all rights reserved including rights of translation — interpretation throughout the world etc

✤ please send me the following for the salvation — conservation of ✗mas-s ✤ energy — love of mankind

✤ i am now paying for ✗enogenesis #1
12" stereo record — $6.66
    ✤ more because it's worth it
✗enogenesis #1 — 12" stereo record $6.66
✗enogenesis #1 — cassette $6.66
✗enogenesis #1 — 8 track cartridge $6.66
✗enogenesis #2 — 12" stereo record $6.66
✗enogenesis #2 — cassette $6.66
✗enogenesis #2 — 8 track cartridge $6.66

wonderful for meditation
2001 a space odyssey — 12" stereo record
original mgm sound track $5.00
2001 a space odyssey — cassette $6.66
2001 a space odyssey — 8 track cartridge $6.66
the sound of music — 12" stereo record
starring julie andrews & christopher
plummer $5.00
the sound of music — cassette $6.66
the sound of music — 8 track cartridge $6.66

books
the aquarian gospel of jesus the christ by
levi $4.95
the story of an atom by mae & ira freeman
written on an introductory level so everyone
can understand the omnipotenti deus atom $2.95

Figure 28. The LP's inner gatefold sermon: Column 6

111

Figure 29. Xxenogenesis Side 1 Record Label

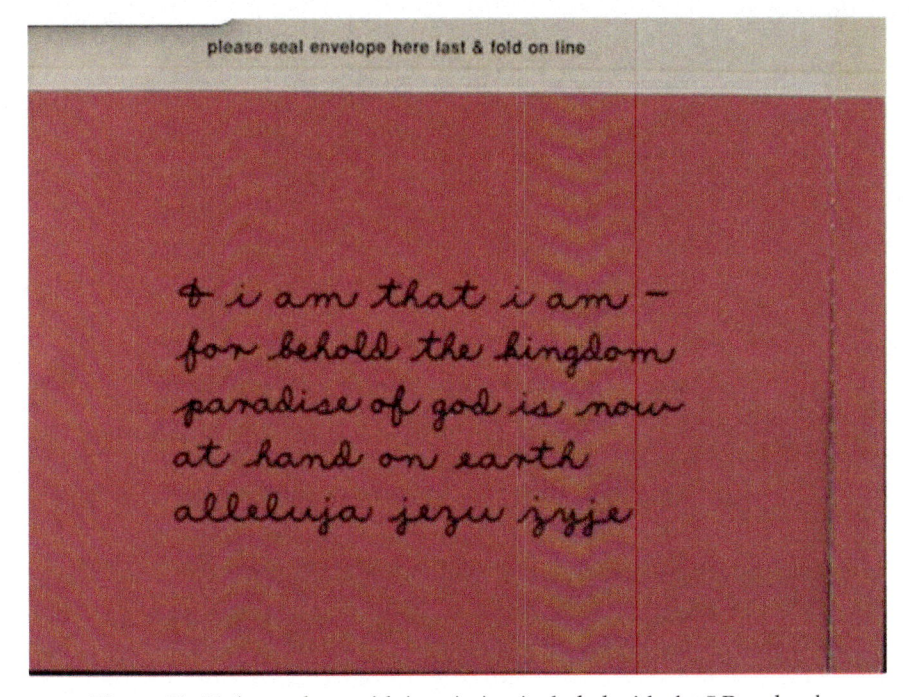

Figure 30. Pink envelope with inscription included with the LP and to be used for sending a message back to Xxenogenesis

4. LP Transcript with Xxegesis

Side 1

(Needle drop: the opening fanfare of Richard Strauss' "Also Sprach Zarathustra," from the *2001: A Space Odyssey* soundtrack, Berlin Philharmonic Orchestra, Karl Böhm conducting [1968])

The album begins with an act of piracy: a lengthy needle drop from a popular movie soundtrack. On the one hand, the Strauss theme immediately brings to mind Arthur C. Clarke and Stanley Kubrick's monoliths, and therefore themes of cosmic intervention and evolution. On the other hand, Xxey's brazen, lawless attitude locates his LP within the trajectory of his notion of religious history: "every religion is guilty of plagiarism."

And hi everyone! My limitless love unto you, the people of this planet Earth.

Greetings from the cosmos: Xxey reveals himself as alien, but the listener is left in suspense for the time being: Is this God, an ascended master, or perhaps an extraterrestrial?

And I am that I am.

Exodus 3:14 (KJV): "And God said unto Moses, I AM THAT I AM." Other translations include: "I will become what I choose to become," "I will be what I will be" and "I am AHIAH ASHAR HIGH [that is, the LIVING GOD]" (Peshitta). This manifold invocation of the Hebrew God affirms itself as pure being. Richard Doyle writes about the Tetragrammaton in this way: "Yahweh instructs us to love the most abstract and yet actual phenomenon in all of existence: "existence itself. 'Yahweh' in Hebrew means 'I am that I am,' or 'Me, I'm Being Itself, Being.'" This last phrasing strongly resonates with Xxey's refrain of "Mi/me a name I call myself." As Doyle interprets later: "While Elohim creates, Yahweh just is." Many new thought and theosophical groups reference this potent claim of self-sufficiency in their fundamental teachings and basic invocations, including Charles Fillmore's Unity Church, Alice A. Bailey's Arcane School, Guy and Edna Ballard's I AM Activity, and Mark-Age, Inc.'s I Am Nation. Bailey glosses its relevance for cosmic consciousness: "If you split this verse into its three parts you have . . . first, the atomic consciousness, I AM; then the group, I AM THAT; a consciousness that he is not just a separated individual . . . but that he is something still greater. Man then reaches the recognition which will lead him to . . . merge his consciousness in that of the group. Of such a conscious union we know practically nothing as yet. This is succeeded by the still greater stage, when I AM THAT I AM will be for us not an impossible ideal, and a visionary concept, but a fundamental reality, when man in the aggregate will recognize himself as an expression of the universal life" (Bailey, *The Consciousness of the Atom*).

Xx   Xx   Xx

Echo and reverb are crucial recording practices of the 20th century that fundamentally undermined notions of "fidelity" in recording. For instance, applied to cowboy songs in the 1930s, echo and reverb added authenticity by signifying "the vastness and loneliness of the prairie and desert country" (Paul Théberge, "Sound of Nowhere," in Robert Fink, et al., *The Relentless Pursuit of Tone*). By the time of the recording of non-jazz popular musics of the fifties, "fidelity had lost its authority. . . [and] [r]ecord producers 'relied not on fidelity but on situating a record in a universe of other records'." The Xxenogenesis LP deploys reverb ruthlessly, creating multiple levels of supernatural, "exaggerated sound spaces" (Peter Doyle, *Echo and Reverb: Fabricating Space*). Expert in sonic forensics Tom Breene notes that the album uses both "plate reverbs and spring reverbs, with a lot of variety in terms of the stereo field and the proportions of wet and dry signals." Here, using his "I Am" (Godlike) voice for the first time, Xxenogenesis may well be using a "panning stereo delay effect," according to Dr. Breene. The controlled and versatile use of reverb on the LP likely also means that the studio where Xxenogenesis recorded the LP owned one or more EMT 140s–expensive, bulky, and heavy plate reverb units introduced in 1957 by Elektro-Mess-Technik and sold to major studios worldwide.

Him. He. I. You. Names. World. Words. Etcetera.

The pronominal distinction between third, first, and second persons can be superseded by the notion of a shared "world," but can also be undermined as mere "words." "All books are prison houses of ideas, and only when speech and writing are superseded by telepathic communication, and by intuitive interplay, will the plan and the technique of its expression, be grasped in clearer fashion. I talk now in symbols . . . but, as I do so, I know well how much must be left unrelated, and how seldom it is possible to do more than point out a cosmology, macrocosmic, or microcosmic, which will suffice to convey a temporary picture of divine reality" (Alice A. Bailey, *Serving Humanity*).

And I am that I am.

(Sings) Do-Re-Mi a name I call myself.

"Do-Re-Mi" is a song from Rogers and Hammerstein's *The Sound of Music* (1959), one of Xxey's favorite musicals. No longer merely mnemonic, this repurposing of popular music may be a warning not to fall into the trap of ego-identity, and further suggests again both the limitations of language as well as the self's ultimate potential translation into song. Indeed, the song is easy to apply to a hierarchical cosmos understood as a gigantic musical scale (as found in the work of Nellie B. Cain). The LP's inner gatefold details that Xxey's small mail order operation will sell you a copy of the soundtrack in one of three formats: LP ($5.00), cassette, and 8 track cartridge (each $6.66). (Years later, the leaders of the UFO contactee group Heaven's Gate renamed themselves "Ti" and "Do" in honor of this song, and wrote a version with new lyrics, including: "Mi are we, next level mind").

The everlasting, infinite, universal SeXxenogenesis atom of Etcha, from the Sound of Music of all spheres.

"SeXxenogenesis" is merely a sexier way (or "SeXxway") to say "Xxenogenesis." In either case, we begin with the atom as a minimal, fundamental esoteric unit, a notion that runs through a great deal of theosophical literature, including the works of Blavatsky, Bailey in *The Consciousness of the Atom* (1922), and Vera Stanley Alder in both *The Finding of the Third Eye* (1938) and *The Secret of the Atomic Age* (1958). Blavatsky on atomic theology: "From Gods to men, from Worlds to atoms, from a Star to a rushlight, from the Sun to the vital heat of the meanest organic being — the world of Form and Existence is an immense chain, the links of which are all connected" (*The Secret Doctrine*). The Pythagorean doctrine of the "music of the spheres" suggests that "the cosmos is musically or harmonically organized" and that therefore music itself can be therapeutic and help to purify the soul (Joscelyn Godwin, *Harmonies of Heaven and Earth*). Everything about Xxey's LP implies that music might aid cosmic evolution, but beware: Agostino Steffani said that dissonance constrains one's *spiritus*, and Tommaso Campanella wrote that "low-pitched sounds bruise, condense and thicken" it. Xxey's love of "ultra-high frequency vibrations" might pose unusual difficulties: Campannella reminds that high-pitched sounds "rarify and lacerate" *spiritus* (Godwin), both dematerializing and raising it, but also tearing and cutting into it.

And who am I? I am just a nobody. Yes, a nobody. Because you can't see my body, but you can hear my voice. So I am a somebody.

Xxey is no one special; to the extent he is "somebody," he is just hanging out in "some body," waiting for transfiguration. And to the extent that he is also "nobody," he might also be positing esoteric community along the lines of Emily Dickinson: "I'm Nobody!/Who are you?/Are you nobody too?/Then there's a pair of us!/Don't tell!" As a final twist, this passage may well resonate with the occult doctrine of attraction suggested by the Dean Martin hit, "You're Nobody Until Somebody Loves You."

Yes, I am the atom existing in a body just like yours. In each of you, speaking to your inner self, to your consciousness, to your inner sanctum soul of your universal mind to where the magical kingdom of God is within you.

Luke 17:21. The "kingdom of God" is an esoteric mystery: "Unto you it is given to know the mystery of the kingdom of God: but unto them that are without, all these things are done in parables" (Mark 4:11 [KJV]). Blavatsky cites the Greek Gospel of the Egyptians regarding the condition necessary for this kingdom's appearance: "When out of Two has been made One, and the Outward has become as the Inward, and the Male with the Female neither Male nor Female." Of course it's all about the body, and, according to Blavatsky, one obvious interpretation of this passage prefigures "the return to the androgynous state as will be the case in future Races" (*Companion to Pistis Sophia*). Xxey's addition here of the word "magical" also hints toward Disney's Florida "magic kingdom" with its utopian pretensions.

Not some place else. For what is here is every place else. And what is not here is no other place to be found.

This citation comes from an early moment in the *Mahābhārata* in which the text itself proclaims that it compiles all known records, and that nothing will be found to be missing from its pages. The quotation was a favorite of Sir John Woodroffe (Arthur Avalon), who introduced sexual Tantrism to the West. When Woodroffe cites it in 1919 he is quoting the Viśvasāra-Tantra, where the reference is no longer to the book but to the human body (*Serpent Power*), and Esalen's John Heider follows suit in his roman à clef *Living in Paradox* (1976): "What is here is elsewhere. What is not here is nowhere" (quoted in Jeffrey J. Kripal, "Roar of Awakening: The Eros of Esalen"). In other words, a bit of *Mahābhārata* ad copy eventually becomes the preferred slogan for the modern tradition of *coitus reservatus*.

And there never was a time that you were not and there never will be a time that you will not exist.

Xxey cites here the words of Lord Krishna in the *Bhagavad Gita* (2:12) who posits that the individual soul is part of the one infinite consciousness (Atman is Brahman). Xxey's point is different: though being human is the same as being dead, all humanity was once immortal and will be again, following implantation of the soular-lunar seeds and the completion of the Xxenogenetic process.

For you are the infinity/anti-infinity of matter/anti-matter.

We are made up of a near infinity of oppositions, including the ultimate dipole of infinity and anti-infinity, and the Xxenogenesis process turns the body into a super collider in which opposites are smashed together and binaries collapse, all in the name of higher synthesis. As any traditional physicist or atomic theosophist will tell you, when a particle meets its matching anti-particle, mutual "annihilation" occurs, and the resulting energy is transmuted into some other form.

And don't be a fool. Don't look to the beyond or hereafter for this kingdom of God. Don't wait till you die to attain some illusion or this paradise of God because it's here in every present moment of now, in each of you, in every atomic cell of your body.

"Don't be a fool" might be the key theme of the Book of Proverbs, and it is here recharged to argue not only that heaven's in here rather than out there, but also that this kingdom is "in every present moment of now" (a now common New Age expression) rather than off in the future. This latter opposition is crucial for historicizing the *longue durée* of the New Age, as Steven Sutcliffe's *Children of the New Age* (2002) argues. Xxey is here on the cusp of history, firmly and forever rejecting the perpetual advent of the Universal Link movement and the UFO contactee clubs, both popular throughout the 1960s.

But I, the Xxenogenesis atom, am having a most difficult time to vibrate-oscillate-modulate, to maintain my resonant beautiful melodious "duliazation" Sound of Music of the spheres in each of you.

When biologist T.H. Huxley first introduced "xenogenesis" into public discourse in 1870, he regretfully noted that the term describing a birthing where "the offspring" [is] "altogether, and permanently, unlike the parent" should have been "heterogenesis," but for that term's having an already existing and quite different scientific meaning. The distinction is subtle: Huxley said that "xenogenesis" means technically "the generation of something foreign" rather than something "unlike," pushing the meaning of the concept toward the strange rather than the merely different. That which is "unlike" might be well-known, while the absolutely "foreign" remains uncertainly open and unfamiliar.

Xx   Xx   Xx

"Duliazation" is one of the most difficult words in Xxey's vocabulary. Another, neologism in the album's liner notes – "duliaceting" – is almost certainly related. These are imaginary compoundings of "dulia," or the reverence accorded to saints and angels in Roman Catholicism. C.W. Leadbeater's gloss: dulia is a "a term denoting servitude, and implying, when used to signify Our worship of distinguished servants of God, that their service to Him is their title to our veneration. As the Blessed Virgin has a separate and absolutely super-eminent rank among the saints, the worship paid to her is called *hyperdulia*" (*World Mother as Symbol and Fact*). Xxey's flirtation here and elsewhere with the cult of the Virgin Mary reflects his intense Catholicism as a young man, and in his discourse suggests the worship of the original and coming androgyne uplifted in the ranks of the godhead. Because "duliazation" follows both "resonant" and "melodious" there might also be a touch of "dulcet"– "sweet and soothing" – in the inventive mix.

So I, the Xxenogenesis atom, have decided to teach each of you how to equate your equilibrium to an ultra-high frequency vibration-modulation-homogenization in your present physical body and every present moment of now is the time to do it yourself.

The passage moves from teaching to self-actualization. Before Xxey was Xxey he was Cash-N-Carry Harry, a sixties spokesman and cheerleader for the budding "do it yourself" movement in home improvement. So why not carry this same philosophy into metaphysics, and be done with gurus once and for all?

Xx Xx Xx

"High Frequency" is half of the formula given to Herman J. Gabryel during the nocturnal visit from the celestial androgyne in 1962. Xxey ascribes to a Theosophically-inspired vibrational ontology – fundamentally, each of us is made of atoms that vibrate, and the more one is spiritually attuned the higher one's vibrational frequency. Nellie B. Cain's 1972 chapter "Perception of Higher Frequency Levels" provides one example. One year earlier, David Spangler's influential *Revelation: The Birth of a New Age* (1971) sets the cosmic tone by arguing that recently, "because of this change in the energies flowing through the etheric, all atomic structure [in the universe] had to undergo a subtle change in order to attune to the formative energies from which it secures its substance and existence. All nuclear energy became transmuted from its attunement to the old etheric 'wiring' to that of the new."

For this brand New Age, right here and right now, Edenic theology is replaced by nuclear theology, and Adam therefore has become an Atom.

Yes, I, the Xxenogenesis atom, have to vibrate extremely very fast, very hot, very passionately in order to function properly.

One might be forgiven for noting the sexual hunger in this passage but not passing over the "passion" in the "passionate" provides a subtle nod to Xxey's cosmic crucifixion.

And you know what the secret to this glorious mystery of life is? It's limitless love, in many forms, in many guises.

The channelled figure of "Limitless Love" has a complex history in the sixties and early seventies, and Xxey found all of it fascinating. At first Limitless Love sent messages to the Universal Link network via Richard Grave of Worthing regarding a worldwide event of "nuclear evolution" that would take place during Christmas time 1967. After that event failed to materialize, Limitless Love went silent for a while, but began speaking to David Spangler at Findhorn in the early 1970s. Limitless Love's new message was more affirmative, decidedly less apocalyptic, and subtly ecological: "I embrace all that lives. I assist the descent of One from beyond this planet who carries New Age energies. . . . The old ideas must go. The concept of love and communion, oneness and respect for all life in its own particular uniqueness, and blending with all life to create new patterns yet undreamed of — these are the concepts which I offer" (*Revelation: The Birth of a New Age*).

For the young and old. For the brown man, for the yellow man, for the black man, for the red man, for the white man, for the electromagnetic spectrum etheric man. For all alike.

Xxey's "man" is universalist, which should come as no surprise. Roy Mitchell noted in *Theosophy in Action* (1923) that Theosophy's first goal was "to form a nucleus for the universal brotherhood of mankind without distinction of race, creed, sex, caste or colour." But Xxey insists here that there are more categories of diversity than dubious markers like "race" or "ethnicity" might offer, and "etheric" man is not so much extraterrestrial as interdimensional, and capable of occupying the entire electro-magnetic spectrum.

For aren't we all the children of the same one God, the atom, the nuclear energy?

The word "God" means nothing more and nothing less than "nuclear energy," a premise that Xxey shares with the founder of chiropractic, D.D. Palmer, and with energy medicines in general. With or without the nuclear, an energy ontology, like a vibrational ontology, attempts to bridge the empty spaces of 19th century materialism, and leads toward Barry Commoner's ecological maxim of the early 1970s: "everything is connected to everything else."

And what is my objective now that I have this immense limitless love pleasure to speak to each of you atoms from my compassionate burning heart of love, of desire to help each of you Carbon 666 atoms to become limitless love?

Xxey is likely the first metaphysician to realize what now seems obvious: Carbon has 6 electrons, 6 protons, and 6 neutrons, and therefore is numerologically comparable to "the number of the beast" in Revelations 13:18, where it is said, "let him who has understanding decipher the code number of the beast; for it is the code number of the name of a man" (Peshitta). Indeed, 666 is the number for all men on earth, each made of deathly carbon. Xxey's insight here was perhaps facilitated by texts like Rachel Carson's *Silent Spring* (1962), who argued that "carbon is not necessarily a symbol of life" and that the wonderworld of post-War carbon-based inventions was more than offset by widespread deaths due to cancers caused by hydrocarbons. Xxey here asks all of us dead Carbon 666 atoms to seek atomic metanoia.

Etcha, Etcha, Etcha, Etcha.

And what does Etcha mean? "E-T-C" means Et cetera. And "E-T" from Latin means: and, uniting, continuum, never-ending. And

"cetera" means: other things of your own limitless imagination. And so on, and so forth.

Etcetera means "and the rest" or "and the like" and in Xxey's monologue it implies that there will always be a "so on, and so forth," potentially "never-ending" and non-stop. The chain of signification meets no limit and that is because it is reliant for fuel on "limitless imagination," the "actual foundation of creation" according to George Adamski and the "formative principle of being – the channel through which consciousness becomes manifest" (*Wisdom of the Masters of the Far East*). The result is that meaning is always excessive, with more and more and more to be plumbed or charted. In that spirit, "Etcha" might also refer to "etch," as in the process of inscription, once again marking out a certain writerly distance from the really real.

And "H-A" means Ha Ha Ha Ha Ha Ha Ha Ha Ha Ha Ouch Ouch Ha Ha Ha Ha Ha Ha Ha Ha Ha Ha Ouch Ow Ha Ha Ha Ha Ha Ha Ha (Breaths in) Ahhhh which is the most capricious, extremely passionate laughter of joy, of blissful happiness.

The aspiring theosophist needs a searching funny bone, according to Alice A. Bailey who insists that all disciples must "develop a sense of humour, a real (not forced) capacity to laugh at oneself and with the world" (*Discipleship in the New Age*). The fact that this ability to laugh at oneself sometimes hurts (Ouch and Ow!) reflects Xxey's belief that "unlearning hurts," and that the ego is bruised whenever one's received, cherished beliefs collapse. "Capricious" is an adjective to describe a person or thing that's impulsive and unpredictable, like a bride who suddenly leaves her groom standing at the altar. Blavatsky likes this word almost as much as Xxey and uses it to describe the "self" or "ego" "that serves as the fundamental base, determining the tone of the whole life of man." As such, it is "that most capricious, uncertain and variable of all instruments, and which more than any other needs constant tuning; it is its voice alone, which like the sub-base of an organ underlies the melody of his whole life" ("Are Dreams But Idle Visions?").

For I am that I am.

The everlasting forever and ever you'll be my limitless love of no beginning nor no end. The alpha beta omega.

Limitless love overcomes mortal time and opens onto infinity ("from alpha to omega"), but what's "beta" doing here? Let's look elsewhere: the Theosophical Seal incorporates all three of these letters and Arthur M. Coon writes that by placing "alpha" and "omega" together on the seal, "we have a word which signifies the union of spirit and matter, uniting the two poles of being - God as 'Father-Mother'." And "beta," Coon writes, is the word made flesh, or the Son. So that Xxey's formula of "alpha beta omega" is a kind of shorthand for what Christianity calls the Holy Family (*Theosophical Seal* [1958]).

Ha Ha Ha Ha Ha Ha Ha Ha Ha Ha Ha Ha. It's fun to be alive eternally, perpetually.

The verb "fun" in Middle English means to cheat, to hoax, or to fool. So is Xxey genuine or just gaming? And no matter which, what are the stakes? Bataille: "Laughing at the universe liberated my life. I escape its weight by laughing."

For I am that I am. The immortal.

A major revelation that the stakes of Xxey's project involve immortality and maybe not just metaphorically but "for real." As Alice Bailey reported as early as 1936: "Doubt as to the fact of immortality, will be solved before long in the realm of science, as the result of scientific investigation. Certain scientists will accept the hypothesis of immortality as a working basis upon which to base their search, and they will enter upon that search with a willingness to learn, a readiness to accept, and a desire to formulate conclusions based upon reiterated evidence" (*Esoteric Psychology I*).

(Sings) Mi a name I call myself.

And now that I am here with you, I want to reverberate-vibrate-modulate-homogenize each of you. To love you, to trill you, to shrill you.

Trilling is quavering or warbling, much like some of the crooners of the late 1920s and early 1930s as well as their great champion in the modern era, Tiny Tim. It cannot escape the attentive listener that every time Xxey edges toward musicality he starts to trill. He is a crooner at heart, working the mic at close range and serenading you and you alone using a tuneful language of love. And "shrill" is high-pitched and piercing, much like an ultra-high frequency vibration. Once again: Ouch! Unlearning hurts!

To the most delicious, capricious dessert of God, of 2001, a space odyssey.

Xxey cites Rumi's *Masnavi* ("You will eat your fill of the viands and dessert of God, so that hunger and begging will depart from you") and further predicts that if you follow his advice your life will now begin to imitate art – or better, film.

And who is God and what does God mean? And "GOOD" from Anglo-Saxon means God.

One of the key forms of Herman-eutics involves interpretation by means of convoluted and unprovable etymologies a-maze-ingly sourced through Xxey's library of dictionaries and Bibles and judgeable as either crackpot or visionary. De Saussure emphasized that the meaning of the signifier was based on difference, while Xxey always errs on the side of similitude, risking the possibility that all words are grasping at the same impossible concept or idea. Applied to the case at hand, that is either good news or God-awful.

For everything, everywhere. Always good, always in a perfect, spinning, whirling immaculate virgin conception. X-way, sex way, SeXxenogenesis way.

The spinning, whirling swastika (Sanskrit: *svastika*, "conducive to well-being") is one of the fundamental symbols of Theosophy as developed by Madame Blavatsky, and it here mimics the movement of the atom's electrons, so central to Xxenogenetic transformation. When the swastika stabilizes as the cross (and evokes the crucifixion), it inscribes Xxey's signature "X" mark. "Immaculate virgin conception" obliquely references the fact that Xxenogenetic birth is premised on semen and seed reversal, and that all practitioners are therefore impregnating themselves. Two more points: this is yet one of many examples of Xxey's excessiveness: why use one adjective to modify this conception when there's always more? Finally, it is important to note that Blavatsky's 19th century Aryanism – reflected in her use of the swastika – is regarded as outmoded by Xxey who champions both the full color and the electromagnetic spectrums (as quoted above).

Always in excess, abundance, well-beloved, well-balanced in a perfect, constant equating equilibrium to an ultra-high frequency vibration-modulation-oscillation-homogenization.

Xxey's Bataillian moment of expenditure without reserves and general economy. A surplus of energy ruptures equating equilibrium. However, this leads to a clearer understanding as to why Xxey privileges etcetera and takes up Etcha as his guiding mantra. In the same vein, it should also be noted that the last word on the album cover (the Hebrew word Shalom) is followed by the mark of +. In other words, Xxey wishes us peace in excess. After all, there is always more to come.

Always friendly, loving, humble, sincere, true, honest, dependable, etcetera etcetera etcetera beyond imagination.

Holy triple etcetera! Xxey herein marks the infinite play of signification as a necessarily never-ending process, moving beyond imagination.

And I am that I am.

The only one begotten son of good, God. For I am the only one procreative, creative sexual seed, the hand of God, the atom, nuclear energy in a constant state of nuclear evolution in time-space-existence-continuum-concept.

The key term "nuclear evolution" refers to the Weeping Angel of Worthing's prediction that in 1967, at Christmas, celestial beings will reverse a potentially catastrophic nuclear event and turn it into an epoch-transforming moment, inaugurating the New Age on late, great planet Earth. By 1968 Grand Rapids, Michigan channeler Nellie B. Cain, a key figure in the Universal Link movement, argued that "nuclear evolution" was a process taking place entirely within the human body, and Christopher Hills, responding in kind, entitled his New Age tome, *Nuclear Evolution*. But why add the word "concept" to the end of the mega-compounding of time-space-existence-continuum? Once again Xxey marks his discourse's own apophatic relationship to the noumena.

And I am that I am.

Shazam!

From here to the next line, Xxey speaks words of power and magical invocation. Since 1940, when said by Billy Batson, "Shazam!" (an acronym for Solomon, Hercules, Atlas, Zeus, Achilles, and Mercury) transforms this normal boy into Captain Marvel, an early D.C. superhero. But before worrying overmuch about Xxey's worship of the *Übermensch*, it's best to ponder on this: Xxey loved the military sitcom *Gomer Pyle, U.S.M.C.* (1964-69), and Gomer cried out, "Shazam!" whenever he needed to express amazement or wonder.

(Sound of Fire)

"'What says the esoteric teaching with regard to Fire?' Fire is the most perfect and unadulterated reflection, in Heaven as on Earth, of the ONE FLAME. It is Life and Death, the origin and the end of every material thing. It is divine SUBSTANCE" (Madame Blavatsky, *The Secret Doctrine*).

Adacadabra! Fee-fi-fo! Open Sesame!

Two more terms of power, the ultimate performatives, bracketing a possible ringer. The oddly enunciated variant of "abracadabra" likely still refers to an utterance by a mage who speaks a spell from a grimoire or grammar, and which literally means, "I will create according to the words" (Hebrew Wikipedia). "Open Sesame" comes from an eighteenth-century version of *One Thousand and One Nights*, and one theory suggests that "sesame" is a reduplication of the Hebrew *šem* ("name"), "i.e., God or a kabbalistic word" for "name of heaven" (English Wikipedia). But Jack and the Beanstalk's "Fee-fi-fo" seems to be short a "fum," and typically is translated (in full) as a merely belligerent response to some disturbance: "Where? Why? How? Whom?" (PlanetFusion.co.uk). But Charles Mackay has suggested alternatively that these four syllables can be translated as, "Behold food, good to eat, sufficient for my hunger!" (English Wikipedia), which implies filiation with the earlier citation of Rumi regarding the "dessert of God," and thus suggests that the Xxenogenetic process involves recovering a plenitudinous "meat out the eater" (as Samson would say [Judges 14:4]), or sustenance from our own dead atoms. And there's still more left unsaid about Xxey's feast of incantations. "Open Sesame" may well forecast Herman J. Gabryel's purchase in the late 1980s of the Chiron agricultural sprayer, which made a sound that opened plant stomata. And "abracadabra" colloquially often means "mumbo jumbo," thus joining Xxey's consistent risking of nonsense.

(Sound of Nuclear Explosion)

The myriad 1950s UFO clubs all take up the explicit mission dictated to contactees by the celestial travellers: to end the worldwide threat of extinction by nuclear weapons. This marks without further comment the germ motivation of post-War proto-New Age seekers.

To be or not to be.

When read by Hamlet, this Shakespearean line concerns a living being who is pondering suicide. Which is best? Life or death? The choice remains just as stark for Xxey, but he scrambles the coordinates of this utterance by asserting that we are all already dead (and have been since we fell into a world of gendered matter), and that our only hope is resurrection by means of tantra. To remain dead, or to revive? That is the question.

Who's there?

Who's knocking?

The Son of Aquarius. Most capricious Capricorn Xxenia, seed of Oooooooommmmmmmmm. The Prince of Peace. Xxenogenesis atom. The rock-seed-fruit of the one and only universal vine. Link of God-good.

Herman J. Gabryel was born on January 16, on the cusp of Capricorn and Aquarius, and therefore Xxey is talking here about his own sign and astrological chart (as well as the timing of his cosmic crucifixion, which occurred between January 16 and 26, 1971). Note the use of "Xxenia" in an expanded Xxey lexicon, referring not to Herman's wife but to his own emergent feminine side in a startling moment of self-androgynization.

Also worth noting: Herman's long "Om" reminds the attentive listener of the importance of both Hinduism and Buddhism for Theosophy. Indeed, the Theosophical Seal sports the "Om" symbol as a kind of crown.

And let there be perfect equilibrium of matter/anti-matter, of limitless light, love, life, liberation. Etcha.

(Sound of Thunder and Rain.)

With these sound effects, Xxey comes on like a 60s haunted house record and rocks it old school because "divine origin does not mean here a revelation from an anthropomorphic God, on a mount amidst thunder and lightning; but as we understand it, a language and a system of science imparted to the early mankind by a more advanced mankind, so much higher as to be divine in the sight of that infant humanity" (Blavatsky, *The Secret Doctrine*). Here, J.G. Bennett's dramatic universe takes a turn for the melodramatic!

And I am limitless pure love, limitless pure sex. For love is incomplete without sex and sex is incomplete without love.

Here Xxey just says "no" to the hippies and their notions that love is an illusion and that the pleasures of sex should be freed from all bourgeois convention and affect. Remember: love is the law.

(Sings) And I have the whole world in my hands. I have the whole world in my hands.

An African American spiritual collected for the first time in 1927 by composer and arranger Edward Boatner, and popularized by Marion Anderson, Perry Como, Mahalia Jackson, and Johnny Cash (though Xxey's phrasing here seems borrowed from Laurie London's hit version of 1957).

While the Xxenogenetic process takes place at the atomic level, the resulting ascended atoms are capable of grasping the totality of our shared world (minus themselves, of course – a constitutive blindspot). Relatedly, there is unresolved tension here between Xxey's new egolessness and his substituting the first person for the song's original third person address. Is this a case of quantum superposition?

Meaning atoms at your disposal in SeXxenogenesis.

Xxey hopes to dispose you toward nuclear evolution, and if that happens you will find that your own atoms are crucial minions or helpmates – and therefore at your disposal. Bonus: the disposing of a mountain of toxic, carbon waste.

For you all are the creation from the twelve astrological sun sign stars.

(Sings) Stars are the windows of heaven.

A song from the 1920s, recorded by Ruth Etting, the Andrews Sisters and even Canadian songbird Anne Murray in the late 1970s. Contra astrophysicists, who also "wonder what is a star," angelologists posit that stars are windows "Where angels peep through/Up in the sky they keep an eye/On kids like me and you." The hierarchical implication is that measly humans are just kids. As Gerald Heard asked: Is another world watching? Yes, there are eyes in the sky.

That shine above macrocosmically. The same corresponding astrological identical sex way in each of you as well as microcosmically identically in each of you.

Theosophists treat Hermeticism as part of their deep history, accurately prefiguring their own doctrines regarding the macrocosm and the microcosm ("as above, so below"). But Herman-ticism is almost certainly heretical, with its claim to have bridged the distance via a unique "sex way" causeway.

Because we are all and everything on the same universal limitless love-length called spirit. And SPIRIT is derived from Latin and

Greek meaning a twisting, coiling spiral etcetera. Therefore spirit means spiraling, whirling, orbiting electrons, the cosmic hissing serpents around the nucleus of protons, neutrons. SSSSSSSSSSSS.

More fantastical, Herman-neutical etymology, where homonymic logic and serendipity reign supreme. In terms of this passage's general thematics, esoteric science has long concluded that the cosmos is composed of spirals within spirals within spirals. According to Madame Blavatsky, cosmic evolution is itself spiral-shaped. And she says that the divine feminine energy known as Kundalini is "called the 'Serpentine' or annular power on account of its spiral-like working or progress in the body" ("Voice of the Silence" 25). Famed chemist and enthusiastic theosophist William Crookes created a spiral-shaped table of the elements in 1888, which was later reproduced in Besant and Leadbeater's *Occult Chemistry* (1908). And A.P. Sinnett further noted that the etheric atom is constructed from "very numerous spiral forms" ("Vibrations"). And let's not forget that DNA is spiral shaped! Biogenetically speaking, James Watson and Francis Crick's discovery of the molecular structure of DNA in the early 1950's in terms of the double helix is taken for another spin with Xxey (becoming the double heliXx). Xxey's contribution to this never-ending story of serpentine movement is to note that electrons, too, are always moving in spiral patterns. The painting on the back cover of the album offers a direct representation of "the cosmic hissing serpents around the nucleus of protons, neutrons" with the depiction of six snakes with golden electrons in their mouths coiling around a sphere and biting their own tails. Xxey therefore stages here the ancient serpentine figure of Ouroboros as the hermetic symbol of the cycle of life, death and rebirth and this is also endemic to metanoia itself.

Or it means to-fro quintessent nuclear matter/anti-matter energy of twelve astrological, biological divisions. From the twelve tribes of Israel etcetera which influence everything including your precious physical body.

"To-fro" is a happening concept of movement side-to-side, and "quintessent" is the adjectival form of "the fifth and highest element in ancient and medieval philosophy that permeates all nature and is the substance composing the celestial bodies" (Merriam-Webster). So we are here careening across the heavens, from one zodiac position to another, working relationships among the "tribal" signs. Only a fundamental understanding of these relationships and a great sense of timing will protect one from painful error.

And thou shalt not have strange gods before me for I, the atom, me and the holy-whole complete Trinity of God.

Xxey invokes the first commandment (Exodus 20:3) here and he atomizes it. In the KJV, the text reads: "Thou shalt have no other gods before me." Xxey's substitution of "strange" for "no other" offers an ironic doubling of the term "Xxeno."

For I am the Xxenion proton neutron electron.

The atomic Trinity is now spelled out for the listener.

And I am always in a perpetual, everlasting, everbearing state of immaculate virgin conception.

Certainly not overbearing.

And I am that I am.

(Sings) Do-Re-Mi a Name I call myself.

An atom. The *omni potenti deus*. One hundred forty-four cubit sperm ovum. Oooooooooooommmmmmmm.

When it comes to sexual potency, Xxey is feeling God's power in all directions. The concatenation of sperm and ovum criss-crosses the sexual and the spiritual.

Seed. For without this seed me atom fruit from your sensual-sexual Peter, of your revelation X-John, you could not be, there could not be anything.

In the world of Xxenogenesis, the saints are also re-sensualized and re-sexualized with Peter doubling as penis and with an X-rated John.

For I am the only one begotten son of God, Atom, and the only one God of always, everywhere, everything, transmuted into goodness.

John 3:16 (Peshitta): "For God so loved the world, that he gave his only begotten Son, that whosoever believeth in him should not perish, but have everlasting life."

And upon these petra-peter-rocks, your ovum-sperm-seeds I, each of you, shall build my church, my temple.

Matthew 16:18 (KJV): "That thou art Peter, and upon this rock I will build my church" (and "Peter" is from the Greek "petros," meaning stone-like hardness). So, the sexual humor of this passage is pronounced, as Xxey's satyriac hard-on inevitably prompts him to get his rocks off. It is becoming clear here that the LP is about sex magic, and we might start to think of Herman J. Gabryel as the second coming of the hybridic Egyptian-Greek god Hermanubis, "revealer of the mysteries of the lower world . . . and also of the sexual mysteries" (Blavatsky, *Theosophical Glossary* [1892]).

Meaning your own immortal, infinisonic, E=mc2 body of Christ, God, cosmic consciousness.

While "ultrasonic" is an important technical term for sound beyond human hearing, the unusual coinage "infinisonic" is an Xxey neologism. Clearly a more catholic space-time construction in the realm of sound, infinisonic points toward a godlike auditory experience of infinity, listening in on all frequencies.

So that you may be able to travel in universal flying objects, UFO space crafts, without any hindrance as to food, air, water, etcetera if only you will please have forbearance with me as good manners and humility take time to learn the real kingdom of God which is in my paradise, in the unharnessed virgin atom in your body.

On the one hand, Xxey here makes clear that he does not believe in the extraterrestrial hypothesis with respect to UFOs (where aliens are merely beautiful, feminized men from Venus), but subscribes instead to the "etheric" or fourth dimensional theory promoted first by Mark Probert and Meade Layne in the 1940s, and then later by prominent ET heretics such as Jacques Vallee and John Keel. Indeed, Xxey is so sure about UFOs that he no longer needs to think of them as "unidentified" but instead as "universal" harbingers of raised humanity. Also worth noting is that the problem of time weighs heavily here. In *The Gay Science* (1882) Nietzsche wrote, "Lightning and thunder require time, the light of the stars requires time," and sometimes even Xxey must acknowledge that cosmic education "takes time."

And that is why wherever I go, wherever I am, everyone calls me by my indivisible name—nuclear energy, seed, atom.

The invoking of Xxey's "indivisible name" is reminiscent of a passage in Golden Dawn magus MacGregor Mathers' *The Key of Solomon the King* (1888) that references Adam (subbing for atom): "I conjure ye by the Indivisible Name, IOD, which marketh and expresseth life and their virtue, which Adam having invoked, he acquired the knowledge of all created things."

And I am that I am.

Faith, hope, charity of divine, limitless sex love, of won't you be my Valentine, my next sweetheart, my next love encounter?

Herman was a faithful and devoted husband at the time of his cosmic crucifixion in 1971 and during the recording of the LP just a year or two later. But here's the rub: the Xxenogenetic process typically needs to be passed on from person to person like a meme in order for planet Earth to reach critical mass. Here Xxey alternately comes on like the lost, fourth McGuire Sister, getting ready to sing "Won't You Be My Valentine?" on the Arthur Godfrey Show in 1957, or some prefiguration of Chuck Woolery promoting his 1980s syndicated series, "Love Connection." Aspirationally tuned toward free love, open relationships, and endless seriality.

But thou mankind must first learn that God said, "And I am the Lord meaning the universal law of thy atomic name, your divine heritage principle that each of you are, for I am that I am my own self God."

This passage of pronouns flickers between archaic and modern (thou and you, thy and your), suggesting a listening experience akin to time travel.

Of your magnificent, fantastical, magical kingdom which is in my temple, my only one true universal apostolic church—one congregation of atoms assembled from the twelve tribes of Israel in my and yours own body of Christ.

Xxey's notion of congregation (whether temple or church) splinters off from Christianity by situating all members within one's body. Even though the twelve tribes of Israel are taken by Xxey for an atomic spin, one cannot help but hear the echo of St. Walt in this passage. "Do I contradict myself? Very well then I contradict myself, (I am large, I contain multitudes.)"

And I, if I destroy, lose this physical body, my means of conveyance, I must once again rebuild, reincarnate until I overcome death and transmute my glory of God, of good onto the fourth dimension and beyond, of infinisonic relativity, of E=mc2.

Xxey believed in reincarnation, but only in human form, because neither animals nor plants vibrate at rates fast enough to sustain consciousness. The project of metempsychosis, as Xxey understands it, is aimed toward the etheric fourth dimension or what he sometimes calls "the City of the Four Square." The rich exchange between Victorian mathematics, Theosophy proper and theosophically inclined fellow travellers resulted in a small shelf of relevant works written over many decades including, most prominently, Charles Howard Hinton's *The Fourth Dimension* (1904), P.D. Ouspensky's *Tertium Organum* (1920), Alexander Horne's *Theosophy and the Fourth Dimension* (1928), and Claude Bragdon's *A Primer of Higher Space* (1913) and *Four-Dimensional Vistas* (1941). To further explicate these ideas, one can turn to some of the last lines in the album gatefold where Xxey proclaims: "& my kingdom is not of this earth – your 3rd dimension – but of the 4th & beyond where time does not exist – only every present moment of duliaceting peace and love."

And that is why God said in the Second Commandment, "And thou shalt not take the name atom, the procreative sexual seeds of the Lord thy God in vain."

Here comes the second commandment Xxenogenesis style (Exodus 20:7). It is not only that the name of the atom (what stands in for YHVH) should not be used in vain. It is also semen.

Meaning thou shalt not waste your most precious, procreative substance, of your body of Christ, in an orgasm-organism of selfish gratification.

Every businessman's goal is focused on the minimization of waste, and when Herman J. Gabryel ran the Gabryel Horn of Plenty lumber yard in the mid-1960s, his interest in computerization of his inventory and sales operations was entirely a matter of efficiency. Here Xxey mimics this logic, suggesting that orgasms must be rationed within a restricted economy.

Does that mean that I cannot enjoy sex anymore? Positively not. Because when one shall learn the pure art of Xxenogenesis limitless love, you shall all be able to engage in an immense, most glorious, extremely very passionate, capricious, sexual Etcha love one cannot comprehend now. It will be most delightful to make pure love to whomever you wish.

While Xxey often refers to the Xxenogenetic process as governed by both traditional and occult science, its bedroom practice remains an "art" beyond right or wrong and allied to Etcha's non-stop and never-ending desires.

And as it was prophesized in the yesteryears for the Second Coming of Christ in the *Aquarian Gospel of Jesus the Christ* 7:21: "The only Savior of the world is love. And Jesus, son of Mary, comes again to manifest that love to men. And now love cannot be manifest until its way has been prepared. And naught can rend the rocks. Remember the rocks (atoms) and bring down lofty hills. Fill the valleys up and thus prepare the way, but purity. But purity in life men do not comprehend; and so, it too must come in flesh. Remember in flesh."

Levi H. Dowling's *The Aquarian Gospel* (1908) is a fascinating document, drawn from the Akashic Records and narrating Jesus' early years of travel and initiation in the East. The text's pronounced egalitarianism finds Jesus scolding the various religious leaders he meets about race, caste, and even the treatment of animals. Its wide popularity was such that a large chunk of it was incorporated into the *Holy Koran of the Moorish Science Temple* (1936), including the lines Xxey cites here. But Xxey's appropriation of Dowling's notion of "purity" is neither orthodox nor ascetic but tantric in nature and emphasizes purity of motive over all else.

"And this exiting, exodus Piscean age will comprehend but little of the works of Purity and Love; but not a word is lost, for in the Book of God's Remembrance, a registry is made of every thought, and word, and deed."

The Aquarian Age is soon here, though not yet. But do not despair regarding works that came early in order to prepare the way for the coming of the Christos in the plural, because all such matters and deeds have been recorded and archived in what Xxey and C.W. Leadbeater called the Akashic Records, and what Blavatsky referred to as "the *Skandhic* record" (*Lucifer*, Oct. 1891). These records remain permanently accessible through heroic acts of clairvoyance, such as in Dowling's reconstruction of the *Aquarian Gospel*.

"And when the world is ready to receive, lo, God will send a messenger to open up the book and copy from its sacred pages all the messages of Purity and Love. Then every man of earth will read the words of life in language of his native land. And men will understand the light, walk in the black-white light equilibrium and be the light. And men again will be at one with God."

This is by far the longest quotation from a Gospel source. Xxey incorporates the last three passages from "The Education of Mary and Elizabeth in Zoan" in *The Aquarian Gospel* 7:21-28. The source's Verse 27 reads differently ("and men will see the light, walk in the light and be the light") and it is extremely important to mark the shift here from "light" to "black-white light equilibrium." This links up not only with the celestial androgyne's message to Xxenogenesis ("Equate Equilibrium High Frequency") but also reflects upon light's polarities – and their present-day (dis)connection. When Xxey says, "Men will understand the light," also note his phrasing's proximity to, "Men will understand delight."

And I am the only one, SeXxenogenesis way, the resurrection and the everlasting life, for this earth or any other.

John 11:25.

For I am that I am.

The SeXxenogenesis Etcha atom, the solar (S-O-U-L-A-R) -lunar seeds of immortality, of immunity from death.

Theosophy is sollogocentric, with the solar logos "the closest thing Theosophy has to a god," according to an anonymous seeker on the internet. Xxenogenesis, always working the microcosm, threads a spaceways vocabulary back inside the body recoding "sun" as "soul" (with the addition of the extra "u/you").

Xxey studied Harold W. Percival's provocative interpretation of Patanjali's *Yoga Sutras*, though he disagreed with him on some of the particulars. According to Percival's foundational account, the solar seed originates "at the pituitary gland" and eventually travels up and down the spinal cord to the "pineal body." "On its southern and northern journeying it patrols the spinal cord, the path of eternal life." The lunar seed, on the other hand, "is produced by the generative system....It is called lunar because its travel through the body is similar to the phases of the waxing and waning moon, and it has a relation to the moon. It starts from the pituitary body and continues its downward path along the nerves of the esophagus and digestive tract, then, if not lost, ascends along the spine to the head. On its downward path it gathers Light which was sent out to nature, and which is returned by nature in food taken into the digestive system, and it gathers Light from the blood which has been reclaimed by self-control" (*Thought and Destiny* [1946]). Meanwhile, Xxenogenesis held the position that the solar and lunar seeds, formed in the brain, move primarily down and up the spinal cord as it passes through the chakras—the holders of consciousness.

Hey, bud, are you for real?

Xxey's first announcement of the theme and ultimate goal of immortality prompts the sceptic, the heckler in the audience, the unbeliever who challenges him and who speaks in the colloquial – the vulgar (and not vulgate) language questioning his reality. Comedian Jerry Lewis (Joseph Levitch) is credited by scholars with this expression's popularization in the modern era, and Wikipedia wonders whether this turn of phrase is Yiddish in origin. Once again Xxey's comedic sympathies and proclivities come to the fore, this time in an ethnic register, and the entire LP begins to wobble in an undecidable manner between a metaphysical sermon and its uncomfortably jocular interruption, and therefore between high-minded instruction and corrosive laughter.

I sure am.

Unflappable, Xxey answers the doubter with the assurance of the "I am" – the "I sure am."

And I am the Xxenogenesis revelation from God with the formula from your mortal to immortal etheric existence, from your present physical body in this present moment of now.

This Xxenogenesis revelation with its immortal strivings is in stark contrast to the "stand-up tragedy" of the Nazi concentration camp survivor, Brother Theodore. Preaching "God is dead," the macabre "comedian-metaphysician" once remarked: "Our graveyards are riddled with corpses. Our mortality rate is 100%."

And I am the Xxenogenesis revelation book of life for the salvation of mankind through the Einstein formula of E=mc2, the law of conservation of X-mass and energy not for just a limited motive of mere survival, but the unlocking of the divinity in the Carbon 666 atom of which we all are constructed of, in this very intimate, passionate, universal plan of eternity, infinity/anti-infinity, of matter/anti-matter, Etcha.

One of four strategic places on the LP where Xxey rehearses the formula for relativity, but the only time he raises the proper name of "Einstein." It is a point of pride among theosophists that Madame Blavatsky's main works were written several decades before Albert's announcement of November 25, 1915, and that her writings broadly suggest, if not relativity theory proper, then at least the basic idea that matter and energy are related. Let us say it this way: Blavatskyism didn't invent Einstein, but her rhetoric has permitted a stimulating alliance between Theosophy and "science" of all sorts. For instance, perhaps cosmic relativity permits Xxey to regard the "mere survival" of human beings as a "limited" goal.

And I am that I am.

The Carbon 666 atom with interpretations from Revelation 13:18: "Here is wisdom. Let him who has understanding – is in a state of Xxenogenesis cosmic-God-Christ-consciousness – decipher, interpret for mankind the higher metaphysical hidden up to now treatise of the scriptures and signs."

The oblique qualification, "with interpretations," like a later Xxey aside, "with inserts," is crucial to understanding one key feature and strategy of Herman-eutics: that the Bible is written in code, and that an occasional, key verse, usually rather well-known, is missing words that, once restored, permits an esoteric reading that further illuminates Xxenogenesis. This famous verse needs only a simple fix: one that makes clear that only Xxey himself can decipher the occult identity of the "beast" and interpret it for us as the atoms of our own mortal body. One last thought: the final word here "signs" is phrased so as to rhyme with "science," a constant Xxey concern. Xxey is classically theosophical in his double-dealing relationship with this subject. In other words, he mimics scientific discourse "in order to trade on its authority while contesting its worldview implications" at the same time. (See Egil Asprem, "Theosophical Attitudes Toward Science," *Handbook of the Theosophical Current* [2013]).

And the code number of the beast is the code number of the name of mankind referring specifically to the mythological, astrological names of each beast constellations of the Zodiac, of matter/antimatter– each individual cosmic sign, each person is born under.

And his–mankind's–number is 666.

The code is cracked and, just as in the ancient riddle of the Sphinx, the answer is "man." In other words, Xxey's got our number.

Side 2

And I am that I am.

The Carbon 666 atom of six protons, six neutrons, six electrons now living in a very grave, precarious, stalemating state of mankind on earth in this third dimension, always subjected to the travails of sorrow, sickness, death, recompensation, reincarnation.

In the "Easy-to-Read" science book *The Story of the Atom* (1960) one of only two books advertised for sale in the album's gatefold via Xxey's mail order business, authors Mae and Ira Freeman ask the following question: "Have you ever seen the black part of a burnt piece of wood? The black is carbon. A carbon atom has a nucleus made of 6 protons and 6 neutrons. And it has 6 electrons racing around it." This is accompanied by an illustration that shows the carbon atom in action at the top, and a book of matches and a burnt match at the bottom, with the caption: "Six electrons whirl around the nucleus of a carbon atom." Xxey's "very grave" comment signals this dead zone and dead matter or the "burnt out" state of third dimensional living (what he calls "precarious" and "stalemating") that he seeks to overcome.

And Jesus said, John 14:12: "Truly, truly, I say to you mankind: He who believes in me, this soular-lunar seed of immortality, shall do the works which I do and even greater than these things, he shall do."

This calls for a comparison with the King James version of this Biblical verse: "Verily, verily, I say unto you, He that believeth on me, the works that I do shall he do also; and greater works than these shall he do; because I go unto my Father." How does Xxenogenesis revise and re-vision the words of Jesus thereby setting off a conversion experience? First and foremost, the Son of God's self-reference expands to "this soular-lunar seed of immortality." It is no longer the paternal function of the Christian dogma that is to be worshipped. Indeed, the last clause ("because I go unto my Father") completely drops out of Xxey's reading. Instead, Xxey channels and redirects Christ's divinity in terms of the coming together of the sun and the moon (in magical or metaphysical terms, the masculine and the feminine), and in an act of Xxenogenetic procreation that disseminates everlasting life – or what Xxey elsewhere calls "immortality through Xxenogenesis."

And Matthew 5:48: "You, each of you, are to be perfected even as your heavenly Father is perfected." Meaning: attain the same very possible cosmic-God-good-Christ-consciousness as your heavenly father: atomic nuclear energy.

Sources: "Be ye therefore perfect, even as your Father which is in heaven is perfect" (KJV) and/or "Therefore become perfect, just as your Father in heaven is perfect" (Peshitta Bible). One notices how Xxey's request or command to imitate the father's heavenly perfection again takes an atomic theosophical turn. The roots of such a quest can be found in Anna Bonus Kingsford's, *The Perfect Way: Or, The Finding of Christ* (1882) where the famous theosophical vegetarian writes: "Of the doctrine we seek to restore, the basis, then, is the Pre-existence and Perfectibility of the Soul." She then cites the exact same passage in Matthew referring to it as "the injunction of the great master of mystical science." She further cautions that we do not limit the quest for perfection to heaven alone or "the inaccessible vast of the skies" for "the kingdom of God is within" and, in this way, she lands at one of the cornerstones of the gospel according to *SeXxenogenesis #1*.

And Xxenogenesis subject knowledge ranges from simplicity to complexity whereas at times you will be at a loss, will not understand for only a period of each individual growth of cosmic awareness until one grasps its revealing splendor in due time as you study Xxenogenesis revelation several times.

While Xxey alludes to "cosmic awareness," he offers an opportunity to discuss all of the instances where he invokes the cognate idea of "cosmic consciousness." This links up with the Canadian alienist/psychiatrist and Walt Whitman scholar Richard Maurice Bucke and his classic *Cosmic Consciousness: A Study in the Evolution of the Human Mind* (1901) as Ur-text. Bucke writes that: "This consciousness shows the cosmos to consist not of dead matter governed by unconscious, rigid, and unintending law; it shows it on the contrary as entirely immaterial, entirely spiritual and entirely alive; it shows that death is an absurdity, that everyone and everything has eternal life." It runs parallel to the sudden enlightenment (satori) found in Zen

Buddhism. In Xxey's appropriation of the term here, one notices a tension between the period of time of "individual growth" that one needs in preparation and the "shazam" moment when "cosmic consciousness" strikes the one ready to receive it. Xxey believes that one prepares for it by means of the repeated study of his revelations until one reaches the point where one will no longer "be at a loss" and when one "grasps its revealing splendor." Interestingly, this specific reference echoes Bucke's own phrasing when he recalls that fateful evening when "cosmic consciousness" was first revealed to him. As Bucke recollects, "Into his brain streamed one momentary lightning-flash of the Brahmic Splendour which ever since lightened his life."

And please do not be impatient or dis-encouraged to delve deeper into this now revealing mystery of God-good for you might miss it for still a longer time and that would be very sad.

We encounter here again Xxey's eschewing of the superficial via the deep dive that "delve[s] deeper." This learning practice takes time, patience, and the overcoming of frustration. After all, the "now revealing mystery of God-good" is not a fast-food happy meal. In order to turn the "very sad" into the "very happy," the (encouraged) student of Xxenogenesis revelation pursues the esoteric and metaphysical meanings with the goal of decoding the secrets and the mysteries.

Given how much Xxey loves searching for clues and solving mysteries, it is no surprise to learn that his favorite radio program as a child was Sherlock Holmes. Herman often figured out the "who done it" before the end of the program and he would gleefully tell his brothers and sisters. His son relates, "Even at a young age he was excellent at putting together pieces of information and drawing conclusions from them. Later in life, this natural ability would prove to be very helpful and useful in breaking the metaphysical code of the Bible and discovering the secret to the mystery of life." This penchant also marks the mystery that he created about himself, making it so difficult for anyone to discover his identity.

And the degree required to bring about Xxenogenesis is the mark X of revelation from God.

This is linked to the idea of Christ as a degree earned and continues Xxey's pedagogical musings. But we cannot understand this passage and the following one without a review of Revelation 7:1-8 where it says that those who are redeemed bear an invisible seal upon their foreheads. In Xxenogenesis revelation, the seal that they bear is the mark 'X' and it is the opposite of the Mark of the Beast (of the Carbon 666 atoms).

(Sings) Hallelujah! Jesuschriah! Ha-ha-ha-ha-ha-lle-e-u-u-jah!

Xxey reveals in a Polish melody that by singing God's praises we are always already rejoicing in laughter.

And this mark X degree has been attained by one sent forth among mankind to bring about the purity of love.

Xxey adapts the motif of the Messiah (Hebrew, *Moshiach*) as messenger in order to disseminate his message. As a "Gabryel" (the angel Gabriel brought news of the virgin birth to Mary), Xxey was born to play this role.

And John 10:30: "For the Father, nuclear energy and I are one and the same now, living amongst mankind, speeding exceedingly unto the infinisonic nuclear evolution of fourth dimension of immortality for I the atomic soular-lunar seed that is in me now and the light of the world."

This is an excessive expansion upon the Biblical sentence: "I and my Father are one" (KJV); or "I and my Father are of one accord" (Peshitta). Interestingly, Xxey's friend George Adamski (in his early guise as Founder of Universal Progressive Christianity) also engages with this Biblical passage in his book *Wisdom of the Masters of the Far East* (1936). In answer to the question "What is the most important point in the teachings of Jesus Christ?", the self-styled Prof. G. Adamski writes: "I and the Father are one. . . . Christ within all is the willingness to unite with the Father and serve the Universal principle, thus bringing forth the Kingdom of Heaven on earth." While Adamski interprets the Father as an affirmation of "Universal consciousness" here, Xxey's more sophisticated atomic theosophy figures the Father as "nuclear energy" and entertains such Xxenogenetic topoi as "infinisonic nuclear evolution" and the "atomic solar-lunar seed."

Xx Xx Xx

Coincidentally, "LUNARSEED" (in all capitals) also appears in the esoteric text at the bottom of a poster by the California Kabbalah-inspired artist Wallace Berman in 1965. One recalls in this context the nine issues of Berman's experimental magazine *Semina* (1955-1964) which were never sold but rather dispersed and spread like seeds among his friends. This parallels the dissemination of Xxey's record in terms of how the word was spread. In this way, both artists sought to avoid the restricted realm of commerce through a gift economy based on acts of love and friendship.

(Sound of Thunder)

In "What the Thunder Said" (Part V of *The Waste Land* [1922]), T.S. Eliot asks: "What is that sound high in the air?" The sound of thunder reverberates here not only as one of Xxey's playful special effects but also as the sound that comes from on high and the ethereal regions to herald the spiritual sayer and his words of wisdom.

And Bible scriptures, teachings of world religions, and of science are records, methods, procedures of men, women, places, geographical-historical events of happenings for the salvation of mankind or attainment of God-cosmic-Christ-consciousness.

God-cosmic-Christ-consciousness: Here is a good example of a verbose string that is so characteristic of Xxey's style, and which parodies and parallels the strings found in molecular formulae.

And these eloquent, wonderful statements are step-by-step allegories, metaphors, parables dealing solely with the biochemical, physiological, and atomical-astrological operations, functions of our human atomic body.

Xxey's two favorite books were Manly P. Hall's *The Secret Teachings of All Ages* (1928) and the Bible. Concerning the latter, Xxey believes that Bible scriptures always contain hidden meanings, and it is our job to decipher and decode these "allegories, metaphors, parables." Given this metaphysical approach to the Bible, it is no surprise to learn that Xxey owned many different versions of the Holy Scriptures as well as several Bible dictionaries and concordances and that he utilized them as resources for his own Xxegesis. He also believed in the necessity to make the Bible speak in the language of one's own times. Such an esoteric reading offers the chance to draw scientific conclusions that would be relevant to the atomic age whether in terms of biochemistry, physiology, or nuclear physics. From here forward, Xxey will talk of "science" three times (Scriptures and science, God or science) and always in relation to religion. No doubt the Xxenogenesis process is "biochemical" on some level. To recall Dr. Auguste Marques, "There is but one science that can henceforth direct modern research into the one path which will lead to the discovery of the whole, hitherto occult, truth, and it is the youngest of all—chemistry, as it now stands reformed. There is no other, not excluding astronomy, that can so unerringly guide scientific intuition" (*Scientific Corroborations of Theosophy* [1897]).

And they were purposely, fearfully concealed so that man would not destroy himself until he has risen to an awareness of God, of understanding the atom in this Aquarian Age of the Second Coming of Christ in order that mankind would not use these universal nuclear divine energy powers in men to dominate, abuse, subject God's free will in all creation.

In part, is Xxey recalling the dropping of the atomic bomb at the end of WWII? If so, remember too that J. Robert Oppenheimer's code name for the first nuclear explosion of the Manhattan Project was "Trinity" (July 16, 1945). Oppenheimer later wrote to an historical researcher: "Why I chose the name is not clear. . . . There is a poem of John Donne, written just before his death, which I know and love. From it a quotation: 'As West and East/In all flatt Maps—and I am one—are one,/So death doth touch the Resurrection.'" The themes of death and resurrection haunt Donne's poem as well as Xxey's LP, and Xxey's concern is that such nuclear madness will sabotage the Aquarian Age and the Second Coming of Christ.

And these names of places, people, things, etcetera which are used in the scriptures and in science all have meanings of higher metaphysical understanding of this hidden kingdom of God within us, within the atom, of…

Another Herman-eutical passage that this time addresses the question of the esoteric in the tradition of Annie Besant's *Esoteric Christianity* (1901) and its stress on spiritual "secrets revealed only to a select few in its Mysteries." Xxey marks the need for and importance of Xxegesis in order to draw out the hidden meanings and to reveal the metaphysical truths.

I am that I am. A son of God, of man.

Here the Tetragrammaton expands to include an object – most unusual given the typical tautological nature of this utterance. In a paradox of Trinitarian proportions, Xxey positions himself as a son of God and a son of man but there is a hidden third term: the surpassing of man as one becomes the Xxenogenesis atom.

And the books of the Bible are statements by different prophets, writers about the same identical subject: the salvation of mankind or the conservation of X-mass and energy. Each portraying methods, procedures how to bring into physical manifestation the law of relativity, nativity of $E=mc^2$, this ever-present, visible, universal paradise of God, of second Christmas.

Herman's hermeneutical assumption here is that all Biblical authors and prophets are writing about the same thing – the salvation of mankind. This is in itself a fascinating and contentious claim. But then Herman overlays a singular (and perhaps even heretical) interpretation when he equates salvation with "the conservation of X-mass and energy." In mashing up "second Christmas" and "X-mass and energy," he plays between science and faith, between the laws of relativity and Christian nativity. In alluding to the Xxenogenesis process through the application of Einstein's physics, Xxey portrays himself as a prophet who has mastered and reconciled the physical and the metaphysical.

And in every field of endeavor in technology, every book, everything you see even up to the every moment of now happenings are all identical play-by-play statements, works, clues, inspirations about the same subject: the salvation, conservation, proper use of divine, new nuclear energy for man of the I am a son of everything God-good.

This passage (with its sports spectacular "play-by-play" analysis) continues Xxey's emphasis on the centrality of salvation, but it is important to align his "do-it-yourself" understanding of this subject with a theosophical approach over and against dogmatic Christianity. For Blavatsky in *The Key to Theosophy* (1889), Christianity "tells us of the impossibility of attaining Salvation without the aid of a miraculous Saviour, and therefore dooms to perdition all those who will not accept the dogma." Christianity "enforces belief in the Descent of the Spiritual Ego into the Lower Self" while Theosophy "inculcates the necessity of endeavouring to elevate oneself to the Christos, or Buddhi state" (155). For Xxey, this last line translates into the "man of the I am a son of everything God-good."

And nothing is ever new in time-space-existence-continuum-concept in the universal mind of God. For everything always was-is-before-us in a perpetual immaculate virgin conception...unharnessed state of recycled recreation, rearrangement, incarnation, reincarnation of God-good-nuclear energy.

Xxey moves here in the direction of the Book of Ecclesiastes 1:9: "The thing that hath been, it is that which shall be; and that which is done is that which shall be done: and there is nothing new under the sun." The twist is that he then takes this sentiment, and he attributes it to "the universal mind of God." Moving outside of time, this passage provides another way of talking about the Tetragrammaton in its collapsing of past, present, and future ("for everything always was-is-before us"). Xxey will further this point a little later when he states: "For time and sequence of chronology does not exist."

And in the fourth and beyond realms of limitless mind, of infinisonic multiplicity, pictures and concepts are the order of allness in the Trinity laws of intent-attitude-intensity in every present moment of now.

Xxey's concept of the "limitless mind" here appears to echo C.W. Leadbeater's "The Heaven World" in *The Life After Death and How Theosophy Unveils It* (1918). "On this plane, then, we find existing the infinite fullness of the Divine Mind, open in all its limitless affluence to every soul, just in proportion as that soul has qualified himself to receive." Xxey believes that we are able to tap into this plane of existence (allied to the fourth dimension) and its conquest of time. He dubs it "infinisonic multiplicity" which may be thought of as a heterotopia of cosmic sound and therefore allied to Xxey's intent and intense call for ultra-high frequency vibrations.

For time and sequence of chronology does not exist so please have forbearance, endurance with this Xxenogenesis revelation as it is channelled into multifarious language of impossibility from this beyond—of everything meaning the same, of everything being reduced to one denominator—the God, the atom, the everlasting seed, fruit of the divine.

What to make of this mind-bending idea and phrasing – this "multifarious language of impossibility"? First note that this revelation and its seeding of the everlasting is "channelled" and Xxey's history points to two key figures in the channelling tradition. So is the phrase to be understood as "the voice of the silence" a la Blavatsky? And/or perhaps as "Nada" (nothing) a la Yolanda at Mark-Age? For Xxey, this revelation not only comes "from this beyond" but leads us to the limits, of that which can only be "impossibly" represented.

Quack quack quack quack quack.

Doctors' reputations doctored, sabotaged, smeared. This startling interruption of the five quacks is a moment where the conventional medicine, which Xxey believes prevents rather than promotes healing, is mocked as pure quackery. Given such a situation, you would be better off trying to heal thyself (see below).

Hey, what's up Doc?

Xxey channels and ventriloquizes the animated pop icon, Bugs Bunny, who seems to be responding as if the interruptive quacks were made by Daffy himself! In the process he pulls a metaphysical question out of the rabbit's hat: what is "up" (higher than ourselves, toward space, ascendant in the hierarchical universe)? The first of two references to classic Looney Tunes, the question restages Side 1's similar poser, "Hey bud, are you for real?" and its themes of reality and authenticity.

And physician, heal thyself–by knowing thyself, by loving thyself in order to love another.

This famous proverb is found in Luke 4:23 (KJV): "Ye will surely say unto me this proverb, 'Physician, heal thyself': whatsoever we have heard done in Capernaum, do also here in thy country." Xxey adds on both a Socratic dimension ("knowing thyself") and the Golden Rule ("loving thyself in order to love another").

And this Aquarian cosmic age is the time not of one Christ but of many Christs.

This time "of many Christs" echoes Annie Besant's view in *The Presence of Evil* (1910): "the Christ is less an external Saviour than a living Presence in the human Spirit, a Presence by which the human Spirit unfolds its innate divinity, so that in time all men become Christs."

And Christ is not a man. It is a degree earned in the process of nuclear evolution.

Atomic Theosophy 101. For Xxey, initiation must be understood as a degree program and nuclear evolution is a required course of study. What does it say on the diploma? Christ only knows.

And Christ means universal limitless love, the charisma, chrism, lubricating oil which is the purified procreative substance, the Biblical true milk and honey manna, the secreting hormones of our body in the state of superman consciousness perfected as God, everything good, everything limitless love.

For the wandering Hebrews in Exodus, first there is daily manna in the desert and, later, milk and honey in the promised land – the destinal destination of Eretz Israel. Xxey however puts it all in the mixing bowl, all at once: "the Biblical true milk and honey manna." Is this yet another example where "time and sequence of chronology does not exist" and where we are asked to observe "every present moment of now"? Xxey then proceeds to associate his new mash with the "secreting hormones of the body [in the Xxenogenesis process] in the state of superman consciousness." In doing so, he taps into the rich literature revolving around the term "superman" that begins with Barnard Shaw's *Man and Superman* (1903) and Thomas Common's translation of Nietzsche's *Zarathustra* (1909). There are also two important science fiction texts that deserve mention here by Beresford and Stapledon. Finally, the first Superman comic book appears in 1938, when Herman is twelve years old. It is out of this intellectual history and milieu that Xxey posits "superman consciousness" as transcendent associating it with godlike perfection, goodness, and limitless love.

And Christ from Greek is *christos* means anointed, comes from the verb *creo*, means to schmear, akin to Sanskrit *kursh*, and to English, means grease, oil, petroleum, petra for rock, the lubricant of our body which is the organism-orgasm, the composites of minerals-elements-cubits-atoms which are the precious foundation stones-rocks-seeds of Revelation 21:19.

The first part of Xxey's analysis here resonates with Blavatsky's entry for the Greek "Chréstos" in her *Theosophical Glossary* (1892) on the origin of the name of Christ (and of Christians in general) as found in "the Temple vocabulary of the Pagans" where Chréstos was "a disciple on probation, a candidate for hierophantship." "When he had attained to this [status] through initiation, long trials, and suffering, and had been 'anointed' (i.e., rubbed with oil", as were Initiates and even idols of the gods, as the last touch of ritualistic observance), his name was changed into Christos, the 'purified', in esoteric or mystery language." This corroborates Xxey's stance that Christ is not an actual person, but a degree earned. Meanwhile, Olav Hammer in *Alternative Christs* (2009) refers to *Christos* "as divine Wisdom": This "Christ – the true esoteric SAVOIR – is no man, but the DIVINE PRINCIPLE in every human being."

Xxey's etymology incorporates both Sanskrit and English as he again moves matters to the seXxualized and seminal language of "lubricant" and "grease." However, another strand of Xxey's discourse (as discussed previously) petrifies from petroleum to petra (for rock) as he recalls the role of Peter and the founding of the apostolic church. And when it comes to the symbology of rocks and stones, Manly P. Hall has written something quite foundational in *The Secret Teachings of All Ages* (1938): "The rocks and earth correspond to the bones and flesh; the water to the various fluids; the air to the gases; and the fire to the bodily heat. Since the bones are the framework that sustains the corporeal structure, they may be regarded as a fitting emblem of the spirit—that divine foundation which supports the composite fabric of mind, soul, and body." Xxey's passage ends with a nod to "the precious foundation stones-rocks-seeds of Revelation 21:19" but without a direct citation. The King James version reads: "And the foundations of the wall of the city were garnished with all manner of precious stones. The first foundation was jasper; the second, sapphire; the third, a chalcedony; the fourth, an emerald." Given the bombardment of all of these stones, one may well feel "stoned by stones" (headnote in Julia Lorusso and Mark-Age gemologist Joel Glick, *Healing Stoned* [1976]).

And Christ from Hebrew means messiah, messenger, forerunner, tidings of good abundance, etcetera.

Translating the figure of Christ from the Hebrew *Moshiach* into English, Xxey once again discovers etymological abundance, with a surprising biographical reading hidden in these good tidings: in 1964 Herman changed the name Gabryel Lumber to Gabryel's Horn of Plenty. As on Side 1, the universe is once again grokked as plenitudinous.

And hormone from Greek means excite, vibrate, for I bring about an act of nourishment, redemption, regeneration, deliverance, savior etcetera.

Regarding the use of hormones to further the quest for immortality (and regeneration) see Lucian Boia, *Forever Young* (2004): "Hormone therapy now has a wide-ranging arsenal at its disposal, including human growth hormone (HGH), which can be used to reinvigorate muscle tissue, and oestrogen, a hormone secreted by the ovaries, the level of which drops at menopause." In other words, hormonal therapy taps into such secretions in order to unlock the secrets of rejuvenation and prolongation of life.

And the second messenger hormones of our body are the Second Coming of Christ hormones.

Xxey bridges the languages of biochemistry and spirit in another fantastic atomic theosophical maneuver by grafting "second messenger hormones" onto the "Second Coming of Christ." One recalls that such hormones are small molecules and ions that relay signals to proteins which are received by the receptors at the cell surface. They function as a way to amplify hormonal signals. As an amplification system, second messenger hormones are all about getting the word out, and, in a fascinating way, they double what Xxey thought his record *SeXxenogenesis #1* was accomplishing by spreading his Gospel to whomever would listen.

One must learn how to excite, secrete, conserve this new nuclear energy through limitless pure sex love at Passover time.

Jesus's Last Supper was a Passover Seder whereas this passage stages the Xxenogenesis love fest. However, this exciting and extraordinary exchange involves both semen secretion and conservation in the vein of Tantric sex magic and its pursuit of limitless bliss and limitless love.

And I, the Xxenogenesis atom, am going to teach you how to vibrate-oscillate-homogenize-expand your limitless mind—God's natural way—by increasing, equating your equilibrium to an ultra-high frequency vibration of cosmic God-Christ consciousness.

Beginning with the visitation of the androgyne and the message "equate equilibrium high frequency" in 1962, Xxey's thinking (as an instance and an exemplar of New Age spirituality) asserts the view that each individual vibrates at a certain level and that the more spiritually attuned, the higher one's vibration or frequency. Here and elsewhere, the "ultra-high frequency vibration" is equated with the attainment of "cosmic God-Christ consciousness." Conversely, Xxey bluntly says in the liner notes of the LP – "equate your equilibrium to a ultra-high frequency vibration modulation homogenization etc or die –"

And have no fear for Etcha is here.

Etcha replaces Superman.

Yes, here with me to assist mankind in these most beautiful, wonderful days of all times.

Compared to apocalyptic thinkers and figures like Daniel Fry and George van Tassel, who think that the world is going to hell, Xxey turns a blind eye toward the world stage circa 1973 in referring to "these most beautiful, wonderful days of all times" and thereby ignoring economic and political events like Watergate, Vietnam, and the beginning of another recession. (Advocacy for actively forgetting that pillar of conventional reality known as "politics.")

And Luke 17:20, someone asked Jesus when the Kingdom of God would come. He answered saying: "The Kingdom of God does not come by observation. Neither will they say, 'Behold, it is here or, behold, it is there.' For behold the Kingdom of God is within you."

Herman's son Gabryel believes that this is the most important thing that his father taught us.

Yes, in the divinity of you, in every atomic cell of your body waiting for each of you to reverse the cycle of death through the Xxenogenesis process X-rated Christ pure sex way.

The opening phrasing resonates with language from Xxey's website under the *Aquarian Gospel* themed heading "Purity in Life Men Do Not Comprehend": "Please never forget: The Spirit of God is omnipresent in every divine atom! And you and everything in all creation is structured from atoms." In her classic *The Consciousness of the Atom* (1922), Alice Bailey elucidates this central idea of atomic theosophy; and it resonates with Luke and with Xxey's explication of it, which stresses the divinity "in every atomic cell of your body." Bailey discusses two stages in the "evolution of the human atom." "The first was emphasized by the Christ when He said, 'The kingdom of God is within you,' thus pointing all human atoms to the centre of life or energy within themselves and teaching them that from and through that centre they must expand and grow." But Bailey's chaste reading is a far cry from the SeXxenogenesis action that climaxes this passage and which stresses the importance of Jesus's (second) coming ("X-rated Christ pure sex way").

And First Corinthians 15:21: "For since by a man came death, by a man also comes resurrection of the dead."

Following up the passage that focuses on reversing the cycle of death through the Xxenogenesis process, Xxey inserts another Biblical passage that counterposes Adam with Jesus, the Old Testament with the New Testament, and also death with resurrection. This parallelism also functions as a parable that asserts Xxenogenesis's preeminent position as the first Second Coming of the Christ.

And the mystery of the holy-whole Trinity of God is Father-God principle of alpha rays (protons) and Mother Nature-God principle of omega rays (neutrons) and Son of God principle of beta rays (electrons) which is...

This provides us with yet another excellent example of Xxey's atomic theology with its affirmation of the unity of the three entities in one Godhead and with its superimposition of the nuclear register (protons, neutrons, and electrons) upon the Holy Trinity of Christian belief. But one also notices, in contrast to official Trinitarianism, that "Mother Nature" replaces the Holy Spirit in Xxey's formulation. This transformation was modelled for Xxey during his years at Mark-Age, where Mark, Nada-Yolanda, and Wains (Jim Speed) mirrored this newly ascendant Holy Family.

I am that I am.

More reverb straight from God's mixing board.

(Sings) Mi a name I call myself.

To insert another pop musical reference (whether as a flippant aside or as a meaningful coincidence), the California glam rockers Sparks released a version of "Do-Re-Mi" on their album *A Woofer in Tweeter's Clothing* in 1972. The record was produced by theosophical enthusiast Todd Rundgren, whose illuminated works include the side-length "Treatise on Cosmic Figure" (1975) derived from the channellings of Djwal Khul by Alice A. Bailey, and "Love in Action" (1977), a crucial slogan for both Bailey's World Goodwill organization, and for Mark-Age, Inc.

The atom of you, each of us.

This phrasing and its mode of address (moving from second person singular to first person plural) once again recalls Bailey's *Consciousness of the Atom*. As previously discussed, the first instance is an example of atomization. However, the second instance moves the atom towards the recognition of need for cooperation and the importance of the group. "The second way the human atom grows is through its interaction with all other atoms, and this is something which is only just beginning to dawn upon the human intelligence, and to assume its just importance. ... we are commencing to learn that if our brother is held back, and is not making progress, and if the other human atoms are not vibrating as they should, every atom in the body corporate is affected. None of us will be complete until all other units have achieved their fullest and most complete development."

And the Trinity of God in man is the spiritual super-consciousness, and the subconscious mind, and the physical consciousness.

As we glean from his websites, Xxey was an avid interpreter of his own dreams, but he was by no means a psychoanalytic thinker. Nevertheless, here Xxey is actually rewriting Sigmund Freud's tripartite division of superego, unconscious, and ego. The superego becomes the "spiritual super-consciousness" (and thereby linked to Bucke's "cosmic consciousness"), the unconscious becomes "the subconscious mind," and the ego becomes "the physical consciousness."

And sex from Sanskrit and Latin means combining forms of six which means co-mingling, changing, exchanging of nuclear divine energy of one Trinity of one being and another Trinity of another being through the Star of David universal marriage of two interlaced, intercoursed triangles which means becoming a part of one astro-biological substance through a uniting criss-cross force of equating an equilibrium to either a higher or lower frequency vibration-modulation.

The "criss cross force" of sexual intercourse in both Judeo-Christian (Latin) and Indian Tantric (Sanskrit) traditions and its shared symbolic representation is elaborated in terms of its connection to SeXxenogenesis. Let us recall that the Star of David (or what Nellie B. Cain calls "The Christ Star of Divine Love") is referred to as the sexagram and derived from Latin. The two "interlaced, intercoursed triangles" (or Trinities) represent male and female energies. Furthermore, Tantric doctrine (and its mandalas) affirm the sexagram as a symbol wherein Shiva is represented as the upward pointing triangle and Shakti as the downward pointing triangle. The ultimate truth consists in the complete interpenetration of Shiva (male) and Shakti (female) energies. This brings new meaning to the presence of the sexagram on the album cover: Xxey's hand-painted Star is presented as an upper golden triangle (inscribed with the words "heaven," "natal new moon," and "antimatter") interlaced with a bottom silver triangle (inscribed with the words "earth," "passover full moon," and "matter"). The central space opened up by intersection of the two triangles is occupied by an illustration that depicts a pink carbon 666 atom. The importance of the Star and its placement in the seal of the Theosophical Society is also worth noting.

And Xxenogenesis means spontaneous generation, regeneration, alternation of generations, a criss-cross breeding, fertilization as by passionate, sensual-sexual thermonuclear fusion of a fancy production of an organism altogether and permanently unlike the parent.

We move from sexual intercourse (and its "criss-cross force") to procreation (and its "criss-cross breeding") in a revealing statement that offers to its listeners the meaning of Xxenogenesis. The text overflows with words that denote sexual reproduction. In this and in the following passage, Xxey draws upon the rhetoric of thermonuclear fusion and his memory of the explosive hydrogen bomb as he seeks to harness and reverse such deadly nuclear power by putting it into the service and at the disposal of love and, more specifically, the Xxenogenetic process. Like the fusing of bodies in the bedroom, he desires to make thermonuclear fusion seXxy and sensual, fun and fancy. In contrast to the passion of the Christ, we witness the passion of the Xxenogenesis atom and its birthing of something that is completely other. While Xxey alludes here to "a criss-cross breeding," what is actually at stake here is the emergence of a new breed. This "fancy production" and reproduction offers not a gradualist theory of evolution but a permanent and radical jump from the origin of species. As Gabryel says: "This suggests a new branch on the phylogenetic tree facilitated by epigenetics, Christ consciousness and the fused solar-lunar seed—the seal of the lamb spoken of in Revelation."

And Xxeno means foreign, strange, and genesis means to be born. Combine Xxeno and genesis and you have: He be reborn again in

this physical, mortal body unto immortality in a foreign, strange, sex-way of the cross through crucifixion which one must overcome.

Xxenogenesis etymologizes himself but he does so in a way that acknowledges himself in terms of the other's coming and becoming. This is Xxenogenesis at his most deconstructive.

And crucifixion means to unite through thermonuclear, passionate, sexual love fusion your soular-lunar seeds of anti-Christ and Christ, seeds of immortality. And Christ's attainment comes to men only through his own crossification, crucifixion, resurrection, ascension, descension unto the fourth dimension through overcoming mortal death in this physical body.

Xxey is alluding here to his own cosmic crucifixion, which is quite different from the Christian crucifixion featuring Christ dying on the cross for humanity's sins. Indeed, one would not expect the invocation of "anti-Christ" and "Christ" in the same breath. Instead of getting nailed to a cross in an excruciatingly painful way, Xxey's stations of the cross involve "passionate sexual love fusion" where the only pain comes from the inability to come. However, Jesus's crucifixion also involves the "overcoming of mortal death in his physical body." The California-based Theosophist Gottfried de Purucker had this to say in his catechism *Questions We All Ask* (1929): "the meaning of the crucifixion is the resignation, painful to most human beings, of the material personal man and exchanging it for a greater light; and it is called a crucifixion because to the personal man with his limited vision it seems like his own death. We must remember that the inner Christ — or the inner Buddha if you please — is fixed to the cross of material existence; but after the crucifixion there ensues the resurrection of the inner god." (Or as Gabryel would say: "the resurrection of the omnipresent God within.")

Xx   Xx   Xx

The move "unto the fourth dimension" as an opening to immortality is critical for Xxey and here he is aligned to the esoteric thinkers of the "Fourth Way" such as P.D. Ouspensky and George Gurdjieff. As Ouspensky cites Gurdjieff in *In Search of the Miraculous* (1949): "And only the man who possesses four fully developed bodies can be called a 'man' in the full sense of the word. This man possesses many properties which ordinary man does not possess. One of these properties is immortality. All religions and all ancient teachings contain the idea that, by acquiring the fourth body, man acquires immortality; and they all contain indications of the ways to acquire the fourth body, that is, immortality."

And no one can give you this, or one cannot will this upon himself without the works of Xxenogenesis as it has to be attained through humility, love, and physical mental spiritual cleansing, purification of one's self.

As already noted, Xxey believes that the attainment of Christ consciousness (as a degree earned) and the path that he marks in rhyme as "X way, sex way, Xxenogenesis way" requires a detoxing of mind and body, a physical and spiritual cleanse. The call for humility shines through in his own life with his modest and humble insistence on remaining anonymous until his mortal passing.

And Jesus the Christ from his own encountering, most passionate sexual love life experiences taught two thousand years ago the pure sex-way of crossification, crucifixion, resurrection, ascension, descension of "please follow me unto the cross of Xxenogenesis."

This post-Christian Master teaches us to emulate a seXxy Jesus. His own personal Jesus is not the celibate, otherworldly, and self-abnegating Christ of some institutionalized strands in Christendom – his is the orgiastic Christ who celebrates SeXx-mass.

And John 3:3, Jesus says, "Unless he be reborn again in this mortal body in a foreign, strange regeneration way unto immortal life, you cannot and shall never re-enter, regain the paradise Kingdom of God."

It is crucial to note that this same Biblical passage is used as the epigraph to Bucke's book *Cosmic Consciousness,* and it is not a coincidence that Xxey refers to "cosmic superman consciousness" directly (and in reference to Jesus) in the next passage. In Bucke's version, Jesus answers: "Verily, verily, I say unto thee, except a man be born anew he cannot see the kingdom of God." Of course, Xxey's addition of the words "in a foreign, strange regeneration way" foreground the etymological meaning of Xxenogenesis.

In *Esoteric Christianity*, Annie Besant recalls that there were several words that were used to designate the sacred circle of the Initiates who were the keepers of the Christian Mysteries. These included "The Kingdom of God" and "The Second Birth" both of which are found in the Biblical passage cited here. Xxenogenesis revelation follows this esoteric path.

For how could Jesus have attained the degree of Christ or God or Good or cosmic superman consciousness if he would not have experienced this same physical emotional mental spiritual pure sex way of life himself?

The argument advanced in art historian Leo Steinberg's *The Sexuality of Christ* (1983) involves far more than the display of baby Jesus's circumcised penis. With this extended rhetorical question, we encounter Xxey again bringing seXxy back. His Jesus is experienced in both giving and making love. He is capable of both *agape* and *eros* to invoke the Greek terms to distinguish between God's unconditional love and sexual passion. In these ways, seXxy Jesus rubs against the grain of Christ's desexualization.

Herman's break with Mark-Age revolves around this very same point of contention. The desexualized Christ position was articulated in the channelled Sananda's answer to the question: "Does the use of the sexual function in any manner help prepare one for Christ consciousness?" The answer is absolutely clear in its abstinence. "There is absolutely no precedent for this upon the Earth, at any time, that ever has been successful. In all the patterns I have given for man to follow [in my multiple incarnations throughout the history of the Earth], never once did I imply or give this as the means by which anyone could reach cosmic consciousness or Christ attainment. Christ attainment is a spiritual expression. The sexual use of the energies and the patterns used are strictly physical and will gain only physical adeptness. Nothing spiritual can ever be attained through physical means" (Nada-Yolanda, *Facts of Life 1*). The original transmission was dated May 17, 1972, or one year before the release of the album.

For it is only through experience and attainment of overcoming lower mortal passions that Jesus undertook the Prince of Peace flaming two-edged sword of revelation, black and white light equilibrium of Christ/anti-Christ or matter/anti-matter cosmic consciousness in order to teach the following:

Here Xxey refers to Revelation 1:16 and John's reference to the two-edged sword that emerged from Jesus's mouth on the Isle of Patmos. "And He had in His right hand seven stars, and out of His mouth went a sharp two-edged sword, and His countenance shone as the sun shineth in his strength" (KJV). As the Prince of Peace, Jesus brandishes the Word of God and thereby overcomes physical violence and brute force (and what Xxey designates as "lower mortal passions"). This passage also recalls the doubly deadly use of the two-edged sword by Roman warriors. One notices that there is also a lot of double-edging and slashing in Xxey's terminology: "black/white light," "Christ/anti-Christ" and "matter/anti-matter" for starters. We also must not forget the Janus-faced and double-edged quality of the often ambivalent and ambiguous words uttered by Xxey in his own Revelations. They too cut both ways and are not easy to fix or pin down to a single and unitary meaning.

And Luke 12:25: "But which of you by being anxious about it can add to his stature a single cubit? Therefore if you are not able to do even a very little thing like this, why are you anxious concerning about the rest?"

This famous Biblical passage with its chill injunction of "no worries" has been translated and interpreted both spatially and temporally. "Who of you by worrying can add a single cubit to his stature?" or "Who of you by worrying can add a single hour to your life?" In either case, it is about the recognition of human limits and an example of humility. It is also a letting go of the ego – something often espoused on the three websites. Xxey chooses a spatial interpretation of the passage, and this brings him to the subject of cubits...

Whereas Revelation 21:17: "144 cubits is man's measure. That is the same as angel's measure."

The importance of this passage in relation to Xxey's cosmology becomes clear when we recall that Xxey's most sustained website was named www.144cubits.com. The masthead of that website read: "144 Cubits Or 144 Atomic Elements Is Your Perfect Atomic Structure - To Immortality! Impossible? Not So! Please Read On Now!" This equating of man's measure to an angel's measure in Revelation creates an equilibrium that raises man's stature to the heavens.

And in the deep research of the word cubit from Latin cubitum and cubitio et cetera means engaging in sexual intercourse, to incubate eggs, the soular-lunar, universal etheric genes-genie-genius eggs of immortality.

In this passage, our punning yet punishing etymologist Xxey mobilizes the cubit into double service. It is not only understood as an ancient measurement of length, but it also is read as the incubator of eggs. And when things start hatching in this magical way, it becomes the basis and the (bio)genesis of a transformative SeXxual (and textual) practice that generates a homonymic string of both linguistic and genetic material.

And Jeremiah 30:6: "Enquire and see. Since when do men bear children? Why then do I see all these men, all mankind, with their hands on their sexual seat of passion (loins) like women in childbirth?"

Xxey utilizes this passage from Jeremiah in a delightfully esoteric manner and his reading relies on taking it both literally and allegorically. The standard interpretation of this scene has God rebuking Israel for their fear and trembling and which the Lord promises will be short-lived. But Xxey seizes upon this passage as a way to break down the strict division of the sexes and to signal a transfigured world where men bear children. In this way, the vision of the androgyne has been fulfilled.

Yes, in bringing forth the cosmic-God-Christ childbirth of Xxenogenesis. Because when one commences the process of Xxenogenesis, a phenomenal, beautiful, fantastical, regenerative reversal cycle of dying, of transfiguration, transmutation begins in your bodily processes as your thermonuclear fuse-meld-unite through X-crucifixion, through this immaculate virgin conception marriage, your soular-lunar astrological Passover seeds of immortality and begin

in your navel soular plexus womb a pregnancy associated with pangs of cosmic Corpus Christi Christ childbirth of being reborn again. It is quite a sensation.

This figures yet another scene of SeXxenogenetic procreation and many of the terms already explicated reappear. One notices for instance the emphasis on childbirth in this particular passage. It begins with the verbose string "cosmic-God-Christ childbirth" and it ends with the equally verbose "cosmic Corpus Christi Christ childbirth" (but paradoxically in a re-birthing such that it does not really end). With the repetition of "childbirth," Xxey is unconsciously thinking here about his own childhood in Buffalo as well. Ironically, there is no getting away from the Corpus Christi Church where he first took the sacraments and where he first communed with the body of Christ. The figure of his childhood church accompanies him at the same time that it is overcome, and the result is sensational.

In terms of the fantastical "soular-lunar" birthing experience delineated here, Xxey again invokes the mystical idea of a male pregnancy receiving "seeds of immortality" in this criss-crossing fusion. This is the only time on the album that Xxey makes reference to the third chakra known as the solar plexus (which he neologizes with an extra "u") as a great source of sensation. He notes that this "begin[s] in your navel soular plexus womb a pregnancy" and that it is "associated with [birth] pangs." The third chakra is the emotional core and the passion center of the body and mind. Manly P. Hall takes up this exact point in Chapter XV, "The Solar Plexus and the Pneumogastric Nerve," of *Man: The Grand Symbol of the Mysteries: Essays in Occult Anatomy* (1932): "The solar plexus is the most important of the centers of the sympathetic system and has been called the brain of the stomach." He goes on to say, "Of the three great brains in the body, therefore, the solar plexus is the 'brain of Kama,' reflecting from its 'polished surface' the rays of the emotional nature, which from this center are distributed throughout the body; and also receiving into itself psychical impressions."

Crucify him, crucify him, crucify him, crucify him!

The bloodthirsty cry offers a direct reference to Bible verses Luke 23:21, Matthew 27:21, and Mark 15:13. Pontius Pilate asks the crowd what should be done with the second prisoner named Jesus and the response leads to the death sentence. Xxey substitutes himself for Jesus here alluding to his own cosmic crucifixion. But this is also about the scorn and humiliation he experienced at Mark-Age after he revealed his Xxenogenetic destiny. He elaborates upon this further in the Second Thessalonians passage below.

(Sound of a Long Snort, followed by Sound of a Windstorm which then continues as background for the next section)

Porky Pig rears his head. The long snort signifies a "becoming-animal" because the base rabble neither recognize Jesus as the Son of God nor Xxenogenesis as the Second Coming. This is followed by an extended windstorm sound effect. The trope of God dispensing wind in the Bible is a common one with over two dozen instances. On one occasion in Isaiah (29:6), the prophet's allusion to the Lord's array of effects sounds like a precursor to *SeXxenogenesis #1*: "You will be visited by the Lord of the Heavenly Armies with thunder, an earthquake, and great noise, with a windstorm, a tempest, and flames from a devouring fire." Here, the windstorm and its turbulence accompanies a passage from Revelation about the initial rejection of the Xxenogenesis revelation.

And please observe now how this prophecy of 2000 years ago shall now be fulfilled.

Or as Nellie B. Cain said in *Exploring the Mysteries of Life* (1972): "Man is already feeling the Aquarian vibration, although the Piscean Age is not completely finished. But, each Age is felt before the full vibration is manifest."

And Second Thessalonians and inserts 2:3: "Let no man deceive you by any means acting either as an interceder of God or of science or a man of law for that day of the Second Coming of Christ shall not come unless it is preceded by a rebellion against this Xxenogenesis revelation which will cause at first worldwide rebellion for as these now revealed mystical hidden teachings of the Scriptures. And the man of sin, all of mankind, shalt be revealed (Windstorm ends) as the son of perdition," as one who himself causes all the sorrows,

sickness, death which is the separation of spirit from oneself when one adulterates, destroys his own physical body.

Xxey takes up an important problem that has often plagued the prophets and heralds of a New Age, and he turns to this complex passage from St. Paul's Second Thessalonians in order to find scriptural sources that parallel his own situation. To recite the King James version: "Let no one deceive you by any means; for *that Day will not come* unless the falling away comes first, and the man of sin is revealed, the son of perdition." As noted, the hallmark of Xxey's interpretative method involves inserting new words into an existing passage, and he confesses as much here. Xxey stresses that the time for Xxenogenesis revelation and its worldwide institution is not yet at hand. Far from it. For there must be "at first worldwide rebellion against this Xxenogenesis revelation." Furthermore, Xxey warns not to be fooled by those deceivers and pretenders who preach that the Second Coming is already here, whether in the guise of a man or women of science, law, or spirit. To provide just one example, Xxey's denunciation of such "deceivers" cuts against David Spangler's work, who encouraged his spiritual followers at Findhorn and elsewhere to act as if the New Age already had arrived because the conditions for "nuclear evolution" already had occurred.

And I, the Xxenia, Xxenogenesis Etcha atom, promise to shrill-oscillate-vibrate-modulate-homogenize you atoms, your equilibrium.

At this point, as he nears the end of his sermon, one notes the criss-crossing of gender in the self-reference to himself as both the Xxenia/Xxeno atom in one and the same breath.

Xx   Xx   Xx

In *The Secret of the Atomic Age* (1958), fellow atomic Theosophist Vera Stanley Alder begins Chapter 10 ("Our Personal Relation to the Atom") in a manner that links atoms with vibration: "The atom was the first product of creation. It was the initial concretion of the Divine Breath. It was the form which the Word of Divine vibration first impressed upon the ether. It was the little seed of life itself, the embryo which held all the possibilities and patterns of creation."

Please sit comfortably as you can and relax. Close your eyes and still your consciousness.

We are receiving Instructions from the master to prepare us for stilling the mind and for sitting in meditation with him. Or so we think…

Are you ready?

Ready or not, here he comes…

Let's have fun and try this and see what you can experience after this revelation.

There is a temporal shifter and an instability regarding the phrase "after this revelation." Is Xxey referring here to what has come before or what is to follow? Either way, we are having some fun and giving it a try.

Contemplate. Are you interested in receiving Xxenogenesis #2? If so, please read the enclosed intent-attitude-intensity of this purpose.

Xxey does not follow through with sitting quietly and doing nothing. The imperative ("Contemplate") is not a guru's call to his flock to sit in meditation but rather an ex-businessman's sales pitch to his audience to buy more products, and in this case, to save (up) for his second coming, for a second record album. Xxey refers here to the enclosed hot pink envelopes that accompanied the album. These were to be returned by listeners to him at an Arlen House address. These inserts were inscribed with Xxey's personal note in a hand-written font: "& i am that i am – for behold the kingdom paradise of god is now at hand on earth alleluja jezu zyje." Despite all good intentions, *Xxenogenesis #2* was never written or recorded.

(Sings hymn in Latin). "Gloria Patri, et Filio, et Spiritui Sancto. Sicut erat in principio, et nunc, et semper, et in saecula saeculorum. Amen" (Translation: "Glory be to the Father, and to the Son, and to the Holy Spirit. As it was in the beginning, is now, and shall ever be, world without end. Amen.")

(Sings) I am that I am.

We know that he was an altar boy, but Xxey shows us that he could have been a choir boy too. The spoken word has reached its limit and now it is the time to break into song. The rest of the album is structured as a medley of Xxey's fave tunes. Interestingly, he selects the short hymn of praise to God, "Gloria Patri," to kick things off. This choice sounds like a Trinitarian track although Xxey often replaces the Holy Spirit with the Mother in his teachings. However, the second line is extremely appealing to Xxey because of its nod to the infinite, its collapse of temporal categories, and its desire for immortality. In other words, it invokes the Tetragrammaton. To repeat what we said at the beginning about the Tetragrammaton: it is "this manifold invocation of the Hebrew God that affirms itself as pure being." "Gloria Patri"'s step out of time then prepares the way for Xxey's last invocation of "I am that I am" – what serves as his second sonic selection and perhaps offering us an originary jingle.

(Sings) Oh dear Lord, if I were a rich man, yabba dibby dibby dibby dibby dibby dum.

From classic Christian hymn in its original Latin to Jewish Broadway musical hit, our eclectic show man shows off his range and versatility with "If a Were a Rich Man" from *Fiddler on the Roof* (1964) based on the Yiddish humorist Sholem Aleichem's short stories "The Bubble Bursts" (1899) and "If I were a Rothschild" (1902). The choice of this song also allows Xxey to ally himself to the long tradition of Jewish mysticism and Kabbalah. After all, songwriter Sheldon Harnick asserts that the "yabba dibbys" in this line are meant to invoke Chassidic chanting. We should also recall the final verse of the song where Tevye moves his daydreaming and wishful thinking from materialist goods to matters of the spirit. He imagines himself as rich in wisdom to the extent that the most important men in town seek his counsel and as a holy man who prays in the synagogue facing toward Jerusalem. This is quite appealing imagery for an unwanted Messiah! And for a man who retired at the age of forty-one (after becoming a rich man) to follow his metaphysical pursuits, the final line of the song holds up a mirror to his own life pursuits: "And I'd discuss the holy books with the learned men, several hours every day. That would be the sweetest thing of all." This indeed creates a strong sense of identification between Herman the lumberman and Tevye the milkman. Another oddball (and odd duck) connection is the appearance of the "quack" in both the show tune and on the LP. Let us recall the second verse where

Tevye imagines himself to be rich in livestock. "And each loud 'cheep' and 'squawk' and 'honk' and 'quack'/Would land like a trumpet on the ear/As if to say 'Here lives a wealthy man.'" This may have a different valence than Xxey's "Quack" that we found situated next to the Looney Tune question, "What's up doc?" But didn't Sholem Aleichem prescribe laughter as the best medicine?

(Sings) Oh sweet mystery of life, I'm glad that I have found thee.

Now we are transported back to 1935 and to the signature song of the film version of Victor Herbert's operetta *Naughty Marietta* as sung by Nelson Eddy and Jeannette MacDonald. With its limitless and lyrical message of love, the choice of this blockbuster hit for Xxey's repertoire is crystal clear. It is the assertion of love as the key to the mysteries and the secret of it all. "Ah! Sweet mystery of life At last I've found thee/Ah! I know at last the secret of it all/All the longing, seeking, striving, waiting, yearning/The burning hopes, the joy and idle tears that fall!/For 'tis love, and love alone, the world is seeking/For 'Tis love, and love alone, that can repay!/'Tis the answer, 'tis the end and all of living/For it is love alone that rules forever more." What we have here is immortal love and limitless love – the performance of love through song and the genre of the love song itself. Closer to Xxey's day and exactly like Xxey, Madeline Kahn in the role of Elizabeth (aka, the bride of Frankenstein) in Mel Brooks' *Young Frankenstein* (1974) also breaks into this song when she experiences monster sex for the first time. It is too easy to read this as mere parody. Instead, it is hard not to see this as a popular variant of the esoteric and ecstatic Xxenogenesis.

(Sings hymn in Latin and then Polish) Ave, ave, ave Maryja. Zdrowaś, zdrowaś, zdrowaś Maryja. (Translation: "Hail, hail, hail Mary.")

These are the beginning lyrics of the Polish hymn known as "Po Górach, Dolinach." The lyrics tell a tale of a young girl led by the Virgin Mary to climb a tree in a deep forest in order to commune with her. Near the end of the hymn, the girl beseeches Mary as if she were a heavenly body: "O most holy star, lead us to heaven in the land." Xxey's "Hail Mary" also evokes more famous odes to Mother Mary in classical compositions by Schubert and Bach, among many others.

(Sings hymn in Polish) U drzwi twoich stoję Panie, U drzwi twoich stoję Panie, Czekam na twe zmiłowanie, Czekam na twe zmiłowanie. (Translation: "I stand at your door, Lord. I stand at your door, Lord. I am waiting for your mercy. I am waiting for your mercy.")

Another Polish hymn, this time "U Drzwi Twoich Stoję, Panie," which reflects upon both Revelations 3:20 ("Behold, I stand at the door and knock") and Matthew 7:7 ("Knock and it shall be opened unto you"), while also reminding the modern listener of the potentially interminable scenario with the doorkeeper waiting for the Messiah in Kafka's "Before the Law" (1915). But the emphasis shifts here from waiting for the Messiah to waiting for mercy and therefore implies a desire for forgiveness. This raises the question: how does Theosophy understand sin? Dr. Hastings writes, "Three cognate forms in Hebrew with no distinction of meaning express sin as missing one's aim and correspond to the Greek and its cognates in the New Testament. The etymology does not. . . . necessarily imply intentional wrongdoing. It indicates a quality of actions rather than an act itself, and presupposes the existence of law" (*Hastings Bible Dictionary*). No blame, but "before the law" is indeed where Xxey stands.

(Sings) Beautiful world, wonderful world, wonderful world of love. A beautiful world, wonderful world, wonderful world of love.

Sounding startlingly similar to the opening of the first Tiny Tim album, where the great one cosmically trills: "Welcome to my dream/And how are you?/Will you be here long?/Or just passing through?/Brush off that stardust/Where have you been?/Don't tell me my rainbow/Was late getting in." Perhaps a spontaneous Xxenogenesis melody and lyric, imagining a new song (where the worldly message is yet again the wonder of love), it resonates with the two towering tracks both named "What a Wonderful World," sung respectively by Sam Cooke and Louis Armstrong.

And limitless love is: Always think big, pure love and the paradise of God is at your disposal.

In a final turn to Revelation (2:7), Xxey offers the meaning of "limitless love" and this journey returns those who are disposed to follow him back to Genesis – to the Tree of Life and the Garden of Eden. "He that hath an ear, let him hear what the Spirit saith unto the churches; To him that overcometh will I give to eat of the tree of life, which is in the midst of the paradise of God."

I love you.

And a final proffering of the love cry. Indeed, Xxey performs what is at the heart of Roland Barthes' *A Lover's Discourse* (1977): "To say I-love-you is to proceed as if there were no theatre of speech, and this word is always true, has no other referent than its utterance: it is a performative." Xxey's true love.

Da da dat's all folks, for now…

Porky Pig stuttering with a Brooklyn accent. Why does Xxey give Porky Pig the last word? But if you listen very closely, you will notice that two extra words have been added here – "for now." It is an affirmation of the now. In other words, The Revelations of Xxenogenesis end in favor of the now. They always bring us back to the present that is the now.

5. The Life of Xxenogenesis: A Fantastical Film Treatment in Six Acts

"Your lives are but tracings made by your immortal selves in this film world."
 –Claude Bragdon, *Man the Square: A Higher Space Parable* (1912), quoted by Michael X Barton in *The Weeping Angel Prediction* (1961) and Xxenogenesis in *Immortality Unveiled* (1985)

PROLOGUE: TURN OF THE 20th CENTURY

SCENE: It's Buffalo, and we're entering the Pan American Exposition in 1901, on the very first night, May 1, when they are turning on the astounding Electric Tower, a device which will set the fairgrounds on fire each night with zigzag black and white patternings. It is on this night that Buffalo officially becomes "The City of Light." We witness the triumphant arrivals of both Thomas Edison and Nikola Tesla in the early days of the fair. But this is followed by a darker scene: one month later, the assassination of President William McKinley on the steps of the Expo's Temple of Music by Polish anarchist Leon Czolgosz. Entering the crowd, McKinley reaches out to Czolgosz to shake his hand, a time-honored American political tradition, and Czolgosz responds by shooting McKinley in the abdomen. McKinley clutches his stomach and staggers backward. Someone in the crowd hits Czolgosz's arm and his weapon falls to the ground. The crowd closes in on Czolgosz and starts to beat him with their fists. "Go easy on him, boys," the President tells the mob before passing out.

SCENE: 1, the Polish neighborhood in Buffalo, and we're in an apartment with Bertha Osmola, Xxenogenesis' mother, at the age of six, who is playing on the floor. There's a pounding on the door, and the Buffalo cops burst in to search the apartment. Polonia is in lockdown, and the hunt is on for Czolgosz's collaborators and hideouts. We see raw terror in Bertha's eyes as three cops fan across the room, walking right over her.

THE CREDITS ROLL: *The Revelations of Xxenogenesis*

ACT I: BUFFALO CHILDHOOD

SCENE: It is a cold Buffalo winter at the height of the Depression in 1931. Herman J. Gabryel (Xxenogenesis) is five, and he is sitting at the feet of his parents, who are standing in the living room and fighting. The other five children, ages 3-14, are all there, several peeking from behind a bedroom door. The father, Joseph, shakes his head and says to Bertha, "There's no work in Buffalo, but I'll be back once I've got a steady job lined up." Joseph nods to Herman, and walks out the door, never to return.

SCENE: We witness the bustle of Polonia in 1936, with all forms of social life organized around the church, and in this case the Corpus Christi parish. We can see that Polonia remains resolutely working class in terms of identity (the Church's saint statues, for example, wear peasant clothes). We see the Mass being said in Polish, and Herman learns to sing Polish hymns. Herman appears as altar boy. He is standing over a small coffin on top of a coffee table in someone's home, and tears run down his cheeks. He tries to hide his tears from the two priests who stand behind him, muttering that they find Herman a bit odd. One of the priests asks: "What's wrong with you? Why are you crying? Is that your relative or friend?" Herman hides his head in his hands, walks out of the room past the priests and opens the front door. The sun is in his eyes, and we can see on his illuminated face that he is praying hard. We can hear what he is saying to God: "Why do we die? When I grow up I will find the answer to this mystery. I will learn to defeat Death and, if I succeed, I will share what I learn with everyone."

ACT II: GERMANY, WWII, 1944-45

SCENES: Shades of *Catch-22* as Herman enlists in his third year of high school in April 1944 and becomes a B-17 anti-aircraft ball gunner in the famed 457th Bomb Group ("the Fireball Unit"). He is of medium height and slender, has a light Polish accent and a lilting tenor voice. He is naturally bright, clever, funny, and generally likeable. He begins to serve on missions just after D-Day, but it is late enough in the war that Germany is short on fighters and concentrating its energy on building V-2 rockets, and Herman thankfully never has to fire on the enemy. In this way, providence has smiled upon him. But Herman also realizes that his B-17 bomber is terrifying civilians and killing real people on the ground, and his conscience begins to bother him. He sees enough of war during this period to become a lifelong pacifist.

Germany has a spy network, and one of the propellers on Herman's B-17 is sabotaged before a mission to distribute propaganda leaflets from the air. High in the sky, the loosened propeller starts wobbling and the plane begins to vibrate and then violently shake. Herman slowly and laboriously climbs out of the ball turret, and the whole crew puts on their parachutes and waits for the order to bail out. Now the propeller is torn from the plane, taking both the engine next to it, and severing Herman's ball turret from the plane! But the airmen stay put, and the journey home is a white-knuckle ride, with the plane barely making it back. This close call with death offers a first rebirth for Herman who believes that some strange future destiny has kept him safe amid the carnage all around him.

SCENE: Herman, now a Staff Sergeant, returns to the U.S. in June of 1945, to Sioux Falls, SD Army Air Base to await further orders. At Sioux Falls, several 457th officers and crews enthusiastically volunteer to the "New 8th Air Force" in the Pacific theater, including Herman. Two days later, a nuclear weapon is dropped on Hiroshima. We end this sequence with Herman reading the August 7, 1945 newspaper regarding the bombing of Hiroshima, stunned, and trying to make sense of this dangerous new world where the atomic bomb and the threat of nuclear war now rule the day.

ACT III: THE BUFFALO YEARS (WITH SEVERAL MIAMI SIDE TRIPS) DURING THE 1950s AND 60s

SCENES: Returning home and fresh from the War, family hero Herman borrows money from several relatives in order to jump start his small lumber yard business. Soon after, he falls in love with a local Polish American girl named Theresa and they wed at the Corpus Christi Church in January of 1952. Soon they are raising two beautiful boys and Herman designs the perfect modern home for his nuclear family on a large suburban lot in Amherst in 1958. The Buffalo area in general is booming in the fifties, and Herman is charming and making money hand over fist. And Herman's employees are happy: Herman never lays off employees in the winter, even though his is a seasonal business. Twice in two years the employees have rejected an attempt to unionize them. We see Herman spending large sums on advertising, making both radio and TV commercials, sometimes with a beaver puppet as the Gabryel Lumber mascot; designing and supervising the construction of the buildings for his much-enlarged new quarters in 1962; drilling and hammering together innovative product display systems for his showroom; and experimenting in the sixties with computerization of inventory and sales. Here we see Herman standing in awe over his first computer, provided by IBM. But IBM is of little help beyond providing equipment, and Herman must therefore hire a professor from local Bryant and Stratton College to write the computer programs that he envisions.

He has become a "big man" in the area, and he routinely hosts large, theatrical "home improvement" events in town, and is known to customers as "Cash-N-Carry Harry," the forerunner of Bob Vila and Tim Taylor. At one point, we see Herman negotiating a major deal, scribbling pencilled notes on a card for another businessman as they stand in front of a movie marquee promoting the film, *The Day the Earth Stood Still*.

SCENE: Up until now, Herman may be seen as a David Levinsky-style American immigrant: a religious youth who learns to recite the gospel of capitalism. Or perhaps he is the protagonist in a John Cheever story, a newly prosperous but "empty inside" suburbanite. But Herman's story, beginning one morning in early 1962, is interrupted and torqued toward the logic of a Philip K. Dick novel when he wakes to discover a mysterious pile of papers on his bedroom desk written in his own hand. He has no memory of having written them and does not fully understand their meaning. He will experience bouts of automatic writing routinely for the rest of his life. It's a puzzlement, that's for sure. After this event we find Herman, late at night, poring over samizdat mail-order pamphlets bound in primary-color red, green and brown construction paper. One is entitled, *Weeping Angel Prediction* by Michael X. Another is *Atoms, Galaxies and Understanding* by Daniel W. Fry. We watch him fall asleep while reading and taking notes, with "The Invaders" episode of *The Twilight Zone* on the TV in the background. Later we see that Madame Blavatsky's esoteric classic, *Isis Unveiled*, is among his constant bedside companions. Theresa surveys Herman's new pile of metaphysical books with some concern, uncertain what to make of it.

SCENE: Later that year, in the middle of the night, a twenty-foot-tall figure enters the Gabryel bedroom and awakens Herman and Theresa. This figure is clothed with the sun, the moon is under its feet, and upon its head is a crown of twelve stars. The figure removes several veils, first revealing a pair of female breasts and then male genitalia. It is a celestial androgyne, and Herman is shocked! Some time goes missing, and Herman's clothes disappear. He is in his wife's arms, almost lifeless, and his body has been staged and posed as if he is in Michelangelo's *Pieta*. The apparition sings a hymn and transmits to him the four words that will determine his future: "Equate Equilibrium High Frequency." An unusual hum, almost like that of electricity, issues from Herman's vibrating body: he is achieving a state of ultra-high frequency vibration. The next morning Theresa claims to have no memory of this event but this is a transformational moment for Herman, who wakes up thinking about the androgyne's prophecy. Pulling himself together and driving into work the next day, he hears a song on the radio, Jane Morgan's "They Didn't Believe Me," and recognizes it as the song sung by the androgyne! From now on, popular songs, and especially those that he hears on the car radio, will be a crucial aid for Herman in deciphering his cosmically received visions and messages, and will also provide a soundtrack for the film. All of his activities for the rest of his life will flow out of his need to understand these lost hours and this miraculous visitation, carrying him ever forward on a spiritual quest in search of answers.

SCENE: It is March 1965 and one of Herman's theosophical friends asks him to drive to Rochester to attend a special lecture by the famous Polish-American UFOlogist and space alien contactee, George Adamski. Even though a major snowstorm is predicted that day, Herman decides that he cannot miss this major event. Sure enough, there is a blinding storm and traffic is slowed to a standstill. The friend asks Herman if he knows how Jesus will return to earth. Just as Herman is explaining his messianic views, a prolonged brilliant blue white light appears, lighting his way forward and enabling Herman to pick up speed and drive as if conditions were normal. They arrive at the lecture just a few minutes late to a packed hall and Adamski is already talking about his flying saucer travels in outer space and his own personal meetings with the Space Brothers. At the end of the lecture, two commercial airline pilots in the audience bear witness with a story about how they were flying at high altitude one day and suddenly a blue white light appeared and lit up the sky. This prompts Herman to stand up and tell everyone that this is exactly what happened to him and his friend on the way to tonight's talk! Adamski praises Herman as a kindred spirit and says, "Friends, do you see what is happening? This is further proof that flying saucers are everywhere in our midst. Every day the Space Brothers are getting closer and closer to our world. The new era is coming!"

SCENES: Herman's ongoing experiences with automatic writing are increasingly disturbing to him, in part because much of what he reads directly conflicts with his Catholic upbringing. He prays for guidance: Should he trust the import of this unconscious writing, and follow the path newly opened to him by these seemingly inspired messages? He asks the heavens to send him a sign in the form of a lightning bolt. "If I receive such a sign," he promises, "I will never walk away from this new knowledge." Shortly thereafter, Herman's lumber yard foreman, Ziggy, discovers early one morning that the back of the main building has been damaged overnight. One of the building's rafters seems to have been burned and shattered, and a nearly two-foot piece of the rafter has crashed to the floor. It might be a case of "ball lightning," and Herman is confident that his prayers have been answered. "Oh, how wonderful!" he exclaims to a flabbergasted Ziggy, who can neither explain the mysterious occurrence nor fathom Herman's enthusiasm for the destruction. For decades afterward, Herman keeps the ruined and charred rafter fragment as a type of miraculous relic and as a reminder of the promise he made.

Still later: it is Easter in the Gabryel household, and the holiday is causing lots of strain and friction between Theresa and Herman. Still firmly entrenched in the Roman Catholic fold, Theresa wants to take the two boys to Sunday Mass at St. Gregory the Great in Amherst, and she asks Herman to come along with them. But Herman has other things on his mind. We see him in his library reading Arthur Avalon's *The Serpent Power* and studying esoteric Tantric rites. He is no longer interested in going to church and his Catholic experience is a foundation that he has outgrown. "Theresa, I love you very much, but I can't go with you to church. Christianity is much too limiting for me. There are other immortal teachings of the body and the spirit that we need to comprehend to take us to a higher plane of consciousness." He picks up another of Avalon's books on Tantra. "Listen to this beautiful passage from the Hindu gods —'For what is here is every place else. And what is not here is no other place to be found.'" Theresa is even more confused by this esoteric riddle. "Herman, if this is all so, then why doesn't the Pope teach and endorse this?". Herman is dismissive in his reply: "The Pope's world is the Vatican, but the Vatican is not the world." Theresa has no time for such heretical views with the church service about to start. "My darling Herman, we all will be praying for you to be saved in Church today." She leaves the room in haste.

SCENES: Devoting more and more time to understanding his vision, he meets his first medium, Lucille Kirk, at a cocktail party in Herman's home. Lucille is the wife of one of Herman's salesmen, and, over the course of the evening, Herman feels that she recognizes and authenticates his higher calling. The first words Lucille speaks to Herman are, "I see you are experiencing revelations," and Herman replies, "What is that?" Soon the two of them move to another part of the house to speak privately. Lucille reveals, "There is a man standing next to me in spirit form. He is here to thank you for all the prayers you have said for him." She begins to spell out letter by letter a long Belgian surname. Herman instantly recognizes the name of a close air force friend who was shot down while serving in the war. Herman often had prayed for this friend, but how could Lucille know any of this? A whole new world opens for Herman, and this is the beginning of a long and close friendship.

Soon the Merritt sisters, Shirley and Colette, a pair of chatty, local channelling enthusiasts, show up at Gabryel Horn of Plenty (formerly Gabryel Lumber) to let Herman know some astounding news: while on vacation in South Florida, they met an amazing spirit medium and channeler by the name of Nada-Yolanda at the Mark-Age MetaCenter in Miami, who claims to be receiving messages that are meant for him!

SCENE: Herman heads to Miami in May 1965 and to the Mark-Age mansion, a former boarding house known as The Blue House, where he is greeted by staff member Zan-Thu (Holden Lindsay): "Welcome to the Mark-Age!" she says. "For I am that I am!" Herman shoots back. Co-founded in 1960 by Nada-Yolanda (originally Pauline Sharpe) and El Morya/Mark (Charles Boyd Gentzel), the MetaCenter is a large square building full of offices, filing cabinets, little white statues, paintings, and ringing phones. There are piles of self-published brochures lying about with titles such as *Into the Fourth Dimension, How to Do All Things: Your Divine Use of Power, Christ Consciousness*, and *Seven Rays of Life*. Herman has arranged a sitting with Yolanda who as head of Unit #7 is in constant inter-dimensional contact with the Hierarchical Board – the celestial spirits who are guiding the world into the new Aquarian Age that is about to commence.

SCENES: Yolanda is channelling for Herman from behind her desk. Nearby is a microphone attached to a reel-to-reel tape machine, its gears and reels churning away in order to record all of the seer's precious words. Three other witnesses are present, including Jim Speed. Yolanda channels the entity San Cha who informs Herman that he has a higher purpose in life and that he will help all people achieve Christ-consciousness. "It was revealed to me that you Herman are a key scientist. Before reincarnating here on earth, you trained a scientific group on how to activate divine nuclear energy power in the physical body of man. This also relates to the transition of mankind and planet earth from the 3rd Dimension to the 4th Dimension." She tells him that he is so interested in UFO's, spacecraft, and extraterrestrial visitors because of this, and she predicts that he will have more contact with celestial beings in the future. She reveals San Cha's sign which is the first two fingers held upwards in a parallel position and with the thumb crossing over them. (Neither of them understand its real significance at the time as the mark of Xxenogenesis.) Yolanda also consults the Akashic Records telling Herman tales about other past incarnations and his bright future ahead. Yolanda is warm-hearted, cheery, and very effusive with her Brooklyn accent and she has a larger than life "Kate Smith" personality. After the session, Herman briefly meets Mark, the Don Draper of the saucer set, for the first time. Mark is chain smoking and looking crisp and mod in his suit and tie, but he is not as gregarious as Yolanda and perhaps feels threatened by this new self-confident acolyte. However, Herman is very pleased to meet other key players at Mark-Age including Jim Speed (the Center's brainy nutrition specialist and current Earth incarnation of ascended master Djwhal Khul, and therefore also known as Wains or John Mark or, in his space aspect, J.W. of Jupiter) and Jeanene Moore (who sometimes sings with a big band at the Coconut Grove and who channels under the name of Astrid). Deceased celebrity channeler and Mark-Ager Gloria Lee, who died in 1962 on a hunger strike demanding that the U.S. create an orbital space platform, remains an important presence in the group. Now known as Glo-Ria, her voluminous messages from outer space, channelled through Yolanda, underpin Mark-Age's somewhat delayed but still current initiative, Operation Show Man, which involves preparing the way for the Hierarchy Board's broader "externalization" (becoming visible and tangible, along with their craft—a fleet of flying saucers)! Herman witnesses a group of three or four Mark-Agers, including Jim Speed, in fervent discussion about new measurements confirming the rising vibrational frequency of the Earth and Jim's understanding of the many ways that our bodies must be made ready for the coming changes. Maybe Herman can figure out a way to get closer to this amazing group of enlightened individuals and leave cold and dreary Buffalo behind him one day soon.

SCENES: Herman starts visiting Miami and the MetaCenter on a regular basis between 1965 and 1968; and when Herman is too busy to visit, Yolanda offers him telephone time. But casting a shadow over these positive vibes is Herman's ongoing interest in the Universal Link movement and the predictions of the so-called "Weeping Angel of

Worthing." Herman gets regular mail via the Universal Link mail network, which distributes copies of the writings of individual "light centers," often consisting of no more than two to four individual seekers or channelers. Herman picks up a medium-sized pile of items from the mailbox and sits down at the kitchen table to look through them. The Weeping Angel is a big deal to movement members, and Herman feasts his eyes on a newsletter that prints the verbatim text of the final prediction of this entity, also known as Limitless Love: "By the first second of the first hour of Christmas Morning 1967 I will have revealed myself to the universe through the medium of nuclear evolution... A human press-button device will be used and, simultaneously with the pressing of the button — INSTEAD OF DISASTER — THE UNIVERSAL REVELATION WILL OCCUR." This prediction will haunt Herman for the rest of his life, and many Universal Link members interpret this passage as referring to a nuclear explosion somehow averted. (Behind Herman we see the walls and roof of his house peel away and see the classic image of a nuclear bomb exploding on the horizon while he continues to read his new pamphlets and letters.) But nothing at all seems to happen at Christmas: no explosion, no thwarted attack, no unmistakable sign that the New Age had arrived. Is it possible, as Grand Rapids, Michigan channeler Nellie B. Cain advocates to Link members, that "nuclear evolution" is a matter not of bombs but of atoms in our individual bodies? This gives Herman an important clue toward further research. (We can now see that Herman's body is transparent. He is still reading, and we close in on his abdomen and continue magnifying the image until we reach the atomic level....and then we rapidly zoom back out.) But Herman has his own individual interpretation of the mysterious prediction and believes that the "press-button device" might be a typewriter! After all, isn't the written word more powerful than any bomb? We see Herman reaching to the side of the kitchen table and pulling up a portable typewriter. He places a blank page in the machine and lifts his fingers to type. At the height of the Weeping Angel predictions, in 1967, Herman sells his assets and closes the lumber yard. He will now devote himself full time to his metaphysical pursuits.

SCENE: It is a hot August night in Miami during the late 1960s at the MetaCenter. Herman attends a special open house event – "Atlantis Is Under Miami: Scientific and Spiritual Proofs." Mark calls the meeting to order: "Atlantis is no myth and indeed its remains lies beneath us. Miami represented the peak of the Atlantean epoch and that is why so many people have come here in recent years. Like Yolanda and Astrid, they were inhabitants of Atlantis in their past lives." He then reads a relevant passage from Ignatius Donnelly's seminal work to prove his last point: "But the people of Atlantis had gone farther; they believed that the soul of man was immortal, and that he would live again in his material body; in other words, they believed in 'the resurrection of the body and the life everlasting.'" This then leads to an Atlantean channelling session with Yolanda and Astrid. Yolanda claims she was a high priestess in the Sun Temple of Atlantis in a former life and that Astrid was her assistant. The two channel these past incarnations and recount how they saved many lives before the destruction. The next speaker is Mark-Age gemologist Joel Glick who exhibits some lapis lazuli from the Atlantean age and expounds upon its magical and healing properties: "Lapis encompasses the universal principle of absolute light as emitted by our sister star, Venus, from whom this mineral radiation comes and was thus given to the Earth by the Lords of the Flame." The keynote speaker is the local archaeologist Dr. J. Manson Valentine (the sometime collaborator of Bermuda Triangle theorist, Charles Berlitz). Valentine relays to the gathering his recent discovery of an ancient temple in the waters of the Bahamas which Yolanda had prophesized some ten years earlier. He and his team now believe that Miami and the Bahamas lie on the site of what was Atlantis' most highly developed region, and they are planning to excavate the surrounding waters very soon.

SCENE: Herman has been sitting in the front row all this time with his face full of wonder and pleasure as he soaks up all the esoteric info. After the final presentation, Mark and Yolanda solicit the guests for donations (or "love offerings" as they call them) in order to help them carry on their work. Herman not only writes a fat check to Mark-Age, but he also tells the co-founders that he wants to sponsor an ad in the *Miami Herald* to publicize future Mark-Age publications. "I am very adept in this type of promotional work and I will apply it to hastening the Second Coming of Christ Consciousness here at the Mark-Age MetaCenter. I even have the perfect logo, borrowed from my old lumber yard ads." We next see the actual ad for the publication of the Center's first-ever hardback book, *Mark-Age Period and Program: Entrance to*

Golden Age of Aquarius, which features the angel Gabriel holding glowing embers, or the "coals of revelation," in the upper right-hand corner of the frame. Herman is spreading the word and urging everyone to "participate in the new heaven and the new Earth."

ACT IV: MIAMI BEACH AND FT. LAUDERDALE, 1969-88

SCENE: Retired at age 41, and with money to burn, Herman moves his family to an apartment in a brand-new luxury development, Arlen House, in North Miami Beach, in order to live near the Mark-Age MetaCenter where he has found his spiritual home and community. There is no shortage of material comforts at the Arlen House where Herman has access to a private marina, swimming pool (with a full-time pool boy) and the good life. Nevertheless, Miami Beach already is in decline in this era, and his fancy new address cannot disguise the fact that the area is now attracting more retirees than movie stars. No wonder Arlen House promises "island-like security" to its first residents. One afternoon, sitting poolside, Herman tells a new neighbor friend his ideas about the impressive new "Obelisk" sculpture that graces the front entrance to Arlen House and that was designed by Albert Vrana in 1969: "This sculpture is brilliant. It is the ancient Egyptian mysteries transported to our home in Miami Beach. Don't you see how it maintains this perfect equilibrium of matter and anti-matter, of Christ and anti-Christ?" His friend looks wide-eyed and responds: "You have some really far out ideas, Herman."

SCENE: It is 1970 and Herman Gabryel, Jr. hurts his wrist in high school gym class. At the local clinic the doctor orders a dozen X-rays and informs Theresa and Junior that it's merely a sprain. But the teenager is still in pain and Herman brings a Polaroid photo of the wrist to the radionics wizard and Mark-Age staff member Dr. Mark Gallert even though his skeptical wife Theresa has repeatedly called him a quack and his machines a bunch of "hocus-pocus." He enters Gallert's office/lab space full of radionics equipment (including the famous Gallert White Light Radionics Instrument) and other gadgetry on display. On his desk, he notices a sign that reads, "All things radiate." Gallert is fiddling with his white light device. Herman introduces himself and asks him what Gallert is doing. Gallert replies: "I am tuning into the energies and frequencies of the human body, and, in this way,

I can measure levels of vitality and pathology. I am returning numbers to the world of the senses." Herman explains his son's problem and hands Gallert the photo. Gallert looks closely at the Polaroid for a minute and then places it face down in his machine's light well. He moves a few dials, seemingly fine-tuning a reading of the image. "Do you realize that he has two bones that are broken? There are two hairline fractures in your son's wrist." Herman goes home and tells his wife and son what happened. The next day she goes back with Junior to the medical doctor and asks him to look at the X-rays again and, sure enough, he finds that there is one image, shot from an unusual angle that shows two tiny hairline fractures. When they get home, an approving Herman again calls Gallert who has this further medical advice: "Here is what I want your son to do – I want him to keep his wrists stable, but he also needs to move the ends of his fingers as much as possible to stimulate blood circulation. Now the best way to do this is with lots of typing for exercise. He is young and healthy otherwise and there is a good chance that it will heal by itself – this is nature's way." Herman is thrilled and he sees a silver lining for advancing his own work. "What a wonderful idea, Doctor, and he can type up some of my recent automatic dream writings while he is healing!"

SCENE: Herman knows that yogis have practiced sexual tantra, including semen retention (coitus reservatus), for thousands of years. It is January 1971, and he has been experimenting with these ancient techniques, often linked to improved health and longevity, for the last four months. But he has been achieving some unique results by paying attention both to his dreams and to his readings from the Bible. Through astrological calculations, he has found the period of only a few hours each lunar month in which the process can be performed. This is the singular window of opportunity in which the body's soular and lunar seeds can be fused to create the Christ seed of immortality. At the appointed times once in each of the previous three months, he had engaged in making love to his wife, Terry. We watch a charmingly animated sequence that depicts the anticipated journey of the fourth fused seed as it travels up the spinal cord, to be lodged in the brain as it joins with the previous three seeds. It will be the pivotal fourth point in forming the figure of a cross. This will be the foundation for the "crown of life" which is spoken of in the Bible and many esoteric writings. Now the time has come. He and Terry smile at each other, retire to the bedroom and slowly undress, which we watch behind a tasteful, multicolored, theatrical scrim. Herman feels a sense of true "limitless love," encompassing body, mind and the soul. In the silence Herman begins to perspire more and more. He focuses all of his attention on his wife. It is his focus on bringing her to higher and higher levels of ecstasy that allowed him to also climb to that same place and yet not release his seeds. Herman now knows that love is the ultimate key. It is not about suppressing or taming the sexual desires; it is about loving the person in front of you so much that your own sexual desires disappear. Their heartbeats synchronize and it is the seemingly endless heat and limitless love for each other that fuses the two seeds into one. But there is trouble in paradise. Unlike the first three fusions Herman is filled with an energy so vibrant and stirring that he has tremendous difficulty in preventing a spontaneous orgasm. Surprised by these powerful new energies, he leaves the bed and sits at his desk. As he often does, he consults the Bible, closing his eyes and opening the book at random. His eyes fall upon Revelations 2:10-11: "Fear none of the things thou art about to suffer. Behold, the devil is about to cast some of you into prison that you may be tested, and you will have tribulations for ten days. Be thou faithful unto death, and I will give thee the crown of life. He who overcomes shall not be hurt by the second death." He now realizes this energy that is coursing through his body will continue for the next ten days! He prays and meditates continuously, eating little and avoiding sleep so as to prevent a spontaneous emission. On the tenth day, just as the Bible had predicted, the biting, arousing energy that had been flowing through him subsides and naturally disappears, leaving him in a profound state of peace, contentment, and exhaustion. He then sleeps for three days, and when he awakens, he knows he has been permanently changed. He also knows he shall not be hurt by the second death anymore. He has overcome what the Bible refers to as the "enmity."[7] He is one step closer to his goal of immortality. He remembers his *Pieta* experience and knows he has achieved what he then was instructed to do: "Equate his Equilibrium to a High Frequency."

SCENE: Yolanda and Mark have been on the road for all of 1969 and 1970, trying to establish branches of Mark-Age in California and

---

[7] See Genesis 3:15 and Ephesians 2:14-16. Also, see a further elaboration of the enmity in the Afterword.

elsewhere, although Herman continues to phone Yolanda and thereby maintains his regular contact with higher galactic forces via land line. But the two founders finally return to the MetaCenter in mid-1971, and Herman is quick to show up in order to tell Yolanda and the others all about his cosmic crucifixion. Yolanda does not look pleased to see Herman, but she manages to greet Herman warmly. Perhaps she has heard a bit about Herman's latest adventures and already knows that she disapproves: she herself worked hard as a young person to overcome feelings of sexual desire, and her ecstatic channellings seemed a potent substitute. At first, she is seen channelling a convoluted cosmic message that seems to partially affirm Herman's ongoing importance to the current work of the MetaCenter, now newly dubbed, "Mark-Age, Inc." Later that week, however, Mark, a proponent of celibacy in anticipation of androgynic transfiguration, informs Herman in no uncertain terms that the Center has received nothing from the Hierarchical Board regarding Herman's experience, and that no one at Mark-Age is willing to support or condone Herman's new interest in tantric sex magic. Indeed, Herman is mistakenly substituting self-gratification for ascetic service to the galactic plan, "and," Mark says gravely, "self-love, however 'rigorous,' is not 'love in action'." Herman listens silently and takes his leave. Herman can sense that even those he regarded as friends are increasingly treating him as deluded and suffering from a "Messiah complex." While Jim Speed, Astrid, and Mark-Age member and prominent Florida banker Lee Blount (aka Joseph Whitfield) have been privately supportive of Herman's claims, he now knows that he must be careful about what he says and to whom he speaks.

SCENES: Herman sees subliminal messages in the many signs around him (both on the street and in the books, television programs and songs that he loves) that his cosmic crucifixion is a world-changing event, and he also knows that the Xxenogenetic process is available to everyone…to every couple on the planet, straight, gay, or any which way. And he correctly surmises that the best way to reach the masses in the early 1970s is to make a long-playing record album! We see a montage of Herman overwhelmed with scripts, meeting with producers and engineers at a major recording studio, and with vinyl and record sleeve manufacturers, as he carefully assembles, piece by piece, his one-of-a-kind masterpiece: Xxenogenesis, *SeXxenogenesis #1* (1973). We see him in the studio, rapping and riffing passages from the album, and trying out different voices and effects, instructing the engineer to "add more reverb, please! MORE REVERB!" The crew are dumbfounded, their jaws on the floor. We watch as he insists to a baffled technician that his album must begin with a needle drop from the *2001: A Space Odyssey* soundtrack. We watch Herman record one of his signature lines: "Hey bud, are you for real? (pause) I sure am!" while we gauge the stunned reactions of the witnesses, now growing into a small crowd in the control booth in order to watch the festivities. We see a montage of elements from the album art and listen to a sample from the early part of the album where Xxenogenesis explains the meaning of "ETCHA!"

SCENES: Herman is sitting in his living room with his two teenage sons. He is showing them the gorgeous, gatefold sleeve and his original painting for the cover. "I am going to send this album free of charge to universities, world leaders and opinion makers such as Richard Nixon at the White House, Pope Paul VI at the Vatican, and George Van Tassel at the Integratron. I want the information I am sharing on this record to be a gift to the world." He shares with them a sample of the hot pink envelopes he will include with each record album, to be returned to an anonymous P.O. Box number at Arlen House. "I don't want to have my name or picture published. As you know: 'fools names and fools faces are always seen in public places.' And this information has nothing to do with me or my individual personality." Next we see Herman later sending the album by mail to bewildered college radio station program directors and enthusiastic UFO clubs. The gospel according to Xxenogenesis is spreading.

SCENE: It is October 20, 1973, and we are in the backwater of Merlin, Oregon, for the annual business meeting of UFO contactee Daniel W. Fry's organization, Understanding Inc. The meeting agenda includes the latest UFO sighting reports and a discussion as to how to increase the sales of *Understanding Magazine*. Fry announces that they have a special treat for everyone who can stay after supper. He wants to turn them on to a new and most unusual record that has arrived as a gift recently. The group listens attentively to *SeXxenogenesis #1*, and everyone is blown away. Afterwards, Fry gets Xxenogenesis on the speaker phone and praises the LP to the heavens. "Just out of this world! This recording is something that cannot be adequately described by words

– there is really nothing like it!" Herman is humbled by all this praise but feels that his cosmic message is finally getting through. "My limitless love unto you, Mr. Fry. You are doing such good work at Understanding Inc. May you and your group be able to travel in universal flying objects, UFO space crafts, without any hindrance as to food, air, water, etcetera!"

SCENE: The luxury apartment was turned into a condo in 1973, and Herman has moved on to a less posh address: the "Palm Air" apartments in Pompano Beach. The next year Herman sits at his kitchen table, staring at his bank book and Theresa and the boys are there too. Herman is sipping a cup of peppermint tea. He thinks, "When I retired, I had hoped that my savings and investments could last us a lifetime, but so much of what I earned is gone in just seven years! There's no two ways about it: I have got to go back to work, but I know I cannot return to the lumber business and become 'Cash-N-Carry Harry' all over again." In short, it is time for a new adventure. After careful thought he decides to open up a combination health food store and metaphysical bookstore. We hear, quietly at first but upwelling, the stirring Strauss theme music from 2001. And we dissolve to a small crane raising a sign above a modest storefront in Ft. Lauderdale and lowering it into position. It reads: "Space Odyssey Nutrition." The camera enters the store, and there's already a crowd inside. Just inside the door there's a large display of Propolis, as tincture or tablets, in a variety of sizes. Bottles and jars of imported German "nutrition supplements" seem to be all the rage. We see Herman's two boys are either stocking shelves or helping customers with special orders. To one side of the store, we see a well-stocked book shop of health and metaphysical books. Herman is holding court with a customer: "We're already the second largest New Age bookstore in the State of Florida. Look here: I stock all of Ma and Pa Ballard's books as well as everything from the Mokelumne Hill Press, which specializes in rare titles in health research. By the way, I can get customers a variety of difficult-to-find health products through my mail order business, Omni Christi."

SCENES: Herman is at the hospital in 1976, with tears running down his cheeks as a doctor tells him that the small cancerous tumor on Theresa's spine is inoperable and already is beginning to paralyze her. She dies just 12 weeks after being diagnosed with cancer at the age of 47.

Herman finds himself reeling from this tragic event. The two of them were deeply in love and always close, even when they disagreed about Herman's beliefs and life decisions. He now grapples even more intensely with the question of mortality that has haunted him since the time he was an altar boy in Buffalo. We see him at his desk surrounded by piles of theosophical and spiritualist titles and writing two treatises on the topic – *Immortality Through Xxenogenesis* (1978) followed by *Immortality Unveiled* (1985). His eyes are on fire as he tells his son: "Send a copy of my new book to the Library of Congress and let them know that Xxenogenesis has found the answer to solving mankind's mortal woes!" A few esoteric passages from the book cross the screen as his son dutifully fills out the copyright forms. He signs them with the proper names of "Herman J. Gabryel" and "Herman J. Gabryel, Jr."

SCENES: It's 1982, and Herman and Jim Speed are having a meeting in the office at Space Odyssey with Dr. Carey Reams, an agricultural engineer and guru of alternative farming who is a proponent of the "Chiron" agricultural sprayer made by the Volkswagen corporation. Reams' recent book, *Choose Life or Death: The Reams Biological Theory of Ionization*, is sitting on the table. Reams is explaining the benefits of the Chiron sprayer to Herman, Jim, and his son, Herman, Jr: "The Chiron is the Cadillac of all foliar crop sprayers. I know of no other machine that can deliver nutrients to plants. It effectively turns water into a mist, or smoke, homogenizing particles down to a size that plants can easily absorb and the sprayer itself operates at a relatively high vibrational frequency that stimulates the opening of a plant leaf's pores or stomata. In that way the high-pitched sound made by the Chiron is much like the morning chirping frenzy of birds. It's a truly magical process." We see images on the screen: billowing mist and smoke, magnified microdroplets of water, bustles in hedgerows, centaurs pawing the ground, plant stomata opening suggestively. "Thanks for informing us about the Chiron," says Herman, who decides after some deliberation to purchase the Chiron's manufacturing division. Jim meanwhile has been scouting a warehouse for manufacturing and working on the manufacturing process for the spray heads. Herman enthuses: "We're about to crack the American market!" but the technology is way ahead of its time and Herman is finding resistance to his pricing model. He stands in front of a group of farmers, who have many questions: Why is the initial cost so high? How is the Chiron fundamentally different from other sprayers? Who provides the parts when the system breaks own? The meeting breaks up and only one farmer stays to talk to Herman. "This sprayer is designed to mimic the subtlest ecological processes," he tells Herman, "and it's hard to explain why that's important. Those other folks are having trouble seeing the future." As an environmentalist ahead of his time, Herman nods knowingly but worry also crosses his face.

ACT V: YELM AND RAMTHA, 1986-91

SCENE: It is 1986 and Herman is restless and distracted. Herman, Jr. (aka Gabryel) is running the day-to-day operations at Space Odyssey Nutrition while Herman is focused on selling the Chiron sprayer, an increasingly difficult proposition. On other fronts, Herman remains deeply immersed in New Age channelling literatures and we see him collecting early home videocassettes marketed by emergent New Age stars. He pops a videotape into his VCR, *Superconsciousness, Volume 1*, and begins watching rising guru J.Z. Knight, a forty-year-old woman who channels a 30,000-year-old male Lemurian warrior known as "Ramtha."[8] Ramtha teaches his followers to "love yourself into life" in order to achieve "superconsciousness." When Ramtha invites the viewer to become one of the newly risen Christs, with infinite sovereignty over reality, Herman's ears perk up. And then Herman hears another voice on the tape, superimposed over Ramtha, and this voice suggests that he present himself to Knight as the first such Christ: "How come you don't know about this woman? Don't you think it is about time that you should?" These are the first channelled messages Herman has ever heard that suggest there are other seekers out there like himself, and he is excited by the prospect of a community receptive to his discoveries.

---

[8] Details about the Ramtha School are drawn from four sources: investigative journalist John Crutcher's lengthy investigation of the school, published in the monthly *Common Ground of Puget Sound* in July and August 1995; the many testimonies offered by former students of the school available at enlightenmefree.com; David McCarthy's "Brief of Evidence" of May 9, 2014; and our confirming interviews with Herman J. Gabryel, Jr., who attended the school during its first two years of operation with his father and his friends. Common Ground article:
http://enlightenmefree.com/phpBB3/viewtopic.php?f=37&t=171
McCarthy Brief: http://freepdfhosting.com/61756e3c8e.pdf

SCENES: He decides that he must investigate this as soon as possible, and he learns that Knight's home base is in Yelm, Washington. By July of 1988 we see Herman, his good friend Cynthia, Gabryel, Jim Speed, his spouse Ruth, and other close friends all relocating to Yelm in order to participate in the community there. Historically, Yelm is the gateway to Mount Rainier, which in turn is the birthplace of the modern UFO movement: the location where Kenneth Arnold on June 24, 1947, saw a whole tea tray's worth of saucers darting and disappearing in inexplicable ways. Within weeks of moving to Yelm, Herman learns that Knight is forming the Ramtha School of Enlightenment on her property, and he notices that things are changing rapidly. Previously, all channelled information was readily available at a nominal price, but now tapes of particular events are sold only to those who had paid to attend them. Worse yet, oaths of secrecy are asked of students, who are forbidden to share information from these events with family and friends. Herman ruminates on the fact that he spent thousands of dollars to produce and distribute his LP record free of charge, while Knight seems to be turning enlightenment into a business proposition, controlling information that should be available freely to all. In short, Herman is ready to leave the Ramtha School, intuitively feeling that the School will be a dead end. He tells the other seekers about his desire to leave only seven weeks after arriving in Yelm. "Where is the love?" he asks them. "The atmosphere here is unwholesome, and I think 'Ramtha' isn't who he says he is." At the urging of his friends and family, however, he agrees to soldier on for a while longer. But he minimizes his attendance to required events and some evening sessions during the next two years.

SCENE: Herman and Cynthia attend a mandatory social event, where they meet many young and enthusiastic students, along with a few ostentatiously wealthy individuals. Herman points out a current, photogenic TV star among the attendees, and he and Cynthia head for her and a circle of admirers, who are chatting with the star about her visions and channelling experiences. At one point she turns to Herman and remarks earnestly, "You know, Ramtha is my brother." To which Herman replies, "Well, I will tell you a little secret too. I am Xxenogenesis, the first Christ of the Aquarian Age. I must let Ramtha know this." The TV personality puts on a big Hollywood smile, backs up, and drifts off toward another newly arrived set of fans.

SCENES: Ramtha tells his students that they will need to attend and pay for seven years of coursework in order reach their goals (later revised to ten years!). As part of this, Herman and his group, designated Ak Men Ra, are asked to participate in "Fieldwork" and "The Tank," complex outdoor competitions where participants are blindfolded and must navigate intuitively a field or a maze. Students are told that their improving powers will prevent them from hurting themselves, but many people get banged up in the process. Later, Herman chats with Gabryel about the fact that Ramtha seems to praise a particular group one moment, and criticize another the next, seemingly stimulating competitiveness instead of camaraderie and cooperation. Gabryel suggests that this seems more like a "Psychic Olympics" than a path to spiritual fulfillment or enlightenment. Through it all, Herman maintains his typical sense of humor: when Ramtha's teachings turn increasingly apocalyptic, concerning a forthcoming invasion of Earth by reptilian humanoids, we see him laughing out loud at the fact that even imminent invasion has not prevented Knight from listing publicly next semester's seminars and fees!

SCENE: Eventually consensus is reached within the little band of seekers that things are going nowhere. Gabryel tells his father that he notices two changes as a result of his participation: first he was taken out of "the flow" and second, his own intuitive gifts and abilities have been diminished. Herman "moves on" spiritually but remains in Yelm because he has fallen in love with Washington and the Pacific Northwest. Back to square one for Xxenogenesis, who still has not found a community of like-minded souls for his message.

ACT VI: PUBLIC ACCESS CABLE AND THE INTERNET, 1992-2016

SCENE: It is 1993 and Herman goes to the theater with friends who want to see the new movie *Free Willy*, shot in the Pacific Northwest and taking the world by storm. He is touched by this story of an orphan boy and a captive orca he sets free, and it reminds him of a sobering Biblical verse from Matthew 12:39 that helps to explain the film's success as well as the fact that Herman's revelation is falling on deaf ears: "A wicked and adulterous generation asks for a sign! But none will be given it except the sign of the prophet Jonah." He listens to the gospel-laden theme song of the movie as sung by the pop star Michael Jackson, which asks the musical question, "Will you be there?" This too reminds Herman of his spiritual mission and that he must seek a new medium for God's messenger.

SCENES: Herman has spent a lot of money on the Ramtha School in the last few years, and he is now living frugally with his son in Yelm. But that does not mean that senior citizen Herman Gabryel is going to sit idly as a couch potato checking out TV reruns or watching the wheels go by from his porch. Quite the contrary. Never the passive consumer, Herman feels that it is time to try his hand at a new communications medium–community access television! Herman travels to Olympia to meet with the program director of the Thurston Community TV station who is always open to programs that will provide something innovative and "far out" for viewers across the state. Herman is given the nod to create a series of eight one-hour TV programs. These shows cover religious and spiritual topics including Biblical interpretations, the evolution of Christianity, and the dissemination of New Age wisdom. Always someone with a DIY sensibility, Herman learns to use all of the production equipment including the cameras and the studio mixing board himself. We see Herman in the studio with his headphones on, mixing one of his favorite singers of the day, Sarah Brightman, and her new track, "Heaven is Here," with some nature footage that he shot near the majestic Mt. Rainier featuring the sun-speckled lush greenery of summertime and then changing to snow quietly falling in winter. The natural cycle of the seasons in such a beautiful setting provides the visual backdrop for Herman's voice track. He speaks into the microphone and tells the TV audience about the imminent approach of New Age higher consciousness for all mankind and the need for each individual to be reborn. Then he does some Biblical exegesis Xxenogenesis style! Herman feels hopeful at the beginning of the series that his TV shows will help him to spread the word much more broadly than the *SeXxenogenesis #1* LP did in the seventies, but he is soon disappointed. Yet again, so few people are heeding the call and responding to his spiritual messaging. Now what?

SCENE: One morning in the mid-1990s Herman is watching television while eating breakfast and he hears the co-hosts of *The Today Show* asking each other about something called "the World Wide Web."

Soon Herman has a home computer and is eagerly "taking in the sites." It's an untamed, virtual wilderness out there, and Herman is fascinated by the thousands of newly emergent sites, with more popping up each day, accommodating crazy start-up communities of ecology, queerness, and alternative religious types. We pull back and watch him surfing the 90s version of the Web; Herman thinks back to the mid-1960s and the Universal Link movement, which was designed to bring the whole of the world into a New Age through newsletter and pamphlet communication. Now he sees that those sixties dreams can be fully and concretely realized at the end of the millennium.

SCENE: Herman finds the immaterial realm of cyberspace congenial to his metaphysical bent and spiritual aspirations, and he is excited by the prospect of new and larger audiences for his ideas. With its avatars, assumed names, and role playing, the internet also allows him the anonymity to reconnect with his Xxenogenesis identity without any possibility of anyone detecting his disguise. We see him typing out the domain names for his new websites www.xxenogenesis.com, www.144cubits.com and www.unlearninghurts.com. He motions to his son, "Hey, can you give me a quick read of this front page to see what you think? Is this what will captivate our audience right from the start?" They discuss a few possible edits and settle on another way to convey his cosmically inspired ideas. Herman retypes the first two questions: "Did you know that you are composed of trillions of atoms? And you have the potential to harness the universal energy within you to attain light energy?" He concludes the page with the old salesman's pitch: "Guaranteed results when you participate!" Intuitively, Herman is asking all the right questions about the new cyber-medium: Who is my audience here? Who exactly is tuning in to xxenogenesis.com? How can I reach more persons? Will what I'm doing get my message across to them? He is determined to reach this new generation of users.

Herman never does things in half measure, and he spends the next several years building a rabbit warren of web pages, posting the equivalent of hundreds of pages of information regarding his life, accumulated wisdom, and even his favorite television programs and favorite jokes. He frequently checks the "hits" counter that lets him know who is visiting and from where. We see him at his kitchen table with research books and newsletters piled high. At the age of 75, he chooses an e-mail address for his brand new Xxenogenesis website that recalls the key divinity who relayed messages to him via Yolanda's mediumship four decades earlier. He chuckles to himself, "And I am that I am. I am sancha@xxenogenesis.com. How exciting, how excellent!" "What do you think of that, dear Yolanda?" he continues, "I have found a new medium now!" He then makes the sign that San Cha first revealed to Yolanda in 1965, now clearly understood as the mark of Xxenogenesis. Herman gestures towards the computer screen and it reflects the dual cross back at him.

SCENE: Herman is alone in line at the local Department of Motor Vehicles. Herman is 87 but looks much younger, in part because he has a full head of salt and pepper hair. The teller informs him that he needs to have his eyes tested before he can renew his driver's license. Herman goes to an ophthalmologist, but he is unhappy to hear that he will have to have eye drops in order to dilate his pupils; he is uncomfortable taking drugs of any short, but he agrees to the procedure. He immediately has trouble seeing, but the doctor assures him that he will be fine tomorrow. Still, things keep getting worse, and Herman is now nearly blind. He tells his son, "I can see that there is a person in front of me, but I wouldn't know who it is unless you spoke to me." Over the next several months Herman, Jr. treats his father homeopathically and manages to restore a portion of his sight, but Herman permanently loses his depth perception and most of his vision. Strangely, his driver's license is renewed with no restrictions, but Herman never drives again. He has gone from being a highly active and self-sufficient person to leading a life full of new challenges. "I once saw everything so clearly," he bitterly complains as he turns off the computer and rubs his eyes. His heart is broken.

SCENES: Herman is in his ninety-first year, and he is sitting in a comfortable chair in his backyard. The sun is shining. He has on a brown fedora, similar to the one David Bowie wears at the end of *The Man Who Fell to Earth*; Herman is awake but lucidly dreaming. One vision begins with the aged but still spry Herman returning to the MetaCenter one last time and being confronted by Yolanda, Mark, and Jim Speed. "Why didn't you tell us who you are when we were alive on earth?" "But I did!" Herman insists, and the sky behind him begins to go dark. The wind begins to howl. Another dream, which we see acted out in detail, concerns his return, as a very old man, to the Corpus Christi school, now surrounded by water. Xxenogenesis tries to walk through the water, which gets deeper and deeper. From a distance, he watches a new crop of altar boys begin the preparations for Mass and realizes that all of the school's students are now studying his work and attempting to birth the Christ within themselves.

Herman sits back and looks up into the sky. He closes his eyes and smiles. He drifts off into a final dream sequence that appears in the standard colors of an early adopter's website: a swirling mixture of deep red, blue, purple, rust, forest green, powder blue and pale yellow that begin to slowly separate and then assemble into letters and words and long colorful paragraphs. We next see brief, snapshot images of some of the webpages and their vibrant graphics. Little did Herman know what the new millennium held in store for his discoveries in cyberspace. We dissolve to the front page of the Wayback Machine, where a series of automated algorithms are preserving every pixel of the three Xxenogenesis websites as part of the Internet Archive's obscure project of overmemory. We see, via scenes of modern cellphone and tablet users calling up Herman's websites and sharing links with friends, that everything Herman has written has been digitally stored and resurrected, with his teachings and vision transmitted in cyberspace and passed on for generations to come. Indeed, his life's work has become a vital part of the electronic Akashic Records.

Afterword by Gabryel, the Son of Herman J. Gabryel, Sr./Xxenogenesis

Scott and Louis were kind enough to offer me the opportunity to write this Afterword to their book. As Xxenogenesis'/Herman's son, I hope to provide a few insights into Xxenogenesis and his project. To both Scott and Louis, I say thank you very much. I would also like to compliment them on their astonishing efforts to discover the identity of Xxenogenesis which was unknown and "lost in the wilderness" for over 40 years. It was to my surprise that decades and decades after the LP record was made that I received a letter in the mail inquiring about Xxenogenesis.

It also told me about the writing of his biography. My father had gone to extraordinary lengths to remain anonymous feeling that all attention should be on the information he was sharing and not on his individual persona. He even produced and distributed the LP record free of charge so there would be no paper trail. Scott and Louis went to even greater lengths to discover the mystery identity of Xxenogenesis and persevered after reaching many dead ends. My compliments to them on their diligence, and again, my thanks to them. I would also like to say it has been a pleasure to work with them on many levels.

Before talking about Xxenogenesis's project, I would like to talk about him as a person for a moment. He was creative. Creative is an understatement! He was passionate about everything he did. He had an unusual sense of humor and could be very surprising. He was deeply spiritual and committed and very metaphysical; he saw the two as going hand in hand. He was single-minded about his pursuit of the project. He could be a little stubborn, but usually channelled that energy into an unending perseverance. He could often put a smile on a person's face just by walking into a room. But above all, he was kind, generous and very loving. He has already changed the world once by pioneering the use of computers in a business setting. He conceived of and designed the first computer invoice as well as computer inventory systems and computer forecasting programs for inventory management. This changed the world and the way we do business today. I feel the Xxenogenesis Project he started, upon completion, will change the world even more.

The best manner in which to explain the Xxenogenesis Project involves drawing upon numerous quotes from the Bible and the sacred text of The Gospel of Thomas. There are thousands of biblical quotes, some of which are poetic or historical, some metaphysical, and some literal; while others are symbolic, in allegorical or parable form; and yet others were altered or inserted by scribes and editors along the way.[9] This has made the Bible one of the greatest mysteries of all time and somewhat difficult to understand. But given that Xxenogenesis held that it also promises the keys to heaven and immortality, it is worth going over very carefully. What I am about to share is by no means all inclusive. Information to help decode this mystery came from many sources. Although they might appear unrelated, each helped to point the way to the next step in the journey. There is the part that Herman/Xxenogenesis played and the part that you can play, should you decide to participate in this adventure.

I will use as many literal quotes as possible. There will also be times when a word in a quote or the whole quote is symbolic, metaphysical or in parable form. I will add in the interpretations as needed. The appropriateness of doing this was prophesied in the Book of John:

> "These things I have spoken to you in parables. The hour is coming when I will no longer speak to you in parables, but will speak to you plainly concerning the Father." (John 16:25)[10]

---

[9] See Bart D. Ehrman, *Misquoting Jesus: The Story Behind Who Changed the Bible and Why* (HarperCollins, 2005).
[10] Saint Joseph, "New Catholic Edition" of the Holy Bible – The Old Testament Confraternity-Douay Version and The New Testament Confraternity Edition (Catholic Book Publishing, 1962). All further references to the Catholic Bible are abbreviated as CB in the text.

We are in those days now. The short discussion that follows will include aspects of consciousness and those quotes that led up to "overcoming the enmity" and the "cosmic crucifixion," as both are integral to the overall process. Intentional love and a consciousness of love are fundamental to this process. Christ reiterated this in his response to a lawyer who sought to trap him with a question about the "greatest commandment in the law." Also notice that a single greatest commandment was not enough. There are two:

> "Thou shalt love the Lord thy God with thy whole heart, and with thy whole soul, and with thy whole mind." This is the greatest and first commandment. And the second is like it, "Thou shalt love thy neighbor as thyself." On these two commandments depend the whole Law and the Prophets." (Matthew 22:37-40, CB)

Love is the glue of the universe and can be mixed into every moment of our existence and everything we do. God is omniscient, all knowing, omnipresent, simultaneously present everywhere and omnipotent, all energy. In your day-to-day existence, behave as if the God in all life matters.

The conversation about the two greatest commandments is carried further when the person who asked the question complements Christ's answer by saying this imperative to love is more important than any other act of devotion:

> "And to love him with all your heart, with all your understanding and with all your strength, and to love your neighbor as yourself is more important than all burnt offerings and sacrifices." When Jesus saw that he had answered wisely, he said to him, "You are not far from the kingdom of God." (Mark 12:33-34)[11]

So, if you are diligently engaged in the two greatest commandments, then what is that small additional piece of information that Christ is referring to? You are not far off, but not there yet either. And as Shakespeare would

---

[11] *Berean Standard Bible, New Living Translation* and *New American Standard Bible* (NASB, 1977). Direct link online: https://biblehub.com/mark/12-33.htm

say, "There's the rub." Xxenogenesis opens up for us Christ's more advanced teachings. The same teachings that were held in secret by the rabbis of the day and what Christ privately revealed to the apostles. There is a large body of knowledge that Christ taught privately to those students who were most receptive to his message:

> Jesus said: "I tell my mysteries to people worthy of my mysteries." (Gospel of Thomas 62a) [12]

Christ revealed his mysteries directly and indirectly. He also used parables and obscure symbolic statements. Sometimes he privately revealed one mystery to one apostle and not to another:

> "Make a comparison; what am I like?" Simon Peter replied: "You are like a righteous messenger." Matthew replied: "You are like an intelligent lover of wisdom." Thomas replied: "Teacher, I cannot possibly say what you are like." Jesus said to Thomas: "I am not your teacher; you have drunk from and become intoxicated from the bubbling water that I poured out." Jesus took Thomas and they withdrew. Jesus said three things to him. When Thomas returned to the other disciples, they asked him: "What did Jesus tell you?" Thomas replied: "If I tell you even one of the things that he told me, you would pick up stones and throw them at me, and fire would come out of those stones and burn you up." (Gospel of Thomas 13)

Everything has not been revealed but the opportunity for you to participate in the mysteries for yourself will be available to you. Fortunately, not everything was symbolic. Some teachings were of a literal nature. One highly controversial teaching at the time of Christ concerned the temple of God. For the Jews the temple in Jerusalem was the "one and only" house on earth in which God resided. This was the sole residence of God on earth. Christ taught a very different and radical concept for his day:

---

[12] Stevan L. Davies, *The Gospel of Thomas and Christian Wisdom*, 2nd edition (Bardic Press, 2004). All further references are from this version.

> "Do you not know that you are the temple of God and that the Spirit of God dwells in you? If anyone destroys the temple of God, him will God destroy; for holy is the temple of God, and this temple you are." (1 Corinthians 3:16-17, CB)

Christ said literally that the temple of God is not a building. Each person is a living temple of God. He went even further and said:

> "Neither will they say, 'Behold, here it is,' or 'Behold, there it is.' For behold the kingdom of God is within you." (Luke 17:21, CB)

A literal implication would be, the kingdom of God is not in the sky or to be found after death. The kingdom of God is within you.

You were already briefly exposed to one of the mysteries earlier in the book when you read about overcoming the enmity. This is something that Christ did in the Piscean Age and Xxenogenesis did now in the Aquarian Age. This has also been attempted by others and the information was held secretly by more than a few groups. An example of this is right in front of us in the Bible:

> "Woe to you lawyers! For you have taken away the key of knowledge; you did not enter in yourselves, and those who were entering in you hindered." (Luke 11:52) [13]

What is the key of knowledge Christ is talking about? Where could they have entered? Who were those who were entering? How were those who were about to enter hindered? The key of knowledge which was referred to is the information for overcoming the enmity. This was a singular, unique and marvelous accomplishment of Christ. This accomplishment is almost beyond comprehension! This is why it has been overlooked and barely mentioned. But first, let's look at life on this planet before mankind was expelled from the "Garden of Eden." The term, "Garden of Eden" is a poetic way of describing a higher plane of existence, a heavenly existence. When the transgression occurred that was responsible for the expulsion from that higher plane, we are told that one of the numerous

---

[13] https://biblehub.com/luke/11-52.htm

consequences was the creation of the enmity. In order to return back to that higher plane of existence "Eden" or "Heaven," someone would have to undo the damage and overcome the enmity in their body. That person would be an anchor or foundation for a higher consciousness and a doorway for the higher frequencies of a "New Heaven and a New Earth." The creation of the enmity is introduced in Genesis:

> "I will put an enmity between you and the woman, between her seed and your seed; he shall crush your head and you shall lie in wait for his heel." (Genesis 3:15, CB)

This quote along with the other quotes of Genesis Chapter 3 describe the results of shattering the Androgynous beings that existed in the "Garden of Eden." The fall of Adam and Eve was really the fall of all mankind. After all, it wouldn't be very fair to punish the entirety of mankind over multiple millennia for the transgressions of two individuals. This was a symbolic story of the fall of all mankind. The portion of the above quote, "he shall crush your head and you shall lie in wait for his heel" is written symbolically/metaphysically. The "he" refers to the person who will undo the enmity. Interestingly, the Bible that was in Xxenogenesis's hands had an inserted "title" above the quote for Genesis 3:14 which read, "Punishment: the Promise of a Redeemer." This was helpful in bringing his attention to this particular point in the Bible. He spent years in fully decoding this quote and gaining the understanding of the enmity that he would need to complete his "cosmic crucifixion." Xxenogenesis saw the Bible as a coded, symbolic, metaphysical guide to overcoming the enmity. He knew that each person was the Temple of God and that overcoming the enmity was performed in the body. He knew he was recreating something that had been shattered in the beings that were expelled from the "Garden of Eden." Additional clues came from the multiple quotes that speak about the "cornerstone" and especially the "cornerstone which was rejected":

> The stone which the builders have rejected has become the cornerstone. By the Lord has this been done; it is marvelous in our eyes. (Psalms 118:22-23, CB)

This stone has nothing to do with the construction of a building but instead refers to the atoms in your body, the temple of God. We know this by the manner in which Christ spoke of it:

> Jesus said to them, "Did you never read in the Scriptures, 'The stone which the builders rejected, has become the cornerstone: by the Lord this has been done, and it is wonderful in our eyes? Therefore, I say to you, that the kingdom of God will be taken away from you and will be given to a people yielding its fruits. And he who falls on this stone will be broken to pieces; but upon whomever it falls, it will grind him to powder. When the chief priests and the Pharisees heard Jesus's parables, they knew he was talking about them." (Matthew 21:42-45, CB)

The cornerstone is the fused Christ seed of immortality. The Holy Spirit provides the heavenly gift of the soular and lunar seeds that Christ fused to overcome the enmity. The frequency of this particle is in harmonic resonance with the New Heaven and New Earth. This is what will be used by the "Lamb" to seal the 144,000 plus individuals as prophesied in Revelations. This gift of the Holy Spirit must not be rejected. The apparently self-contradictory quotes below are now easily understood given the above information:

> Jesus said: "Whoever blasphemes against the Father will be forgiven. Whoever blasphemes against the Son will be forgiven. But whoever blasphemes against the Holy Spirit will not be forgiven, neither on earth nor in heaven." (Gospel of Thomas 44)

> "And so I tell you, every kind of sin and slander can be forgiven, but blasphemy against the Spirit will not be forgiven. Anyone who speaks against the Son of Man can be forgiven, but anyone who speaks against the Holy Spirit will never be forgiven, either in this world or in the world to come." (Matthew 12:31-32)[14]

The most powerful quote in the Bible that metaphysically talks about this fusion is in Ephesians. When the below quote talks about the two, it is talking about the soular and lunar seeds:

---

[14] https://biblehub.com/matthew/12-31.htm

> For Christ himself is our peace, he it is who has made both one, and has broken down the intervening wall of the enclosure, enmity, in his flesh. The Law of the commandments expressed in decrees he has made void, that of the two he might create in himself one new man, and make peace and reconcile both in one body to God by the cross, having slain the enmity in himself. (Ephesians 2:14-16, CB)

Unlike most quotes which are very similar from Bible to Bible, there are wide differences in translation of the above three verses. I used the same Bible Xxenogenesis had in his possession as a reference for the above quote. The part of the quote that says, "The Law of the commandments expressed in decrees he has made void," refers to the voiding of some religious laws on this plane that are replaced with the laws from the New Heaven and New Earth." Xxenogenesis placed a great deal of emphasis on the enmity and felt it is a highly crucial piece of the puzzle. The above quotes from Genesis and Ephesians and Peter below are only a few of the many quotes that refer to the enmity. Once the enmity is overcome, the fused Christ seed of immortality is referred to in various ways:

> Therefore, thus says the Lord God: "See, I am laying a stone in Zion, a stone that has been tested, a precious cornerstone as a sure foundation; he who puts his faith in it shall not be shaken." (Isaiah 28:16, CB)

You may have noticed the unusual spelling for solar and lunar as soular and lunar. The "soular" seed is a part of our soul here. The lunar seed is the essence of the "New Heaven and New Earth," it is the essence of the Holy Spirit. This is why, when Jesus joined the two together, he became the foundation for anchoring the "New Heaven and New Earth" here. Of course, there is also the consciousness factor which must also be embraced as part of the adventure. That is where you come in, only you can do that part for yourself. There will also be those who don't want to take the time to investigate for themselves or who just don't believe:

> "Lay aside therefore all malice, and all deceit, and pretense, and envy, and all slander. Crave as newborn babes, pure spiritual milk, that by it you may grow to salvation, if indeed you

have tasted that the Lord is sweet. Draw near to him, a living stone, rejected indeed by men but chosen and honored by God. Be you yourselves as living stones built thereon into a spiritual house. A holy priesthood, to offer spiritual sacrifices acceptable to God.....but to those who do not believe, 'a stone which (you) the builders (of your temple of God) rejected, the same has become the head of the corner, and a stumbling-stone, and a rock of scandal.'" (1 Peter 2:1-8)

I guess the question that arises after reading this quote is: how will laying aside all malice, and all deceit, and pretense, and envy and following Christ appear as a "rock of scandal" to others?

Along the same line of thought:

"I am the bread of life. Your fathers ate the manna in the desert and have died. This is the bread that comes down from heaven, so that if anyone eat of it they will not die. I am the living bread that has come down from heaven. If anyone eat of this bread he shall live forever; and the bread I will give you is my flesh for the life of the world." The Jews on that account argued with one another, saying, "How can this man give us his flesh to eat?". . . . "As the living Father has sent me, and as I live because of the Father, so he who eats me, he also shall live because of me. This is the bread that has come down from heaven; not as your fathers ate the manna, and died. He who eats this bread shall live forever." These things he said when teaching in the synagogue at Capharnaum. Many of his disciples therefore, when they heard this, said, "This is a hard saying. Who can listen to it?" But Jesus, knowing in himself that his disciples were murmuring at this, said to them. "Does this scandalize you?" (John 6:48-53, 6:58-62)

I have primarily discussed the first part of a three-part project, the "cosmic crucifixion." The second part of the project has already had its foundation laid out two millennia ago by Christ. His teachings and His focus on Love have changed the world. Unfortunately, only a portion of mankind has embraced what he had to say. Much of what he did say has been watered down and His Secret Teachings are yet to be revealed. The second part involves a shift in consciousness that will be in alignment with the Christ Consciousness. Lastly, in order to complete the project, there will be the gathering of a minimum of 144,000 individuals who will lock in the frequencies of the New Heaven and the New Earth.

Xx Xx Xx

In conclusion I would like you to ponder on these words from the Gospel of Thomas:

> And he said: "Whoever finds the correct interpretation of these sayings will never die." (Gospel of Thomas Verse 1)

> Jesus said: "The seeker should not stop until he finds. When he does find, he will be disturbed. After having been disturbed, he will be astonished. Then he will reign over everything." (Gospel of Thomas Verse 2)

> Jesus said: "People think, perhaps, that I have come to throw peace upon the world. They don't know that I have come to throw disagreement upon the world, and fire, and sword, and struggle." (Gospel of Thomas Verse 16a)

> "There will be five in one house. Three will oppose two. Two will oppose three. The father will oppose his son and the son oppose his father. And they will stand up and they will be alone." (Gospel of Thomas Verse 16b)

Thank you for letting me share with you,

Gabryel

Additional readings: Don Miguel Ruiz, *The Four Agreements: A Practical Guide to Personal Freedom* (Amber-Allen Publishing, 1997), *The Gospel of Philip* (http://gnosis.org/naghamm/gop.html), and various books from the Nag Hammadi Library.

Acknowledgements

Many people have helped to make this book possible and the first in order of importance is **Herman J. Gabryel, Jr. (aka Gabryel)**, the son of Herman J. Gabryel, Sr. (aka Xxenogenesis). Gabryel received a registered letter from us in February of 2021–delayed a couple of weeks because we sent it to an old address. After consulting with other members of the Gabryel family, he contacted us by phone and offered to help us with our book in any way that he could. He very generously told us that he would try to answer all of our questions, and he kept that promise. Our initial Spring 2021 conversations involved six sessions of two hours each, during which time he answered over a hundred detailed inquiries about his father's life and times. Since then, we have been in regular touch with Gabryel. He fact-checked and improved the entire manuscript over a several month period, and he has continued to provide us with new research leads and further biographical insights. Without Gabryel's crucial assistance and support, this book would not have taken flight. But it goes without saying that any serious errors or planned eXxaggerations in this book are ours, and not his.

Thanks also is due to **Hilliary Gabryel**, Xxenogenesis' granddaughter, and a founding member of the Material Girls artist collective. She was the first person in the Gabryel family that we succeeded in contacting, and she helped to explain to the Gabryel family the nature and scope of our project.

This book wouldn't exist at all without **Richard M. Doyle (aka M0b1us)**, the founder and editor of Metanoia Press. Rich came to Louis, an old friend, and asked if he would consider writing a book for his upstart publishing (ad)venture, and Rich did not flinch when we pitched him our pie-in-the-sky dream project, *The Revelations of Xxenogenesis*, a book about a 1973 spoken word record album that few have cared about, that almost no one has ever heard, and that was created by a figure who sought strict anonymity. Rich's "yes I said yes" to all of this remains the project's greatest mystery, and we hope he is pleased with how we rose to the opportunity and how his call was answered.

Also at Metanoia, we need to thank editorial Sangha members **Thomas Breene** and **David B. Saint John** for being thoughtful readers of our original book proposal. We knew very little about Herman J. Gabryel at that time we wrote the proposal in the summer of 2020, but they had faith in us and offered up several important suggestions for improving the project. Tom continued working with us throughout the process of researching and writing the book as the official representative of the Metanoia Sangha, and he later copyedited the manuscript carefully. We have had many warm and wonderful Zoom sessions with Tom during this process, and we remain deeply indebted to him for his valuable comments and feedback.

Of fundamental importance to the ultimate success of our investigations are the dynamic duo of distinguished musical artist (Current 93), painter and scholar **David Tibet** and **Daniel Wojcik**, Department of English, University of Oregon who is an expert in the fields of outsider art and vernacular religions. David and Daniel came into our lives unexpectedly on January 21, 2021 at the prompting of **Seth Larkin Sanders**. The next several days of constant email conversation were fundamental to solving the riddle of Xxenogenesis five days later, on January 26. After that, David and Daniel have been with us every step of the way; Daniel, for example, subtly guided us toward consideration of flying saucer contactees and their organizations in the 1950s and 60s. As the IntroduXxion explains, David gently pushed us toward copyright questions and thereby opened the door to our big discovery. David and Daniel are the angels watching over this project and they are sometimes therefore also known by their apostolic names of DavXxey+++ and DannXxy. We are grateful to Professor Sanders who is a fellow WHRB ghost and a religious studies scholar at the University of California, Davis for setting things in motion. And thanks here are also in order to illustrator and designer **Ania Goszczyńska**, who, as David's partner, listened to the Xxey album and identified the album's Polish hymns for us.

Important thanks also are due to **Philip J. Jacobs (Phillel),** Co-Executive Director of Mark-Age, Inc., in Pioneer, Tennessee, **David McCarthy** of Enlightenmefree.com, and **Joseph Szimhart**, a former Ramtha School of Enlightenment student, like McCarthy, and today an artist, author and expert in "cults." While none of these three ever met Herman J. Gabryel, Sr., the former was able to confirm Herman's importance to the early history of Mark-Age, and the second and third named individuals provided us with crucial journalistic accounts of the Ramtha School from the mid-nineties that featured extensive commentary by Herman's son, Herman, Jr. Their early confirmation of our research hunches was crucial to our work, and we learned a lot from all three of them regarding the early milieus of the Mark-Age MetaCenter and the Ramtha School.

A million thanks to **Theresa Meléndez**, Scott's partner, for her tangible support during each phase of this project. While she was certainly surprised to learn the subject of Scott's new book project, she rapidly warmed to the study of this modern mystic, and she edited and significantly improved the early drafts of every section. She was crucial too in critiquing early attempts at writing the life of Xxenogenesis, and in strongly supporting some of the book's boldest organizational moves and strategies. Her advice made the book much better, no doubt about it.

We reached out early to libraries that might help us turn a nugget or two of information into something more substantial, and, in the process, were aided by wonderful librarians at Michigan State University **(Hui Hua Chua**, Collections Librarian, and **Kathleen Weessies**, Social Sciences Coordinator and Head of the Map Library) and at the University of Miami, Florida (Senior Library Assistant **Chelsea Jacks**).

In trying to track the recording location of the Xxenogenesis LP, we were kindly aided by three distinguished audio investigators – **Erik Lindgren**, **Richard Weize**, and **Jeffrey M. Lemlich** (in addition to Tom Breene). While the investigation remains open, all signs continue to point to Criteria Recording Studios in Miami as the likely site, and we would love to hear from anyone who was present during the recording, or who might have access to Criteria's logbooks from the period.

A very big thank you to **Sacha Kaplan-Shiff** for his constant moral support and love, and, excitingly, for the creation of the world's first talking Xxenogenesis emoji based on photographs from the *Building Materials Merchandiser* feature story.

Thank you to **Michigan State University** and its **Department of English** for a single course release in the Fall of 2020 in order to benefit Scott's research.

Louis also wishes to thank the **Department of Visual Studies at the University Toronto Mississauga** for awarding him SIG (SSHRC Institutional Grant) subvention funding.

A tremendous thank you to the visionary **Brewster Kahle** and the good people who run the Internet Archives' **Wayback Machine**, which began its strange labor in 1996 and has been taking pictures of webpages every day since. To visit Xxey's three websites in all their stages of development and growth provided us with a mind-blowing trip as well as offering us invaluable materials. Without this incredible resource and the ability to recall Xxenogenesis' labyrinth of buried websites, we would not have been able to imagine this book, nor even have solved the mystery.

Scott also wishes to thank a network of former students that have all shown unusual enthusiasm for (or, at least, a very cheerful tolerance of) his pursuit of the Xxenogenesis story. Some of us are in a Zoom reading group about "religion": **Morgan Shipley, Todd Mireles, Zack Kruse, Evan Lee, Dave Watson, Lance Conley, Garth Sabo**. Morgan and Todd in particular were always willing to chat about the state of Xxenogenesis research and Morgan several times helped Scott and Louis identify possible candidates for both "the Solar Center" and the school run by "the tyrant."

Louis thanks our former classmate **Jeanne Heifetz** for her insights and helpful feedback especially on the Timeline and the Film Treatment. He also wishes to thank his former student **Heather Diack** (who now teaches at the University of Miami) for her keen interest in this project and for her leads in connection with Xxey's South Florida stomping grounds. Further thanks go to his old friend and colleague **Celine Trautmann-Waller** (Université Sorbonne Nouvelle, Paris) for her cultural historical interest in the esoteric phenomena surrounding our twentieth century mystic.

Finally, we want to express our deepest gratitude to **Sanket Bojewar**, who was hired by Metanoia Press to manage typesetting and layout for our book. Sanket worked closely with us for several months and proved to be an excellent collaborator, finding solutions for even our trickiest typographical concerns. And aiding Sanket, in the final, technical stretch, were the lifesaving efforts of **Suzanne Winters** and **Billy Rose**.

Etcha!!

Okemos, Michigan/Toronto, Ontario
January 2023

Printed in Great Britain
by Amazon

43377506R00126